The Black Churches
of Brooklyn

THE COLUMBIA HISTORY OF URBAN LIFE

KENNETH T. JACKSON
GENERAL EDITOR

The Columbia History of Urban Life
Kenneth T. Jackson, GENERAL EDITOR

for Marsha

and to the memory of
my Mother, Mamie

The Black Churches of Brooklyn

CLARENCE TAYLOR

COLUMBIA UNIVERSITY PRESS
NEW YORK

Columbia University Press

New York   Chichester, West Sussex

Copyright © 1994 Columbia University Press
All rights reserved

Library of Congress Cataloging-in-Publication Data

Taylor, Clarence.
The Black churches of Brooklyn / Clarence Taylor.
p.   cm—(The Columbia history of urban life)
Includes bibliographical references and index.
ISBN 0–231–09980–0
1. Afro-American churches—New York (N.Y.).
2. Brooklyn (New York, N.Y.)—Church history.
3. Afro-Americans—New York (N.Y.)—Religion.
I. Title   II. Series.
BR563.N4T38   1994   277.47′ 23′ 008996073—dc20
94–5546   CIP

Printed in the United States of America

c 10 9 8 7 6 5 4 3 2 1

CONTENTS

ACKNOWLEDGMENTS

I am grateful to many friends and colleagues for helping to make this work possible. I would like to acknowlege the debt I owe my mentor, the late Herbert G. Gutman, for instilling in me a vision of how to write about the past. It was in Herb's classroom at CUNY's Graduate School that I learned to appreciate the richness and importance of social and cultural history. His enthusiasm, research, and writing and his lectures inspired me to write about ordinary people as historical actors.

I wish to thank Jonathan Birnbaum for the months he spent reading and editing my manuscript and for his helpful changes. Without Jonathan's painstaking work and patience, this book would not have been possible. I deeply appreciate his friendship.

I am extremely thankful to David Garrow, Carol Berkin, Eric Foner, and David Rosner. They guided me in my journey to uncover the rich past of Brooklyn's black churches. I also thank George Cunningham and Janet Bogdan for reading parts of this work and for their useful suggestions.

I am indebted to my colleagues and friends Ed Judge and John Langdon for their careful reading and editing of the work and for their tremendous support.

I wish to give special thanks to Sharyn Knight for her guidance.

At Columbia University Press I want to thank Kate Wittenberg, who first read the manuscript and helped me shape it into a book, and Roy Thomas for his scrupulous copyediting.

This work could not have been possible without the numerous people who opened their homes in order to tell me their stories. Their contribution has been immensely important.

Last, I wish to thank Marsha for her unending support and immeasurable help. She has spent years reading, typing, editing, and patiently listening to my ideas. She has been by my side every step of the way. There are no words to express how much she means to me. I am eternally grateful for her love and devotion.

SELECTED LIST OF CHURCHES

Antioch Apostolic Church of God in Christ
Antioch Baptist Church
Berean Missionary Baptist Church
Bethany Baptist Church
Bethel Baptist Church (*see* Tables)
Bethel Tabernacle African Methodist Episcopal Church
Bethlehem Healing Temple
Beulah Church of Our Lord Jesus Christ
Bibleway Temple
Bridge Street African Wesleyan Methodist Episcopal Church
Brooklyn Tabernacle Church
Brown Memorial Baptist Church
Caldwell AME Zion Church
Church of Christ Holiness USA
Church of Our Lord Jesus Christ of the Apostolic Faith
Concord Baptist Church
Cornerstone Baptist Church
Deliverance Evangelistic Center
Ebenezer Baptist Church
Elect Church
Evening Star Baptist Church

Fire Baptized Holiness Church of God
First African Wesleyan Methodist Episcopal Church
First African Methodist Episcopal Zion Church (*formerly* Fleet
    Street AME Church)
First Baptist Church of Williamsburg (*later* First Baptist Church
    of Crown Heights)
Free Church of God and Christ
Friendship Baptist Church (*see* Tables)
Greater Good Will Baptist Church
Holy Trinity Baptist Church
House of Prayer for All People
House of the Lord Pentecostal
Institutional Baptist Church
Jesus Christ's Triumphant Church of the Apostolic Faith
Life and Time of Jesus Pentecostal Church of the Apostolic Faith
Messiah Baptist Church
Morning Dew Baptist Church
Morningstar Baptist Church
Mount Calvary Baptist Church
Mount Calvary Holy Church of America
Mount Carmel Baptist
Mount Hope United Holy Church of America
Mount Lebanon Baptist Church
Mount Pisgah Baptist Church
Mount Sinai Baptist Church
Mount Tabor Baptist Church
Mount Zion African Methodist Church
Mount Zion Baptist Church
Naomi AME Zion Church
Nazarene Congregational Church
New Hope Baptist (*see* Tables)
Newman Memorial Methodist Church
People's Institutional AME Church (*see* Tables)
Pilgrim Baptist Church
Plymouth Congregational Church
Rose Hill Baptist Church
St. Ambrose (AOC)
St. Augustine Protestant Episcopal Church
St. Leonard's (AOC)
St. Mark's Holy Church

St. Mary the Virgin (AOC)
St. Michael's (AOC)
St. Paul Community Baptist Church
St. Paul's (AOC)
St. Phillip's Protestant Episcopal Church
St. Simon (AOC)
Salem Baptist Church
Sanctified Church in Christ
Siloam Presbyterian Church
Stuyvesant Heights Christian Church
Tabernacle Healing Temple
Tabernacle Prayer for All People
United Holy Church of America, Inc.
Varick Memorial AME Zion
Victory Temple Church
Washington Temple Church of God in Christ
Wright Memorial African Methodist Episcopal Church
Zion Baptist Church

INTRODUCTION

By the dawn of the twentieth century, Brooklyn, New York, had become the home of a large number of churches of various denominations. By the middle of the twentieth century many of these churches had thousands of members, offered a variety of social services to the black community, were important cultural centers, and had nationally renowned pastors. Some of Brooklyn's black clergy had become well-known advocates of civil rights; among them were William A. Jones, Gardner C. Taylor, and Milton A. Galamison. In more recent times some Brooklyn black ministers, such as Herbert Daughtry and Al Sharpton, have gained national attention and prominence because of their political activities. In spite of these facts, Brooklyn's black churches and ministers have almost remained absent from the literature on urban black churches and civil rights. In fact, most works done on New York City's black churches and ministers have focused on Harlem.[1]

Attention needs to be paid to Brooklyn's black churches and ministers because they have been much more than institutions of supplication. The concerns of the black community have remained a central focus of churches and ministers. Throughout their existence they have consistently labored to improve the lives of African Americans, especially in the realms of culture and politics. Churches and ministers have been at the center of culture and politics in the black community, continually attempting to find ways of enriching the lives of black people. Through cultural forms black churches have forged an identity of black people that counters the racist images projected by the dominant culture. For the most part, black ministers have attempted to provide political and moral leadership to the black community. They have not always been successful in their efforts. Nevertheless, because of their efforts, black ministers have become some of the most influential political leaders in the black community.

Anthropologists Hans Baer and Merrill Singer have argued that black churches and ministers have adopted both accommodating and resisting approaches to the customs of the dominant society. Indeed, some black churches have instilled capitalist virtues, cultural practices of the dominant society, and acceptance of the political legitimacy of the state. On the other hand, black churches were not completely dominated by the forces that rule. As Baer and Singer note, black churches have gained a certain amount of autonomy in a capitalist society that enables them to oppose certain aspects of the dominating order. Scholars have failed to see the dual nature of black churches—that they have operated as both accommodating and protest institutions. Accommodation and protest should not be simply juxtaposed, labeling some churches as accommodationist and others as oppositional, but there must be a realization that all churches have both tendencies. At times they willingly buy into the dominant society and at other times they resist the dominant society's customs. The themes of accommodation and protest are central to this book.

My book focuses on African American Christian institutions from their beginnings to the late twentieth century. Although other religious institutions existed in the black community, I limit my focus to the black Christian churches because, unlike any other black religious institutions in Brooklyn, they have a long history, have attracted thousands of members, produced nationally renowned leaders, and played a major role in the cultural and political life of black Brooklyn. This survey also excludes Catholic churches because they did not have a black leadership. My focus is not on the religious practices but on the social, cultural, and political significance of the churches. Throughout this book I attempt to place the churches and ministers in the social, economic, and political context of black Brooklyn and to convey how they addressed the crucial concerns of African Americans.

Several other major themes are the focus of this survey. Specifically, from the nineteenth through the early twentieth centuries Brooklyn's mainline black churches (which included African Methodist, Baptist, Congregational, Protestant Episcopal, and Presbyterian) have taken the cultural forms of the larger society and molded them to benefit African Americans. Although they bought into the cultural practices of the larger white society, they were not merely imitating that society. Instead, they were forging a positive identity of African Americans in a racist environment. By adopting the cultural forms of the larger society, black churches were able to contest popular racist images of blacks, maintain the churches' cultural integrity, and remain economically independent.

Churches where working-class people dominated, such as the Holiness-Pentecostal churches, were more resistant to the values of the dominant society. Through a black Holiness-Pentecostal culture, African Americans challenged the dehumanization of black people and created alternative measures for success that did not exclude anyone on the basis of economic ability. Therefore, they succeeded in winning the loyalty of many blacks. However, they also adapted to some values of the larger society, especially capitalist virtues. They adhered to a capitalist ideology stressing upward social and economic mobility, and consequently, like the mainline churches, the Holiness-Pentecostal churches were both resistant and accommodating.[2]

One important phenomenon affecting both mainline and Holiness-Pentecostal churches of Brooklyn by the 1930s was mass culture. Although much has been written about mass culture and the working class, the relationship between mass cultural forms and black churches remains an unexplored topic. The black churches played a major role in reworking various mass cultural forms. The formation of church clubs and auxiliaries and leisure activities such as dances, picnics, bazaars, and fashion shows were not an indication of a growing secularism among the black churches of Brooklyn but a blending of the secular with the sacred. The churches were responding to a changing black community that was investing heavily in leisure-time activities. The black churches took mass culture and shaped it for their own needs. They used it to remain economically, culturally, and socially independent of the larger society. Although most of the churches adopting mass cultural forms were mainline, some Holiness-Pentecostal churches also embraced these forms.

Although many black churches of Brooklyn were able to incorporate the cultural forms of the dominant society and use these forms to benefit black people, they were less successful in taking advantage of the political order. By the middle of the twentieth century, Bedford-Stuyvesant (often, popularly, Bed-Stuy) was Brooklyn's largest ghetto. Plagued by the problems of poor housing, high unemployment, inadequate health care, a failing school system, and increasing incidence of juvenile crime, Bed-Stuy received little assistance from the federal, state, or city governments. More than any other members of these institutions, pastors and ministers were in positions of great influence in their communities.[3] Several black ministers and their churches were in a strong position to create an independent movement and wage a war against the ghettoization of Bed-Stuy. However, the black clergy of Brooklyn did not take advantage of their strength and resources to challenge an unresponsive city government. Instead, many tried to work with the two-party political system but were unable to use it for the benefit of the black community. These men took on the role of mediators between the community and the state. The black ministers failed to create a militant civil rights movement in Brooklyn that could have challenged the political superiority of the larger society and struggled effectively for African Americans in Bed-Stuy from the 1930s to the 1950s. However, despite several ministers' failure to stop the deterioration of Bed-Stuy, members of black churches did provide services to help alleviate some of the suffering of Bed-Stuy residents.

Not until the 1960s did black ministers act collectively to challenge the dominant political order. Inspired by Martin Luther King Jr. and the movement, and persuaded by more radical forces, some of Brooklyn's prominent black clergy and their churches ignored their friendly relationship with government officials and became revolutionaries for a brief period of time. They borrowed tactics from the Birmingham, Alabama, civil rights campaign and used them in the Downstate Medical Center

Campaign in the summer of 1963. A number of Brooklyn's black ministers stepped out of their roles as mediators and used militant tactics in order to gain economic justice for people of color. It was the first time that Brooklyn's black churches and their leaders had acted collectively and used radical tactics to gain concessions from both the State and City of New York.

Although the activities of male ministers are a major focus of this book, I do not ignore the role of women in Brooklyn's black churches. Despite the effort to exclude women from positions of formal power in the mainline churches, women forged a leadership and helped continue the religious, social, and cultural mission of these churches. By doing so, they helped build the institutional structure of the churches and were able to gain recognition and distinguished positions.

In spite of the fact that some Holiness-Pentecostal institutions attempted to deny women positions of conventional power, some were able to become pastors and leaders. Unlike mainline churches, where scripture was used to justify men's dominance, the universal acceptance of "the call" into a position of authority in Holiness-Pentecostal churches was used by women to advance the idea that God does not set limitations based on sex. In addition, in both the Holiness-Pentecostal and mainline churches women in particular helped shape the social and cultural activities of the church. They managed to present to their churches what Evelyn Brooks Higgenbotham has so aptly labeled a racialized vision of gender.

My main goal in this book is not only to provide a deeper understanding of Brooklyn's black churches but to give a better understanding of the people and community these institutions sought to serve. As W. E. B. Du Bois noted, "It is thus clear that the study of Negro religion is not only a vital part of the history of the Negro in America, but . . . of American history."[4]

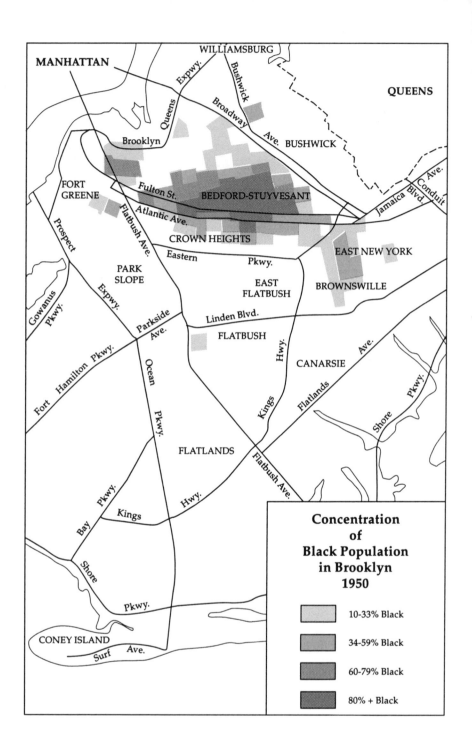

MANHATTAN

WILLIAMSBURG

QUEENS

Queens Expwy.

Bushwick

Broadway

Brooklyn

BUSHWICK

FORT GREENE

Fulton St.

BEDFORD-STUYVESANT

Jamaica Ave.

Conduit Blvd.

Atlantic Ave.

Flatbush Ave.

CROWN HEIGHTS

EAST NEW YORK

Prospect

Eastern   Pkwy.

PARK SLOPE

EAST FLATBUSH

BROWNSVILLE

Gowanus Pkwy.

Expwy.

Parkside Ave.

Linden Blvd.

CANARSIE

Shore Ave.

Fort Hamilton Pkwy.

Ocean Pkwy.

FLATBUSH

Kings Hwy.

Flatlands

FLATLANDS

Flatbush Ave.

Bay Pkwy.

Kings   Hwy.

Shore

Pkwy.

CONEY ISLAND

Surf   Ave.

Concentration of Black Population in Brooklyn 1950

10-33% Black

34-59% Black

60-79% Black

80% + Black

The Black Churches
of Brooklyn

CHAPTER ONE

The Formation and Development of Brooklyn's Black Churches from the Nineteenth to the Early Twentieth Centuries

In November 1885 the Bridge Street African Wesleyan Methodist Episcopal Church (AWME) of Brooklyn gave a concert celebrating the purchase of a new pipe organ. The organist of Brooklyn Tabernacle Church played the "William Tell Overture," the choir sang "As Mountains Around His People," and two members of the congregation performed a violin and piano duet of "Could I Teach the Nightingales." However, the highlight of the evening was the performance by Edward G. Jardine, owner of Jardine and Sons, who built the $3,000 instrument.

Mr. Jardine gave an idea of the calmness and repose of nature and the singing of birds on a summer's afternoon. The pipe of the shepherd is heard in the distance echoed from hill to hill. The peasants enjoy a rustic dance but are interrupted by the distant muttering of thunder. As the storm approaches, the thunder grows louder, the winds moan; suddenly the storm breaks with full violence. Gradually it subsides and the vespers hymn is sung by the peasants as a safe deliverance from the tempest.[1]

The event highlights more than the incorporation of secular elements into the services of Brooklyn's black Protestant churches. From the first half of the nineteenth century, black Brooklynites began to establish religious institutions that would address their needs in an urban society. Parishioners were exposed to classical music and architecture, literature, elocution, fine art, and scholarly sermons stressing intellectualism, self-improvement, and how to cope in the larger white society. However, church leaders and members were not merely imitating the larger white society. Instead they were seeking strategies to address their needs as African Americans. Brooklyn's black churches continually sought approaches to alleviate blacks from the yoke of white oppression. Culture was one important arena used by the churches.

This cultural attitude in the black churches has been attacked by scholars who contend that these institutions did little to oppose racial inequality in the early twentieth century and, rather than lead the struggle, merely promoted decorous religious culture. For example, the theologian Gayraud Wilmore contends that by the end of the first World War the Independent Black churches were becoming respectable institutions. Having rejected the nationalism of [African Methodist Episcopal Bishop Henry McNeal] Turner they moved more and more toward what was presented by white churches as the model of authentic Christian faith and life. The dominant influence of the clergy in the social betterment and civil rights groups helped to keep these organizations on an accommodationist trajectory.[2]

Without a doubt these churches accommodated the dominant society. However, just because churches accommodated the hegemonic order does not mean that they were not useful to African Americans. The significance of black church culture must be understood in its historical context. Until recently, little has been written about the culture of urban black churches in the nineteenth and early twentieth centuries.[3] Here I explore their emergence, with emphasis on their values, sacred worldview, and impact on the black public. I examine how urban African Americans asserted their social, economic, and cultural independence, implemented strategies for moral and economic uplift, and challenged their image in the eyes of the dominant society.

Western nations justified slavery by claiming to save the souls of slaves from damnation by delivering them from the heathen practices. However, many slaveowners refused to attempt to convert their slaves because they thought that blacks did not have the mental capacity to understand Christian principles; they feared Christianity would lead to slave rebellions and cared little about the spiritual life of their chattels. As for the slaves, many rejected Christianity because it stressed literacy (memorization of verses and catechisms), lacked drama, and condemned certain African practices including spirit powers, voodoo, and conjurers or magic men.[4]

But in the Great Awakenings, beginning in the 1740s and antebellum decades, large numbers of African Americans converted to Christianity. During these eruptions of religious fervor, fiery ministers challenged Christianity and offered salvation to all, regardless of social and economic position. These awakeners contended that salvation did not come through a priestly class or through formal knowledge. Instead, one found God through conversion by faith or rebirth, as evidenced by trances, visions, shouting, dancing, "fits," and other ecstatic acts. The conversion experience was appealing to both whites and blacks whose illiteracy limited their involvement in the Episcopal, Congregational, and Presbyterian churches, all of which required followers to be well versed in the Bible. Many African Americans attended evangelical revivals and took part in the conversion experience.[5]

As African Americans embraced evangelical Protestantism, they reshaped its form and content to accommodate their own needs. They accepted the basic doctrine of conversion through faith, but their sacred worldview included a God who could deliver them from slavery; thus the Old Testament was essential because its narratives stressed the theme of faith and deliverance. When singing about the Hebrews' deliverance from bondage because of their faith in God, slaves played out their own deliverance from oppression. Like the peoples of all preliterate societies, slaves made little distinction between words and action.[6]

By seeing themselves in the context of sacred time and sacred space, African Americans in bondage were able to invoke the presence of God anytime and anyplace. Worship was not limited to a church; it could take place in the fields, by a campfire, or when the individual was alone during the day. The sacred time and sacred space created by African Americans in bondage helped keep them permanently in contact with god. Thus they were able to make sense out of a chaotic and hostile environment. Emotional behavior—ecstatic dancing, shouting, moaning, sobbing, fainting, and singing in the fields as well as in places of worship—was seen as proof of the Holy Spirit's perpetual presence in an individual or a congregation.[7]

Moreover, African American services were communal, using these and other practices to involve the entire congregation. One such practice was call and response: when an individual sang or preached, the congregation responded. The response could be a shout, a word or statement, clapping, an emotional outburst, and other forms of replies to the preacher or singer. Another practice was the ring shout, where a group of congregants would dance in a circle, singing a continuous chant. The participants stamped their feet and clapped their hands to the music, usually working themselves into a frenzy. Shouts of encouragement were heard throughout this activity. Blending the individual voice with the communal helped create a corporate identity in which the leader's role was not more important than that of any congregant.[8]

Although sermons were delivered by preachers considered leaders of congregations, the preacher's role in worship did not supersede that of the congregation. Sermons were not scholarly lectures but rituals intended to evoke an emotional response from the congregation. Ecstatic behavior evidenced the presence of the Holy Spirit. Without an emotional outpouring from the congregation, sermons would be meaningless.[9]

The ritual style of African American religion continued after slavery. Many late nineteenth-century observers commented on this highly emotional and communal aspect. For example, the black abolitionist William Wells Brown recalled visits to numerous black Baptist churches in Tennessee between 1879 and 1880:

> In the evening I went to the First Baptist Church on Spruce Street. This house is equal to in size and finish to St. Paul. A large assembly was in attendance, and a young man from Cincinnati was introduced by the pastor as the preacher for the time being. He evidently felt that to set a congregation to shouting was the highest point to attain, and he was equal to the occasion. Failing to raise a good shout by a reasonable amount of exertion, he took from his pocket a letter, opened it up and began, "When you reach the other world you'll be hunting for your mother, and the angel will read from this paper. Yes, the angel will read from this paper." For fully ten minutes the preacher walked the pulpit, repeating in a loud, incoherent manner, "And the angel will read from this letter." This created wildest excitement, and not less than ten or fifteen were shouting in different parts of the house, while four or five were going from seat to seat shaking hands with the occupants of the pews. "Let dat angel come right down now an' read dat letter," shouted a Sister at the top of her voice. This was the signal for loud exclamations from various parts of the house. "Yes, yes i want's to hear the letter." "Come, Jesus, come, or send an angel to read the letter" . . . and other remarks filled the house.[10]

However, when urban black communities developed and the education and socioeconomic position of some African Americans improved, they began to reinterpret religious life. Rejecting "uncultured" antebellum religious practices, many blacks began creating institutions that stressed a worldview different from traditional African American Protestantism. This new worldview is exemplified by the churches of Brooklyn, New York.

Brooklyn's Black Population

People of African origins have resided in Brooklyn since the seventeenth century. During the colonial era, most blacks in Brooklyn were slaves on farms owned by the early Dutch settlers. Harold X. Connolly notes that in the first comprehensive census of New York, taken in 1698, 15 percent of Kings County's population (296) consisted of African slaves. No free blacks were listed in the county's six towns of Brooklyn, Bushwick, Flatlands, Flatbush, Gravesend, and New Utrecht. By the early eighteenth century, the slave population had grown rapidly, making Kings the "heaviest slaveholding county in the state of New York." By the mid-century, one-third of the county's population was of African origin.[11]

Kings County was an agricultural community that relied heavily on slave labor. By 1790, 60 percent of all white families residing in Kings County were slaveholders, and it became known as the "slaveholding capital" of the state. This fact explains why there were so few free blacks in the county. Although one-fifth of New York State's black population was free, by the end of the century only 3 percent (or forty-six) free blacks resided in Kings County, the smallest number in the state.[12]

Between 1800 and 1870 the population of Kings County increased from 5,720 to 419,921. Eventually, Brooklyn would absorb the other five towns. By the second half of the nineteenth century, Brooklyn had come to dominate Kings County with 396,099 residents in 1870. Although it did not grow as dramatically as the white population, the black population increased from 1,811 to 5,653 between 1800 and 1870—and 4,931 of the county's 5,653 blacks resided in Brooklyn.[13]

Connolly points out that by the mid-nineteenth century some blacks were engaged in a variety of skilled and semiskilled occupations such as "barbers, tailors, carpenters, painters, butchers, shoemakers, coopers, and ropemakers, as well as holding employment as domestic servants, waiters, and sailors." Census data show that some blacks were also brick masons, veilmakers, gardeners, cooks, milliners, musicians, cabinet makers, and dressmakers. A small number held middle-class positions such as ministers, clerks, teachers, and doctors. However, census data also reveal that the overwhelming majority of blacks were engaged in menial jobs such as washing clothes and domestic work for women, and as farm laborers, coachmen, porters, servants, waiters, and seamen for men.

Throughout the nineteenth century, no individual neighborhood claimed a majority of Brooklyn's black residents. In 1827 New York State abolished slavery, thus allowing for the development of black communities. During the 1830s, blacks purchased land in an area in the Ninth Ward, founding the communities of Weeksville and Carrsville. These two independent black communities were located within a mile of one another within the boundaries of present-day Bedford-Stuyvesant: Atlantic Avenue on the north, Ralph Avenue on the east, Eastern Parkway on the south, and Albany Avenue on the west. By 1875, 650 blacks resided in the Weeksville-Carrsville communities. There was another large black concentration within the Fourth Ward, which included Fulton Street on the west, Sands Street on the north, and Bridge Street on the south. By the 1830s one-third of Brooklyn's blacks resided in this area.[14]

Formation of Black Churches

Except for the family, the black church became the most important institution among African Americans. Churches helped them to gain independence, met their religious, educational, and social needs, and alleviated the impact of racism; churches also provided a satisfying community life. As Brooklyn's black communities developed, so did numerous churches, the first of which was established early in the nineteenth century. The number of free blacks increased in Brooklyn, both from blacks who had gained their freedom through manumission and blacks who had moved into the downtown area after the building of the first steam ferry between Manhattan and Brooklyn in 1814.

As the black population of the downtown area grew, many newcomers sought places of worship. Some joined the predomi-

nantly white First Methodist Episcopal Church of Brooklyn, popularly known as Sands Street Methodist Church (although the
increase in black membership caused great alarm among the
white membership). Responding to white resentment to the
increase of black members, church officials charged people of
African origins ten dollars per quarter to worship at Sands. In
addition to this humiliation, the pastor of the church, Alexander
McCaine, publicly defended slavery and would later publish a
pamphlet entitled "Slavery Defended from Scripture."[15]

Deciding that it was better to form their own congregation
than endure insults and attacks on their humanity, blacks collectively withdrew from Sands and held religious services in their
homes. This action demonstrated the determination of African
Americans to oppose racism and their desire for independence.
They sent a delegation to Philadelphia to meet with Richard
Allen, the founder of the African Methodist Episcopal Church
(AME), to seek recognition in the African Methodist Episcopal
body and a minister for the new congregation. The male members
of the new congregation selected a trustee board, which applied
for and received official recognition from the state of New York
as the First African Wesleyan Methodist Episcopal Church
(AWME). By taxing each member fifty cents a month, the new
congregation raised enough money in 1819 to purchase land on
High Street and build its first church. In 1854, after moving to
Bridge Street in Brooklyn, the church changed its name to Bridge
Street African Wesleyan Methodist Episcopal Church.[16]

Soon after, other African Methodist churches were organized.
Sometime between 1827 and 1835 the black community of
Williamsburg organized what eventually became the Union
African Methodist Episcopal Zion Church (in 1894), joining with
the newly formed African Methodist Episcopal Zion Church. The
African Methodist Episcopal Zion had broken off from St. John's
(Methodist Episcopal) Church, and its black members had left in
1800 to form their own church because they had been forced to
worship separately from white members. The new body added
Zion in order to distinguish itself from the African Methodist
Episcopal Church established by Richard Allen in Philadelphia in
1796. In 1844 the Mount Zion African Methodist Society was cre-
ated, and in 1847 the Weeksville community organized the
African Methodist Episcopal Bethel Church (later known as

9

Bethel Tabernacle African Methodist Episcopal Church). Union AME Zion moved to Ralph Avenue in 1909 and changed its name to Ralph Avenue AME Zion; in 1949, it assumed the name Varick Memorial AME Zion.[17]

By the second half of the nineteenth century other African Methodist churches had been formed. In 1850 Williamsburg blacks established the First African Methodist Episcopal Church; in 1852 blacks founded an AME church in Flatbush. Fleet Street African Methodist Episcopal Zion Church was founded by fifteen members of an AME church relocating to Atlantic Avenue, who applied for and won recognition as a church body in the AME Zion connection in 1885. The congregation, located on Fleet Street near Myrtle Avenue, was forced to move in 1905 to Bridge Street after the second floor of the Fleet Street church collapsed in 1904, killing ten and injuring forty. Once on Bridge Street, the church changed its name to the First African Methodist Episcopal Zion Church. Incorporation records note the establishment of a Saint Peter's African Church in 1837 and a Metropolitan African Methodist Episcopal Church in 1885, although there is no information on these bodies.[18]

The next largest group of churches established by blacks was Baptist. Although the early black Methodists had gained congregational independence, they became dependent on the bishops of the Methodist Episcopal Church in their ecclesiastical affairs, in order to receive recognition as a part of Methodism. The Baptists did not have any hierarchical structure and therefore were independent in all matters. This independence made it easier to establish Baptist churches. Anyone organizing a group of people could establish a Baptist church. The independence in ecclesiastical affairs may also explain why the Baptists were considered more evangelical and spirited in services than the Methodists.[19]

In 1847 six members of Manhattan's Abyssinian Baptist Church who lived in Brooklyn met at the home of Maria Hampton on Fair Street. Their mission was to create a Baptist church in their own community, eliminating the hardship of traveling across the East River every Sunday to worship. The small but growing band of worshipers hired Samuel White, formerly of Abyssinian Baptist Church, as pastor, purchased two lots on Concord Street near Duffield, and built the Concord Street Baptist Church of Christ.[20] The racially integrated Berean Missionary Baptist Church, located in Weeksville, became the second black Baptist church in Brooklyn when its white membership abandoned the church in the early 1850s. Before the end of the century other Baptist churches had been established, including Mount Calvary in East New York, Brooklyn, in 1875, Bethany in 1883, and Holy Trinity in 1899.[21]

The African Methodist and Baptist denominations made up the largest congregations in Brooklyn, but they were not the only ones. The same year that Concord was established, James Gloucester (son of John Gloucester, the founder of black Presbyterianism in Philadelphia) started a Presbyterian mission on Fulton and Cranberry streets. After moving to Prince Street in 1849, Gloucester was granted permission from the Brooklyn Presbytery to organize the Siloam Presbyterian Church.

Both the Congregational and Protestant Episcopal churches also made inroads in Brooklyn with the founding of a Colored American Congregational Church in 1853 and the Nazarene Congregational Church in 1873. The small black community of Canarsie established the Plymouth Congregational Church in 1888.[22]

In 1875 a small group met at the home of businessman Kellis Delamar to organize a Protestant Episcopal Church. During the first year, services were held in the Delamar home at 417 State Street; Prince T. Rogers, of Fayetteville, North Carolina, was selected pastor. The following year the group received official mission status from the Protestant Episcopal Diocese and named their group the St. Augustine Protestant Episcopal Church. The parishioners received official parish status in 1890.[23]

These nineteenth-century black Brooklyn churches began modestly. Concord, Bethany, Varick Memorial, and St. Augustine all began in founders' homes while St. Phillip's Protestant Episcopal started out in a store at 1887 Pacific Street. Unable to buy or build, both Siloam and Nazarene rented halls on Fulton Street, while the small Holy Trinity Baptist Church rented a building on Claver Place and Jefferson Avenue. Financially poor, many churches were unable to attract or hold on to their leadership or full-time managers. For example, between 1847 and 1863 Concord had five ministers; from 1883 to 1887 Bethany had four ministers. The Reverend William H. Dickerson of Siloam resigned as pastor after church officials were unable to pay the minister the $1,000 annual salary agreed on, cutting it by $200.[24]

Except for Concord Baptist and the African Wesleyan Methodist Episcopal, membership remained small. As late as 1889 many had less than one hundred members, with Berean reporting thirty-five, Nazarene forty-six, St. Varick fifty-two, and St. Augustine eighty-six. Fleet Street AME Zion and Bethany Baptist each reported slightly more than one hundred members.[25]

Despite humble beginnings, many churches survived to become vital organizations. Church trustee boards became more efficient in keeping records and managing accounts, as well as in delivering monthly and annual financial reports to the congregation. A case in point was Concord Baptist Church. While presenting his annual financial report in 1906, Rev. William T. Dixon praised the board of trustees for their "careful and correct accounting" procedures, singling out the secretary, Mr. Graham H. Cooper, for providing excellent services for twenty-three years. "He is exact in his figures and renders monthly and yearly reports to the church," which are "printed and distributed among the members of the church and congregation so that each member may see where the money goes."[26]

The churches employed various techniques to raise revenue. The most common, the Sunday collection, proved a steady source of income. Some churches in financial straits turned to desperate measures. Siloam Presbyterian rented pews to its members, and the AWME imposed a mandatory fee of fifty cents per member. Usually, black churches used more innovative methods to raise money. Both St. Augustine and Siloam charged admission to annual excursions and bazaars. AWME, AME Zion of Williamsburg (Varick), and Siloam held concerts; Fleet Street charged admission to its annual picnic. Bethel AME organized color-coded groups to compete with each other in raising money for the church.[27]

In addition to becoming self-supporting organizations, free from outside pressure, black churches of this era became important institutions in the struggle for liberation. During the antebellum period, Brooklyn's black churches emerged as active agencies in the struggle against slavery. Both Bridge Street AWME and Concord Baptist churches became sanctuaries for runaway slaves, while Siloam Presbyterian Church created a fund for the Underground Railroad.[28] Clergy and church officials participated in the fight for African American freedom. Some became active in black conventions, such as the Christian Union Convention organized by ministers of Manhattan and Brooklyn. The convention met on January 14 and 15, 1861, to "take into consideration of our present oppressed condition and to take measures to invite Christians throughout the United States to observe a day of fasting and prayer to Almighty God for his interposition in our behalf in these times of trial and peril." Among the organizing ministers were Samson White, pastor of Concord Baptist Church, and L. C. Speaks, pastor of Bridge Street AWME.[29]

Brooklyn's black churches also contributed to the drive for literacy. Concord, Bridge Street, and Siloam established Sunday schools whose purpose was educational as well as religious. The *Annual Report of the Board of Managers of the Brooklyn Sabbath School Union* for 1858–59 points out that Sabbath schools were well-organized departments, staffed by teachers and managed by superintendents. Bridge Street AWME had nine teachers, Concord ten, and Siloam seventeen. Bridge Street Sabbath School serviced forty-four, Concord sixty-five, and Siloam 154 students in 1859. The report indicates that the classes were not only for children: ninety-six of the students attending classes at Siloam were adults, with nine at Concord, and with no children at Bridge Street AWME—all forty-four students there were adults. Both Concord and Siloam had libraries, reporting forty-five and one hundred books, respectively.[30]

As black churches multiplied in Brooklyn during the post–Civil War period, they joined in creating Sunday schools. In some cases Sunday school enrollment was more than half the size of the church's membership. Concord reported 696 church members in 1891 and a Sunday school enrollment of 430. Bridge Street AWME had 874 members and 542 Sunday school members. Union Bethel AME had 89 Sunday school members out of 107 church members.[31]

However, many black church schools reported having more Sunday school members than regular churchgoers. In 1892 Mount Calvary Baptist's congregation numbered 354, but its Sunday school membership was 550. Siloam had 175 church members and 210 Sunday school students. St. Augustine had 170 Sunday school members and only 150 church members. In 1886 Berean Missionary Baptist Church had only 60 members, but 165 people were enrolled in Sunday school, while Nazarene Congregational Church reported 1,342 Sunday school members and only 102 church members in 1900.[32]

Sunday schools attracted students outside the churches because they combated illiteracy and gave religious instruction to African Americans. Many in Brooklyn's black communities took the opportunity to gain tools for advancing in an urban society.

The Growing Significance of Brooklyn's Black Middle Class

As the black population in Brooklyn grew, social and economic differences within communities developed. By the end of the Civil War most Brooklyn blacks were relegated to the lowest positions in the labor market with little chance for advancement. As noted, the 1870 and 1880 censuses reveal that the vast majority of African Americans were manual laborers.

Despite harsh discrimination and a rigid class system, urban society offered occupational and educational opportunities denied to blacks in rural life, thus promoting the development of a small yet significant black elite. Some members of this group were from families that occupied high positions among the black population before the Civil War. They were usually the professionals: doctors, lawyers, and educators. Other blacks moved into this group by becoming involved in activities that relied on the support of a black clientele such as business owners, ministers, and skilled workers including a number of dressmakers, undertakers, carpenters, barbers, butchers, gardeners, tailors, brick masons, shoemakers, musicians, and clerks.

It should be noted that the notion of class was not well defined in the black community. The historian Allan Kulikoff notes that "classes are formed when discrete groups of people with similar levels of wealth and similar relations to the dominant means of production come to understand their place in the social order and develop coherent ideologies to legitimate or challenge that place."[33] Unlike the larger society where classes formed coherent ideologies to justify their economic and social position, Brooklyn's black elite did not have such an ideology. They justified their position in the black community by arguing that the race could advance through social, economic, and moral uplift. However, this ideology was not shared by them exclusively. Many working-class African Americans shared this belief. Moreover, unlike the elites of the larger community, the black elite did not create segregated institutions. Although the black elite was identified by churches it attended and by the secular organizations it operated, for the most part these churches and organizations were not class segregated.

Some members of Brooklyn's black elite rose to prominence. Among them was William H. Smith, called by the *New York Times* in 1895 one of the "Wealthy Negro Citizens" of Brooklyn, who was employed at the Bank of New York. Worth more than $100,000, Smith lived in a "handsome house" on Lafayette Avenue and employed several servants.[34] Samuel R. Scottron, a successful businessman during the late 1890s and early 1900s (whose stock included mirrors, looking glasses, wood moldings, and imitation onyx for lamps) reported his yearly income at $25,000. Scottron was active in the Republican Party and in 1894 was appointed to the Brooklyn Board of Education.[35]

Peter Ray (1825–1906), one of Brooklyn's first black physicians, graduated from Castleton (Vermont) Medical School in 1850 and opened both an office on Herkimer Street and a drugstore in Williamsburg. He became a member of the Kings County Medical Society and treasurer of the Brooklyn College of Pharmacy, which he helped establish, as well as a major property owner.[36]

Dr. Susan Smith McKinney-Steward (1847–1918) became the first African American woman to practice medicine in the state of New York and only the third in the country. She attended New York Medical College for Women, graduating in 1870 as valedictorian. McKinney was the founder of the Women's Hospital and Dispensary in Brooklyn, later the Memorial Hospital for Women and Children. She was active in both the women's suffrage and temperance movements. According to the *New York Times*, her house on Dekalb Avenue was located in the "midst of the fashionable quarter of the Hill," and the *New York Sun* asserted that Dr. McKinney had a "handsome bank account." Historian William Seraile notes that she financially supported her husband, stricken with apoplexy in 1890, and six other family members living with her on Dekalb Avenue.[37]

Maritcha Lyons (1848–1929) became one of Brooklyn's most prominent black educators of the late nineteenth and early twentieth centuries. Lyons was the daughter of Abro and Mary Lyons, whose house was a station on the Underground Railroad. Fleeing

15

New York City during the Draft Riot of 1863, the Lyons moved to Providence, Rhode Island, where Maritcha was the first black to graduate from Providence Public High School. In 1869 Maritcha began teaching at Colored School No. 1 (later Public School number 67) under the supervision of the noted black educator Dr. Charles A. Dorsey. Later, she became an assistant principal, training new teachers for elementary school service.[38]

Among the elite were several ministers, including Rufus L. Perry (1834–1895), who was born a slave in Tennessee and later attended a school for free blacks. In 1852 he escaped slavery and began to study theology at a seminary in Michigan. Graduating in 1861, he became an ordained Baptist minister and served as pastor in Ann Arbor, Ontario, Buffalo, and finally Messiah Baptist Church in Brooklyn. He founded and edited the *National Monitor*, a monthly religious publication, and wrote *The Cushite; or, The Children of Ham* (see note 73).[39]

Fredrick M. Jacobs, born in 1865 in Camden, South Carolina, received his B.A. from Wesleyan University in Bloomington, Illinois, in 1884 and a degree in theology from Howard University in 1887. In 1895 Jacobs received a doctor of divinity degree from Livingstone College in Salisbury, North Carolina. Two years later he became pastor of the Fleet Street AME Zion Church. While serving as pastor, Jacobs attended Long Island Medical College and earned a medical degree in 1901. Soon after this, he left Fleet Street to establish a lucrative medical practice in Brooklyn.[40]

William Dixon (1833–1909), pastor of Concord Baptist Church, was born on Elizabeth Street and educated in Brooklyn public schools. He became a school teacher and principal and served as pastor of Concord from 1863 until his death in 1909. He founded the New England Baptist Association and was elected its president in 1900. He was also moderator of the predominantly white Long Island Baptist Association.[41]

T. McCants Stewart (1852–1923) became one of the most prominent and influential citizens of Brooklyn. Born of free parents in Charleston, South Carolina, Stewart attended Howard University from 1869 to 1873 and later the University of South Carolina, where he received both an A.B. and an LL.B. in 1875. After practicing law briefly in South Carolina, Stewart studied at Princeton. In 1879 he was an ordained minister, becoming pastor of Bethel AME Church in New York City. In 1883 Stewart gave up the ministry to become a teacher at Liberia College for two years. In 1885 Stewart moved to Brooklyn, becoming the corresponding editor of the *New York Freeman*; in 1886 he resumed his law practice as attorney for Bridge Street AWME Church. He was appointed to the Board of Education in 1893.[42]

Evidence suggests that intraclass marriage was common among Brooklyn's black elite. For example, in 1874 Dr. Susan McKinney, then Susan Marie Smith, married the Reverend William McKinney, a "modestly wealthy man" who owned a building valued at $6,000. Two years after her husband's death in 1896, Susan married the Reverend Theophilus Gould Steward, who was a well-known minister, chaplain of the Twenty-Fifth U.S. Colored Infantry and professor of history at Wilberforce University in Xenia, Ohio. Susan's older sister was married to famed abolitionist Henry Highland Garnet, and Susan's daughter Annie married M. Louis Holly, son of the Bishop of Haiti.[43]

Brooklyn's black elite also had numerous social affairs, featuring European-style artistic forms including concerts, dances, and literary events. For example, a testimonial was held for M. Albert Wilson. The "leading citizens" from both Brooklyn and New York attended. The event was a "notable artistic and social success. Mr. Walter F. Craig, Mme [first name unreadable] Jones, and M. Wilson were the bright particular stars of the occasion and acquitted themselves in brilliant style, the Li Trovatore Fantasia by Mr. Craig being especially well done." The Henry Highland Garnet Republican Club gave a concert in Brooklyn and "the program was as follows: Part I: organ solo, Mr. Melvelle Charlton; soprano solo, Mrs Estelle Pinckney Clough; piano solo, Miss Bertha Bulkley; selection, Nashville Quartet, Philip Parlock and W. H. Tucker, tenors, and N. B. Collins and J. F. Delyons, basses; violin solo, Miss Marie A. Wayne; and baritone solo, Mr Burleigh."[44]

By the late nineteenth century newspapers had recognized the existence of Brooklyn's black elite. In 1892 the *Brooklyn Daily Eagle* reported on a social affair of the "Colored four hundred of Brooklyn," the "elite of Brooklyn's colored citizens." In 1895 the *New York Times* asserted that Brooklyn attracted a number of wealthy blacks: "As soon as negro men amass a comfortable fortune, they move from this city across the East River, because they can find in Brooklyn more economical and satisfactory investments."[45]

Besides social and cultural events, Brooklyn's black elite was active in a number of activities to uplift African Americans. Businessman Samuel Scottron became an outspoken advocate on the issue of "self uplifting" of African Americans. Expressing a view that blacks must help themselves (a view shared by a large number of the black elite), Scottron contended:

> The Negro has advanced rapidly and seemingly beyond all comparison. He is moving along with the age and it would be impossible for him not to advance. . . . But it remains for him to show that he is contributing to the force that moves things! That he is not dead weight, simple ballast, clinker in the furnaces, but good coal affording light and heat. . . . What can the Negro do for himself and what is he doing? Are the all-important questions, and in the answer of these lies the future of the American Negro.[46]

Scottron was also a crusader for the abolition of slavery abroad. Along with Henry Highland Garnet, Professor Charles A. Dorsey, Rev. William T. Dixon of Concord Baptist Church, and Rev. A. N. Freeman of Siloam Presbyterian Church, Scottron was a member of the American Foreign Anti-Slavery Society.[47]

Maritcha Lyons was an outspoken advocate for women's rights and African American equality. She was active in the Women's Club movement of the late nineteenth century and a member of the Women's Loyal Union. An outspoken integrationist, she attacked the evils of segregation, arguing that denying blacks participation in the larger white society had impeded their progress and jeopardized America's democracy.

According to Lyons there could only be one solution to America's race problems:

> The abuses that exist are the outcome of unscientific, unscrupulous propaganda on the part of those who have abrogated to themselves the right to obstruct the path of the colored American. These obstacles, illogical assertions, preconceived notions, false premises, specious reasoning—must be cut down or dug up by the keen blade of unpreju-

diced opinion; must be burned away by the ardent glow of an unquenchable reverence for humanity.[48]

Many members of Brooklyn's black elite became advocates of educational facilities for blacks. In a speech celebrating the opening of a new building for one of Brooklyn's "colored schools," schools that serviced African American children, Professor Richard P. Greener, who held a degree from Harvard and became a well-known black educator, contended that the colored schools of Brooklyn were needed because they instilled pride. In addition, black teachers made black children aware of their rich heritage, and in order for African American children to become "useful" they "must be trained by sympathetic heads and hearts of their own race."

In 1883 when the Board of Education contemplated closing the "colored schools" in Brooklyn, Rev. Rufus Perry, Charles A. Dorsey, Rev. William T. Dixon, and a number of other members of the black elite spoke out against the board's decision by noting the need for such schools.[49]

By the second half of the nineteenth century, Brooklyn's black elite were operating institutions that attempted to make poor African Americans economically and socially independent. In order to prepare African Americans for success in society, they stressed moral and social uplift, education, and the fight against racism. Two such organizations were the African Civilization Society and the Brooklyn Howard Colored Orphan Asylum. Established in the 1850s, the African Civilization Society was made up of prominent blacks: Daniel Payne, president of Wilberforce; abolitionist Henry Highland Garnet; the Reverend J. Sella Martin, acclaimed by the weekly *Anglo-African* as a most promising preacher; the Reverends Rufus Perry and A. N. Freeman, both Brooklynites. The society's objectives were to "promote civilization and Christianization of Africa and of the descendants of African ancestors in any portion of the earth," to destroy the African slave trade, to make people of African origins industrious "producers as well as consumers," and to elevate "the condition of the colored population of our own country and of the other lands."[50] After emancipation the Society dedicated its entire effort to establishing and maintaining free schools in the South. At its sixth annual meeting in 1865, the Society reported that it had hired twenty-four teachers and supported ten day and night schools, working with hundreds of men, women, and children.[51]

The Brooklyn Howard Colored Orphan Asylum opened in 1866 and was incorporated in 1868. According to the Asylum's constitution, its objective was to "shelter, protect, and educate destitute orphan children of Colored parentage and to instruct them in useful trades." Besides giving shelter to more than three hundred children and educating them with a professional teaching staff, the institution provided the orphans with medical care. Its medical staff included an ear, eye, nose, and throat specialist, stomach and intestine specialists, a genito-urinary specialist, dermatologist, and a dentist.[52]

Although it received financial support from whites until 1902, the Howard Colored Orphan Asylum had a predominantly black board of directors and an all-black staff. According to historian Carleton Mabee, all of Howard's superintendents were black. After 1902 prominent blacks still led the organization. The Board of Trustees included Rev. William T. Dixon of Concord, W. T. Timms, pastor of Holy Trinity Baptist, and L. Joseph Brown, pastor of Berean Baptist Church. The Women's Auxiliary of the Brooklyn Howard Colored Orphan Asylum, established in 1904, was responsible for fund-raising and providing clothes and bed linen and "other comforts" for the children; members included Maritcha Lyons, Mrs. Charles Dorsey, and Verna Waller, wife of physician Owen Waller.[53]

The Black Middle Class and the Black Churches of Brooklyn

The institutions most clearly demonstrating the involvement of the black elite were the churches. Although there are few records for Brooklyn's black churches in the nineteenth and early twentieth centuries, available information strongly suggests that the black middle-class played a leading role in these institutions. Of the twenty officers of Siloam Presbyterian Church in 1899, twelve of the seventeen whose occupations could be ascertained were employed in middle-class and lower-middle-class positions, the majority as clerks. The board of trustees of Bridge Street AWME Church in 1918 was dominated by prominent middle-class men, including a real estate and insurance broker, a machinist, and the treasurer of the Howard orphanage. The secretary of the board, James E. Bruce, was listed by the Brooklyn Daily Eagle as a member of Brooklyn's "Colored 400." Of the twenty-four officers listed for Concord Baptist Church in 1918, only eleven could be identified by occupation. Eight of the eleven held middle-class positions, including six clerks, an undertaker, a realtor, and a carpenter. Of the five trustees whose names appear on the charter of Bethany Baptist Church, at least two had middle-class occupations—engineer and carpenter. Leading members of St. Augustine Episcopal Church included its founder William J. Delamar, Maritcha Lyons, and Mr. and Mrs. Charles A. Dorsey. It should be noted that some men held jobs in the larger community as janitors and servants while acting as officials of the church. This indicates that Brooklyn's black churches became important centers where classes could mix and working-class people in many cases could share positions of power with the elite.[54]

As middle-class blacks gained prominence in Brooklyn's black churches, they used these institutions to develop their own image as rational, urbane, literate community leaders, addressing the demands put on blacks in an urban society. They shaped the religious institutions to reflect the new urban setting, which demanded accommodation to values of the larger society. These churches emphasized a rational understanding of Christian traditions, elaborate ceremonial practices, an appreciation for architecture and music, seminary training for their ministers, and a deep concern for personal success, achievement, and liberal values in the secular world. Hence, secular concerns took on a greater significance.

There is evidence that black Baptist churches carried on some early Southern practices well into the twentieth century—rituals such as revivals, shouting, "falling out," and other ecstatic behavior. However, as in the white-affiliated denominations during the postbellum period, there was a trend toward formality, elaborate services, decorum, restraint, scholarly sermons, and architectural beauty. As Carter G. Woodson observed of African Methodist and Baptist churches in the late nineteenth century:

> Preaching became more of an appeal to the intellect than an effort to stir one's emotions. Sermons developed into efforts to minister to a need observed by careful consideration of

the circumstances of the persons served, hymns in keeping with the thought of the discourse harmonized therewith, and prayers became the occasion of thanksgiving for blessing which the intelligent pastor could lead his congregation to appreciate and of a petition for God's help to live more righteously.[55]

Architectural and interior beauty was an important expression of black church culture—a way to demonstrate an urbane, polished style of worship, identifiable with the European cathedrals. According to the minutes of the twenty-third Quadrennial of the General Conference of the African Methodist Episcopal Churches (1908): "Architecture is the art of building according to principles which are determined, not merely by the ends the edifice is intended to serve, but by consideration of beauty and harmony."[56] This was especially evident in the black churches of Brooklyn.

Through collective efforts, the black churches of Brooklyn organized building committees and sponsored fund-raisers to finance large brick Gothic structures with pointed arches, stained glass windows depicting biblical scenes, lavish outer carvings and interior designs, decorated altars, fancy wooden pews to accommodate hundreds, and elegant chapels.

Sometime between 1890 and 1914, during the pastorship of Rev. L. Joseph Brown, Berean Baptist Church on Bergen Street purchased a brick building with high arches, stained glass windows, and a small garden. Shortly thereafter, the church's building committee adopted a plan to add two elaborate wings to the church. St. Phillip's Protestant Episcopal also purchased a two-story castle with a large tower and stained glass windows. In 1899 St. Augustine Protestant Episcopal Church purchased St. Mary's Chapel on Canton Street, a large brick building with an extended entryway and high arched, stained glass windows. Moreover, at least six churches claimed that they had edifices that could seat three hundred or more worshipers.[57]

One of Brooklyn's most elegant churches was the Bridge Street AWME Church, located at 309 Bridge Street, formerly the estate of Edward and Margaret Pierrepont, who signed the property over to the First Congregational Church. In 1854 Bridge Street AWME bought the building from the First Congregational Church for $12,500. The church had two wooden pillars in the entrance porch and a "spacious gallery." The main hall seated twelve hundred people comfortably. The *New York Freeman* described the woodwork and upholstery as "substantial and neat." By the turn of the century Bridge Street had added a thirty-light chandelier, made of oxidized brass, to its decor.[58]

Great care was also given to the decoration of the churches to establish the proper atmosphere for Sunday morning worship. The *New York Globe* reported that on one Sunday morning the Bridge Street AWME Church had flowers that were "tastefully arranged.... The Bible desk was covered with beautiful white silk cover, trimmed on either side with silk cord and silk moss fringes. In the center was a cross of lilies of the valley. Behind the pulpit was suspended a large cross of choice flowers." The *New York Freeman* proclaimed that the flowers for a Sunday morning service at Siloam Presbyterian Church on Prince Street were "quite elaborate, perfuming the church with their fragrance." The First AME Zion Church of Williamsburg had a lecture room garnished with flowers; the major attraction was the pastor's harvest table located in the auditorium, "heavenly laden with choice fruits, flowers, vegetables, wheat, etc." Many churches established floral committees during the late nineteenth and early twentieth centuries.[59]

Lecture rooms were important cultural features as well as academic centers of the churches. Concord Baptist, Bridge Street AWME, First AME Zion of Williamsburg, Fleet Street AME Zion, and other elite black churches of Brooklyn built lecture rooms, which became centers of cultural events, lectures, literary endeavors, and classical music programs. Concord's lecture room was used for lectures by noted black figures such as journalist Ida B. Wells; T. Thomas Fortune, editor of the *New York Age*; and T. McCants Stewart, noted author, attorney, pastor, and organizer of numerous black literary societies. On several occasions, the Guitar and Mandolin Club of the local YMCA performed in the lecture room of the church.[60]

The stress on architectural and interior design reflected the new secularism of the black churches, an appreciation of aesthetic beauty and wealth. Parishioners saw their churches as places of beauty to be held in reverence, changing the idea of sacred space in black culture. Unlike earlier African Americans who had extended the spatial boundaries of the sacred, the black elite religious institutions limited it to a house of worship, giving the secular a greater role. They deemphasized the mystical and reinforced worldliness, materialism, and aesthetic beauty.

Like architecture, music was also intrinsic to the style of Brooklyn's black church worship. Although information about the music performed during services is limited, newspaper advertisements, announcements of church concerts, and church anniversary books give indications. In traditional African American Christianity, music was spiritual and participatory, involving singing, dancing, and shouting from the congregation as well as the performers: however, Brooklyn's black churches of the late nineteenth and early twentieth centuries incorporated European classical music (which was more temporal than spiritual), shunned congregational participation, and emphasized exactness in performance.[61]

On a Sunday service at Holy Trinity Baptist Church, the choir sang "anthems," while St. Augustine Protestant Episcopal Church began its Sunday service "promptly at 11" with the church choir singing "Onward Christian Soldiers." It was not uncommon for churches to sponsor recitals, cantatas, and concerts featuring prominent artists. During its centennial celebration in 1918, Bridge Street AWME featured two soprano solos and a violin performance. In a benefit concert held for Bridge Street, Nellie Brown, the famed New York soprano, sang "La Stella" by Arditi and the "The Last Rose of Summer." At one of its gatherings, the Concord Literary Circle featured a violin duet and a vocal performance of "Love's Golden Dream." An evening dinner held for the benefit of the Nazarene Congregational Church, featured a solo from C. C. Clarke, a baritone from Denver, Colorado; a performance from Professor Charles Johnson, a tenor from Brooklyn; and Edward Wood, violinist, also from Brooklyn.[62]

Moreover, the black churches relied on musical experts for polished and professional performances. All church choirs were trained by choir masters or musical experts. The *New York Age* noted in 1908 that "Chorister" Charles F. Monroe of Concord Baptist was busy training the voices of the church's choir while the music of St. Phillip's Protestant Episcopal was "making splendid progress under the direction of Mr. D. J. Edgeworth." Some choirmasters were even given the title "professor of music." On some occasions, choirs held competitions for the best performance. For example, in the summer of 1905, Bridge Street AWME, Fleet Street AME Zion, and Concord Baptist competed for the "silver cup" award for best performance. "Choir professor" W. B. Berry of Fleet, "Professor" Albert Myers of Concord Baptist, and "Professor Richardson," leader of Bridge Street AWME, were contestants. "All three choirs showed excellent training, but the honors of the evening were given to Concord."

The churches purchased large pipe organs and hired trained organists; among the best known was Dr. Susan McKinney, musical director of Bridge Street AWME Church, and the organists of the Turner Lyceum and the Siloam Presbyterian Church. The music of Bach, Handel, and Brahms set the tone for Sunday services in some churches. Recalling an earlier period, before gospel music became a dominant force at Berean Missionary Baptist Church, Myra Gregory, a member of the church since 1913, noted that Baroque music was commonly heard.[63]

Music was no longer a participatory ritual but a performance that parishioners appreciated solely for its artistic value. Parishioners responded to performances as though they were attending concerts. Instead of the traditional African American response of clapping and shouting to music, they listened and applauded at the end of the performance. Describing a concert given by the Hyers Sisters at a black church in Brooklyn on August 18, 1884, the *New York Globe* reported that the audience "attentively listened and were enthusiastic in their applause." The *New York Freeman* described a benefit concert for Bridge Street AWME Church as a financial success and noted that the audience was "an appreciative one" and "applause and encores were generously bestowed."[64]

The black churches also moved toward a well-trained ministry. Early on, the black Presbyterian, Episcopal, and Congregational denominations required their ministers to receive seminary training at institutions such as Fisk University in Tennessee, Trinity in Alabama, Lincoln in Pennsylvania, and Biddle in North Carolina.[65]

This educational requirement was later established in the African Methodist churches. As early as the 1840s, AME state conferences passed resolutions calling for the establishment of seminaries. The first significant African Methodist school was Wilberforce in Ohio, established in 1856. Less than three decades later other schools followed, including Allen College in Columbia, South Carolina, Morris Brown in Atlanta, Georgia, and Paul Quinn in Waco, Texas. Due to the shortage of trained ministers, the AME established a rotation policy by which the few educated ministers circulated among the congregations. In 1908 the twenty-third Quadrennial General Conference of the AME called for a well-trained ministry:

> If proper endeavors are not put forth there is great and impending danger of the respectability and influence of our Church being seriously lessened. The constant advancement of culture in the pew renders absolutely imperative the demand for equal advancement of culture in the pulpit. We are persuaded that our ministry is so well aware of these truths that no argument is needed to enforce the admonition to scrutinize with care the candidates for admission to our Conference and to insist on a high standard of qualification.[66]

Although the Baptists did not have general educational requirements for ordination, the elite Baptist churches became discriminating. Before the Civil War, institutions run by other denominations educated the elite. Historian Carter G. Woodson notes that both Lincoln and Biddle (Presbyterian colleges) graduated men who later joined both Methodist and Baptist churches probably because there were more Methodist and Baptist churches, thus less competition for ministerial positions. However, after the Civil War, the Baptists established their own educational institutions to train ministers, such as Shaw University in Raleigh in 1865, Morehouse in Atlanta and Roger Williams in Nashville in 1867, and others.[67]

Among Brooklyn's notable educated Baptist ministers were Francis Blair of Bethany Baptist Church, who received both his B.A. and Ph.D. from Lincoln University; Rufus L. Perry, who received his Ph.D in theology from Michigan Seminary; William T. Dixon of Concord Baptist Church, a former school teacher and principal who graduated from Arkansas University; S. E. Lee of Shiloh Baptist Church, who held a B.D. from Virginia Seminary.[68]

As more educated clergy appeared in Brooklyn's black church pulpits, their sermons became scholarly. A detailed analysis of sermons of the late nineteenth and early twentieth centuries is difficult since virtually none survived. However, the black press of New York did occasionally summarize sermons delivered by Brooklyn black ministers, providing some evidence. These sermons were not impromptu speeches but well-planned, scholarly, biblical lessons based on an exegetical outline. Citing a biblical passage and critically analyzing it, the preacher would usually conclude with practical applications. This approach cut across denominational lines: Presbyterian, Protestant Episcopal, Congregational, African Methodist, and Baptist churches.

A sermon delivered by Rev. J. W. Gloucester at Bridge Street AWME illustrates the style. Selecting his text from the thirtieth chapter of Deuteronomy, Gloucester told the congregation that Moses presented "life with its attendant blessings to people, as the condition of proper obedience to the divine law; or death with its curses as a result of disobedience" and cautioned the parishioners to choose. Gloucester contended that "man possesses the ability to choose right or wrong; to accept Christ or reject him."[69]

The emphasis on scholarship rather than emotion was evident in the weekly press descriptions. The newspapers referred to the sermons as "informative discourses," "scholarly," "practical," "full of instruction," and "eloquent." For example, the *New York Globe* described a sermon given by Rev. C. C. Astwood at Bridge Street AWME as "an intelligent and pertinent discourse." A sermon by Rev. L. Joseph Brown, pastor of Berean Baptist, was described by the *New York Age* as "scholarly and instructive."[70]

Besides being scholarly, the ministers' sermons of the elite black churches possessed a moral and ethical dimension. Unlike early African American Christianity, where one came to God through a mystical or emotional experience, the ministers of these churches stressed that one reached God through knowledge and reason.

In addition, the ministers never lost their zeal for politics; however, they were much more accommodating of the cultural hegemony of the dominant society. Ministers of the elite black churches advocated a mainstream approach: individuals must actively improve their lives in this world. Many preachers focused on proper behavior, ethics, and hard work as a means of improving the moral character of African Americans, not as a requirement for heaven but for a successful existence on earth.

27

Dr. Rufus Perry's sermon at Bridge Street AWME entitled "Our Progress" illustrates this point. Perry contended that, twenty years after emancipation, blacks had made strides in the fields of real estate, business, journalism, and religion through hard work. He urged blacks to continue to work hard in order to progress as a race. In another example, a Sunday morning sermon given in 1886 by Rev. Dickerson of Siloam Presbyterian Church pointed out the progress of blacks. Entitled "Prospects of the Colored People of the South," Dickerson spoke of the "noble men of the race," referring to Richard Allen, founder of the African Methodist Episcopal Church, and John Gloucester, founder of black Presbyterianism. He reminded people of African origins that they had a great historical past, and he encouraged them to improve their status through hard work.[71] While the black church was adopting a Eurocentric culture, the minister's role was changing drastically. In African American evangelical Protestantism, the preacher shared control of the worship with his congregation. The ministers of the black elite religious institutions were for the most part seminary-trained professionals, helping parishioners gain an understanding of the Bible and Christian doctrine necessary for salvation. In some sense, the pastor became an intermediary between God and the individual, thus decreasing the congregation's active involvement in service.

Literary Societies and the Push for Moral and Social Uplift

Some of the most important organizations within the black churches of the late nineteenth and early twentieth centuries were literary societies. The organizers and members of these societies promoted erudition, hoping to challenge the notion of black inferiority and to define blacks as rational human beings, able to appreciate literature, to think abstractly, and to advance socially and economically.

The Brooklyn Literary Union of Siloam Presbyterian Church, organized in 1886, became one of the most well-known societies in Brooklyn. Soon after the establishment of the Brooklyn Literary Union, other literary groups were formed, including Concord Baptist Church's Literary Circle, St. Augustine Protestant Episcopal's Literary Sinking Fund, Nazarene Congregational Church's Literary Society, Union Bethel AME's Young People's Literary

Society, Bridge Street AWME's Turner Lyceum, St. John's African Methodist Episcopal's Star Lyceum, and Fleet Street AME Zion's Progressive Literary Union.[72]

These societies sponsored debates, lectures, elocution contests, recitations, musical recitals, and discussions of pertinent issues facing black America. At a meeting of the Concord Literary Circle, attended by publisher T. Thomas Fortune and Rev. Rufus Perry, attorney William Edwards spoke on "Improvement: The Order of the Age." At another Literary Circle program, the *Brooklyn Daily Eagle* reported that journalist Ida B. Wells spoke about the "Afro-American in Literature." Mrs. E. Saville Jones sang "L'incontra," H. H. Butler sang "I'll Await Your Smiling Face," and Miss Helen Thompson "read a very commendable essay on Patriotism." At the Literary and Sinking Fund Society of St. Augustine Protestant Episcopal Church, a member read from Mark Twain, and a violin solo and singing duets were performed. Referring to Brooklyn's black church literary groups, the *Brooklyn Daily Eagle* contended that "there is no other city in the union that possesses as intelligent a community of young people as the City of Churches."[73]

The Brooklyn Literary Union's constitution and by-laws indicated a high level of organization, sophistication, and intelligence. The group, meeting the first and third Tuesdays of each month from eight to ten in the evening, followed a prescribed agenda that included singing and prayer, reading of the minutes, report of the board of managers, and literary exercises (lectures, reading of papers, debates, and general business). According to its constitution, either the group's president or an invited guest was obliged to give a lecture. Anyone giving a paper or participating in a debate had to follow certain guidelines.

1. No paper read before the Union shall exceed twenty minutes, except by special vote.
2. In stated debates there shall be four disputants, each of whom shall be limited to ten minutes, and there shall be no transfer to time.
3. All papers and stated debates shall be followed by a general discussion, which shall not exceed forty-five minutes: and stated debates shall be decided in the affirmative or negative by vote of the Union.[74]

Brooklyn's black elite was active in the literary societies. The Brooklyn Literary Union included among its distinguished honorary members Frederick Douglass and author and poet Frances E. W. Harper. Its officers included attorney and minister T. McCants Stewart, who was president of the union, and publisher T. Thomas Fortune; the board of directors included Professor Charles A. Dorsey and Maritcha Lyons, both principals of Brooklyn "colored" schools; M. P. Saunders, treasurer of the Howard orphanage's industrial school; Frederick B. Watkins, listed along with Charles A. Dorsey as a member of Brooklyn's "Colored 400"; C. H. Lang, also a member of Brooklyn's "400" and one of its wealthiest black residents; and Dr. Susan McKinney. Other members included Rev. William T. Dixon and Rev. Rufus Perry.

The chairman of the board of the Turner Lyceum was Walter S. Durham, an accomplished singer. The president of the Star Lyceum was R. M. Brown, a general commission and export merchant; and J. Howard Wilson, president of the Progressive Literary Union, was a member of Brooklyn's "400."[75]

The organizers and members of these literary societies saw themselves as part of what W. E. B. Du Bois called the "Talented Tenth," the best and brightest of the race, obligated to uplift the black masses by exposing them to the best literature, music, oratory, and keeping them informed on the issues that confronted the race. The *New York Age*, published by T. Thomas Fortune, a major organizer of New York's literary societies, contended that the masses of blacks were in "need of the superior contact which an intellectual and enlightened mind can give. . . . Those of the race who have had intellectual and mental training are to be the levers with which the masses are to be lifted. A literary society in Brooklyn organized with a view to the mental uplift of the community is an imperative necessity."[76]

Using culture to lift the underprivileged was not unique to black churches but was part of a larger movement in the late nineteenth and early twentieth centuries. A wave of new immigrants, mainly from eastern and southern Europe, as well as blacks from the southern part of the United States, moved to northern cities, replacing a mostly white native-born work force and bringing their own unique cultures into the workplace and urban centers. The period witnessed the formation of labor unions and the rise of dime novels and other forms of popular culture. According to historian Daniel Walker Howe, the American gentry was "mostly middle-class, mostly Whig-Republican, literary men and women," who wanted to humanize the new industrial-capitalist order by "infusing it with a measure of social responsibility, strict personal morality, and respect for cultural standards."[77]

This middle-class esteemed Victorian virtues—hard work, sobriety, sexual repression, and the postponement of personal gratification—as a means of molding the new work force. Lawrence Levine notes that museums, art galleries, opera houses, theaters, and symphony halls became "active agents in teaching their audiences to adjust to the new social imperatives in urging them to separate public behavior from private feelings, in keeping a strict reign over their emotional and physical process."[78]

The churches emphasized that blacks could accomplish the best in art, literature, intellectual pursuits, and music; they went against a wave of opinion contending that blacks were mentally and morally inferior. Through a flood of pseudoscientific literature, songs, magazines, motion pictures, and other forms of popular culture, people of African descent were portrayed as innately shiftless, lazy, childish, stupid, amoral, oversexed, violent, beastly, as natural gamblers, and as dangers to American society.[79]

D. W. Griffith's *Birth of a Nation* (1915) is a good example of this type of propaganda. Based on Thomas Dixon's 1902 novel *The Klansman*, the film portrays Africans liberated from the domesticating influence of slavery as beasts. Once the loyal Black servants team up with the notorious carpetbaggers, they destroy the social fabric of the South. Black Union soldiers beat up decent white Southerners; black brutes lust after and attempt to rape white Southern women, and black mobs kill anyone who stands in their way. Once blacks gain control of South Carolina's state legislature, they make a mockery of the legislative process. Black buffoons eat chicken, drink whiskey, take their shoes off and pick their feet, and horrify whites by passing a bill that legalizes interracial marriages.[80]

The popular image of African Americans as brutish and dangerous had political implications. Southern states disenfranchised African Americans, amending their constitutions and adopting various voting qualifications such as the grandfather clause, the poll tax, and the white primary. States and local governments passed legislation segregating public facilities as a means of excluding blacks from the larger society. These regulations, popularly known as Jim Crow laws, denied African Americans equal access to railroads, schools, libraries, hotels, hospitals, restaurants, parks, playgrounds, water fountains, toilets, and cemeteries. The North also imposed restrictive covenants; neighborhood improvement associations, municipal ordinances, and blockbusting by realtors forced blacks into Northern ghettos.[81]

This pattern was not limited to local governments. Between 1873 and 1898, the U.S. Supreme Court voted to strip African Americans of their constitutional rights. In the Slaughter House cases of 1873, the Court voted to curtail privileges and immunities protected by the Fourteenth Amendment, giving states the green light to restrict the rights of blacks. In 1883 the Court declared the 1875 Civil Rights Act unconstitutional because the Fourteenth Amendment did not grant Congress the power to outlaw discrimination practiced by individuals. In 1898 the Court ruled that separate-but-equal facilities were constitutional in *Plessy v. Ferguson*. Such decisions sent a clear message across the nation that the highest judicial body would not oppose the crusade to lock blacks into a caste system.

Violence was also used as a means to enforce Jim Crow. Between 1886 and 1900 twenty-five hundred people were lynched, the great majority of them Southern blacks. From 1900 to World War I, eleven hundred blacks were lynched in the United States. Moreover, an epidemic of race riots hit both Northern and Southern cities, including Atlanta, Brownsville, Texas, East St. Louis, and Chicago.[82]

To suggest that struggle can take only one form limits our understanding of the human reaction to oppressive conditions. Wilmore and others who argue that black churches did little to oppose racial oppression ignore culture as a mode of resistance. In a racist environment, the black churches promoted social equality and human rights for African people. As arbiters of culture, the black churches attempted to create an image of African Americans as intelligent, scholarly, and artistically accomplished within the terms the dominant white culture had set. This image directly challenged the mainstream racist view of blacks as beastly, lazy, childlike, stupid, and menacing. By making their churches literary and artistic arenas, these religious institutions countered the popular stereotype of blacks. The strategy used by the black churches was a race-conscious solution stressing pride in the ability of blacks to achieve success in the larger society.

In their crusade for a cultural hierarchy, black churches took any deviation as illegitimate and, therefore, intolerable. Insisting on proper behavior and correct leisure activities for the masses, they viewed with disdain many earlier aspects of African American religion, particularly emotionalism. Sometimes they scornfully ridiculed African Americans who still practiced them. This resentment was expressed at the thirty-fifth annual National Baptist Convention:

> Then there is a third class representing quite ten thousand, who are simply cutting didoes and bellowing like an untamed animal of the Balaam specie while their thousands of followers scream like they are being stung by wasps, and shout until the building rocks in self-defence. Men of this type have no business in the pulpit. They split churches, break up homes and demoralize the communities in which they live and move and have their being. The poor people put their money into church property, pay the pastors' salaries, but have no knowledge of the real work of the Church of God. Their dilapidated, ramshackle, greasy buildings are parodies on clean, restful, sacred places, where the people, like David, are glad to go to meet God.[83]

High church culture probably attracted many southern black migrants and working-class blacks. Most African Methodist and Baptist churches increased in membership between 1900 and 1920, while the white-affiliated denominations grew slightly or decreased in membership. However, by the end of the 1920s practically all churches including Siloam, Nazarene, St. Augustine, and St. Phillip's had grown.

When black churches defined legitimate culture through their literary societies, educated clergy, and scholarly sermons, they denied the full variety of religious expression, making many feel uncomfortable and unwelcome. Some sought other religious forms, such as Holiness-Pentecostal churches, the earliest of which appeared in Brooklyn in the early 1900s; they increased dramatically during the heavy black influx of the 1930s.

33

Although the churches stressed uplift and challenged social Darwinism, they failed to provide a stronger critique of an oppressive white society that had relegated most blacks to the lowest economic and social positions in society. The strategy of uplift put the burden of improving the conditions of African Americans on the victims. Social and moral uplift assumed that the reason for failure of black people was because they lacked the ingredients for improvement. This was a no-win tactic, especially for poor blacks struggling in a system that denied them social and economic success. Moral and social uplift was a class-bias solution that could not effectively counter a racist and oppressive society bent on dehumanizing blacks. The churches needed to give a stronger critique of the larger society and to challenge the forces of discrimination collectively. By the 1930s new religious institutions would appeal to the growing working-class black population of Brooklyn by offering them just such a stronger critique of the dominant society.

CHAPTER TWO

The Rise of Black Holiness-Pentecostal Culture in Brooklyn

> But when the Lord saves you He burns out the old Adam, He gives you a new mind and a new heart and then you don't find no pleasure in the world, you get all your joy in walking and talking with Jesus every day.
>
> —Elisha speaking to John in James Baldwin's *Go Tell It on the Mountain* (p. 54)

In 1947 New York City's *Amsterdam News* reported that the Christian Antioch Apostolic Church of God in Christ on Fulton Street had celebrated its sixteenth anniversary. This Holiness-Pentecostal church was the first of many established in the United States by Samuel Williams, who was given the title of bishop by the religious organization.[1]

Eleven years later an *Amsterdam News* article reported the death of Greenwood Dudley of Brooklyn, who had been a deacon since 1909 in the Church of God and Saints on Gates Avenue in Brooklyn. Although the article does not mention a denomination, the church was most likely Holiness-Pentecostal. The name of the Church of God and Saints is usually associated with that denomination, and the article refers to the pastor as an evangelist, a title used by Holiness-Pentecostal groups.[2]

These two news articles point out that by the 1930s Brooklyn's mainline black churches were not its only religious institutions. As the black population increased, the major denominations began sharing space with other religious groups, including Holiness-Pentecostals. Most scholars who write on Brooklyn ignore the existence of Holiness-Pentecostal groups or label them as mere storefronts.

It is a mistake to so label Holiness-Pentecostal religious institutions without making distinctions among denominations. Moreover, many black churches in Brooklyn started as storefronts, in someone's apartment, or as a small operation. Included among those with modest beginnings were Concord Baptist, Cornerstone Baptist, Brown Memorial Baptist, Holy Trinity Baptist, Mount Sinai Baptist, Mount Lebanon Baptist, Bethany Baptist, and St. Phillip's Protestant Episcopal. In his 1931 study, George Hobart uncovered sixty-eight storefronts, including twenty-four Baptists, one Protestant Episcopal, one African Methodist Episcopal, and one Methodist. Yet to label all Holiness-Pentecostal churches as storefronts is misleading, for by the mid-1950s some of these churches in Brooklyn were well-established institutions with large edifices, claiming hundreds of members.[3]

As the twentieth century progressed and Brooklyn's black population increased, Holiness-Pentecostal churches grew dramatically, attracting mostly the working poor. They became the fastest-growing religious institutions in the black community. Their growth raises many questions. What do we know of these organizations? Why did they grow? What was the relationship between these institutions and the socioeconomic conditions of Brooklyn's black working class? This chapter examines these questions and presents the cultural and social significance of black Holiness-Pentecostal churches in Brooklyn. Holiness-Pentecostalism stressed a doctrine of otherworldliness, a belief that members should divorce themselves from secular activities and attempt to live a life without sin. This did not mean that Holiness-Pentecostalism was apolitical. The struggle for power takes place on many levels and in many arenas. The otherworldliness doctrine was used by black people in Brooklyn in order to resist an attempt to dehumanize them by the larger white society. Black Holiness-Pentecostal culture countered the cultural hegemonic order by promoting a theory of human value giving African Americans an alternative avenue to gain status and self-esteem. Although it offered a critique of the values of the dominant society, black Holiness-Pentecostals promoted a strict code of behavior that helped instill certain values of a capitalist society. Black Holiness-Pentecostal culture both resisted and accommodated the dominant culture.

Origins of the Holiness-Pentecostal Churches

The Holiness movement in the United States had its origins in the post–Civil War South. It was sparked by a growing dissatisfaction with the movement toward a refined way of worshiping in the established mainline churches, especially the Baptist and Methodist denominations. Many accused the mainline churches of moving away from God by promoting secular activities. Holiness followers based their belief on John Wesley's notion of a "second blessing" by God. It is the belief that through divine grace and the will of the believer, he or she could reach the state of sanctification or sinlessness.[4] In 1867 a group of white ministers of various denominations, who advocated living a life of holiness, "heart religion," and "spirited congregational singing," modest dressing, and dwelling in the Holy Spirit, held a camp meeting at Vineland, New Jersey, and formed the National Holiness Association. Calling for a return to Christian fundamentalism, Association ministers held revivals that helped spread Holiness beliefs throughout the nation, especially the South. By the 1890s a number of "comeouters" (people who had left the Methodist Church) formed their own denominations, traveled, and held camp fire meetings advocating "theological and ethical purity." They became a significant element in the Holiness movement. Eventually some of these groups became Pentecostals, emphasizing emotional behavior such as shouting, crying, and fainting. They claimed that the baptism of the Holy Spirit, manifested by speaking in tongues of men or angels, was an essential experience in the lives of the faithful.[5]

Anthropologists Hans Baer and Merrill Singer as well as others have noted that the distinction made between white Holiness and Pentecostals may not apply to African Americans.

> Specific Black religions refer to themselves as either "Holiness" or "Pentecostal," but the distinction between the two forms is not clear-cut from a social-scientific perspective. As Washington observes, "Whether they are identified as Holiness or Pentecostal, the roots of these groups are identical." Indeed, within the African American community, there is a strong tendency to lump these two categories together by referring to them as "Sanctified churches."[6]

By the turn of the century, African Americans became a major force in the formation of the Holiness-Pentecostal movement. Several founders of Holiness-Pentecostal sects were former Baptist ministers who complained about the inertia in the religious services of their churches and advocated a personal experience with God. They stressed experiencing the spiritual baptism of the Holy Ghost (the belief that the Holy Spirit dwells in believers). This spiritual baptism was manifested by speaking in tongues, dancing, shouting, uncontrollable body movements, and other forms of ecstatic behavior.

A prominent figure in the Holiness-Pentecostal movement was William J. Seymour, born in Centerville, Louisiana, in 1870. Seymour received little formal education. Although little is known about his early religious development, sometime in 1900 Seymour moved to Cincinnati, Ohio, and came under the influence of the Evening Light Saints, a Holiness sect that traveled through-

out the South spreading its message. After confessing and asserting that he was sanctified, attempting to live a life without sin, he
was baptized by the Evening Light Saints and became a traveling
evangelist.[7]

Seymour was probably influenced by the teachings of Charles
Parham, a white Holiness minister from Kansas who established
a Bible school in Topeka in 1900 and conducted revivals in the
South. Parham later established another Bible school in Houston,
Texas, in 1906. Seymour applied to Parham's Bible school to gain
greater religious training. Parham, a segregationist, refused to let
Seymour attend classes or study with his white students in the
main classrooms. According to a Seymour scholar, E. Myron
Noble, Seymour and other blacks "were sent to an anteroom
where they could hear lessons taught through an adjoining
door." It was probably at Parham's school that Seymour adopted
the idea that speaking in tongues was evidence of the baptism of
the Holy Spirit, an idea advocated by Parham and his students in
1900.[8]

In 1906 Seymour was invited by an acquaintance to preach at a
Holiness church in Los Angeles. Seymour accepted the invitation,
but his advocacy of speaking in tongues caused the church leader
to deny him further access to the building, forcing him to seek
another place to conduct services in that city. After Seymour was
denied access to the church, a husband and wife, members of the
church, invited him to hold services in their home, and several
people claimed to have received the Spirit and spoke in tongues.
Seymour attracted an enormous following and was forced to seek
larger quarters. The preacher found an abandoned building on
Azusa Street where he conducted a huge Pentecostal revival,
receiving press attention and attracting people throughout the
nation. This event, known popularly as the Azusa movement,
although not the first recorded act of the baptism of the Holy Spirit and speaking in tongues among black Holiness-Pentecostals,
was significant because it attracted crowds nationwide, lasted for
three years, and motivated others in the Holiness-Pentecostal
movement to adopt Seymour's message.[9]

Other African Americans, including Charles Harrison Mason
and Charles Price Jones, organized Holiness-Pentecostal churches. Mason, born in Tennessee in 1866, became a Baptist minister
in 1893 and established a Baptist church in Arkansas. Soon after

this, Mason became discouraged with "the strict Calvinistic teachings of the Baptist faith" and left the denomination in search of a closer relationship with God. He traveled to Mississippi, where he soon came under the influence of Charles P. Jones and other black ministers who advocated sanctification or living a holy life at all times, and divine healing. In 1896 Mason and Jones founded the Church of God, and in 1897 the name of the religious group was changed to the Church of God in Christ (COGIC).

Hearing of the Azusa Mission, Mason visited the revival in 1907 and accepted the tenets of Holiness-Pentecostal doctrine, including speaking in tongues, the washing of the feet of the saints (which was a sign of reverence and respect for those considered holy), and divine healing. The doctrine of speaking in tongues divided Mason and Jones; eventually the latter left COGIC and formed a new religious group.[10]

Jones, born in Georgia in 1865, became a Baptist minister in the late 1880s. By 1894 Jones became dissatisfied with his own personal experience and began adopting the beliefs and practices of the Holiness movement, such as sanctification and the outpouring of the Spirit, while attempting to remain a Baptist preacher. His Baptist brethren (at a regional meeting) voted him out of the Baptist Association. After fasting and praying, Jones responded to his ouster by calling for a convention of all those interested in Holiness. Jones eventually merged with other "sanctified" groups from Virginia, North Carolina, Tennessee, and Kentucky and formed the Church of Christ Holiness.[11]

Black Holiness-Pentecostal groups were also influenced by the racial attitudes of white Holiness-Pentecostal organizations. The Church of God in Christ started as an interracial group. However, whites who were ordained as COGIC ministers and who did not want to be under black control formed their own Pentecostal group, Assemblies of God in 1914 in Hot Springs, Arkansas. The Pentecostal Assemblies of the World (PAW) and the Fire Baptized Holiness Church of God of the Americas are also good illustrations. Founded as an interracial body sometime during or right after the Azusa movement, and advocating sanctification and speaking in tongues, the PAW experienced a change in racial composition during the 1920s. Blacks, many migrating from the South, joined the ranks of the PAW. Motivated by racism, many white members left and formed a new organization called Pentecostal Churches, Inc. Although claiming to be an interracial body, by the 1930s the PAW was dominated by blacks.[12]

A racial split caused the formation of the Fire Baptized Holiness Church of God of the Americas. During its early history it was an association of the predominantly white sect, the Pentecostal Fire-Baptized Holiness Church, formed in the last decade of the nineteenth century. According to census records, Fire Baptized Holiness Church of God of the Americas was established as an independent body because of the "growing prejudice that began to arise among the people outside" against the association. In 1908 the association and the larger organization agreed to separate.[13]

By the middle of the twentieth century, there were numerous black Holiness-Pentecostal or "sanctified" groups. Some of the most well known were the United Holy Church of America, Pentecostal Assemblies of the World, Free Church of God and Christ, Church of Christ Holiness USA, Church of God and Saints of Christ, United Holy Church of America, Inc., Mount Calvary Holy Church of America, Inc., the Church of the Living God, House of Prayer for All People, Church of Our Lord Jesus, United Pentecostal Council of the Assemblies of God, Inc., Pure Holiness Church of God, Glorious Church of God in Christ Apostolic Faith, Churches of the Apostolic Faith Association, and Apostolic Overcoming Holy Church of God.[14]

Despite the differences in black Holiness-Pentecostal groups, they adhered to similar doctrine and practiced common rituals. All asserted that the Bible was the highest authority. Like mainstream Protestant denominations, all black Holiness groups claimed that their doctrine, including baptism of the Holy Spirit, speaking in tongues, faith healing, sanctification, and other tenets of Holiness doctrine, was based on the scriptures. Moreover, the Bible was used to justify the restrictive lifestyle that many Holiness groups adopted, including dress codes, dietary restrictions, and the taboo on recreational activities. They attacked practices of mainstream churches, claiming that they were not "scriptural." As the Pentecostal Assemblies of the World note: "The denomination stresses belief in the inspiration of the Scriptures, as the only sufficient rule of faith and practice, and does not practice, and does not emphasize systematic theology." While the Fire Baptized Holiness Church of God of the Americas "utterly opposes the teachings of the so-called Christian Scientists, Spiritualists, Unitarians, Universalists, and the Mormons, it denies as false and unscriptural, Adventism, immorality, antinomianism, annihilation of the wicked, the glorification of the body, and many other modern teachings of the day."[15]

Black Holiness-Pentecostal groups accept the universal Protestant concepts of repentance and conversion with rebirth when a person accepts Jesus as his saviour. They believe that, to be saved, a person must accept the tenets of faith, acknowledge a past sinful life, and resolve to lead a new life. The believer "dies," letting go of his old sinful practices and beliefs, and is reborn as a Christian, beginning a new spiritual life. He is in the world but not part of the world.[16]

Closely related to conversion is the concept of sanctification, a spiritual maturing beyond conversion. In this ongoing process the converted attempt to live a "Holiness-Pentecostal" life, free of sin and the pleasures of this world, and to follow the teachings of the scriptures. The believer becomes "sanctified" or "pure" and prepares for the baptism of the Holy Spirit, to save the soul from eternal damnation.[17]

After conversion and sanctification comes the baptism of the Holy Spirit. The Holiness-Pentecostals claim that the Holy Spirit enters the body of the sanctified. According to Holiness-Pentecostal groups, this is the ultimate level a believer can reach because God has taken over the body as a sacred temple. As scholar and theologian William Lovett asserts: "It is the baptism where Jesus, the baptizer, exercises his sovereign will, control and possession of us through the person of the Holy Spirit." The believer becomes a stronger witness for Christ.[18]

As noted earlier, the manifestation of the baptism of the Holy Spirit is speaking in tongues (or glossolalia). The practice of glossolalia among black Holiness-Pentecostal groups had its origins in the Azusa movement. Groups such as the Pentecostal Assemblies of the World, Church of God in Christ, Church of Our Lord Jesus Christ of the Apostolic Faith, and the Fire Baptized Holiness Church of God of the Americas assert that a sanctified person may be taken over by the Holy Spirit, leading to a trance or an altered state of consciousness. The believer is said to have no control over his body and begins speaking in a foreign language or a language of "angels." The Church of God in Christ contends that "speaking in new tongues" and the gift of healing, proof of the miracles of God, are a consequence of the baptism of the Holy Spirit.[19]

Many other practices and rituals of black Holiness-Pentecostal groups are also very similar. Although the songs of the Holiness-Pentecostal churches were written in the style of hymns and anthems during their early years, they were upbeat, similar in tempo to jazz and the blues, encouraging clapping in time with the music. This music, referred to as gospel music by the late 1920s, promoted participation and recaptured African American Christian rituals practiced during slavery. Call and response, an antiphonal practice, was used (and is still used today). It is a dialogue between singers and their audience. The singer or singers shout, sing, or state a word or phrase, and the congregation responds to the singers by singing, shouting, and dancing. It is not unusual for singers and members of the congregation to claim possession of the Holy Spirit and speak in tongues. In *Protest and Praise*, Jon Spencer notes that singing in the early black Pentecostal churches was "tongue singing":

> During the Azusa Revival the activity that further differentiated Pentecostalism was "singing in the spirit' or singing in tongues. Indeed tongue-singing had occurred previously among such religious groups as the Shakers and Mormons, but only during the Second Pentecost did it procure a well-wrought interpretation that secured worldwide promulgation through Pentecostal publications.[20]

Early Pentecostals contended that the Holy Spirit filled the church, taking possession of the parishioners and leading them to sing in glossolalia. Jennie Moore, a participant in the Azusa Revival asserted that during the Revival she was led by the "Spirit" and sang in tongues. "I sang under the power of the Spirit in many languages, the interpretation both words and music I had never before heard."[21]

Lawrence Levine notes the significance of the music of the Holiness-Pentecostal churches:

> While many churches within the black community sought respectability by turning their backs on the past, banning the shout, discouraging enthusiastic religion, and adopting

more sedate hymns and refined, concertized versions of the spirituals, the Holiness churches constituted a revitalization movement with their emphasis upon healing, gifts of prophecy, speaking in tongues, spirit possession, and religious dance. Musically, they reached back to the traditions of the slave past and out to the rhythms of the secular black musical world around them. They brought into the church not only the sounds of ragtime, blues and jazz but also the instruments. They accompanied the singing which played a central role in their services with drums, tambourines, triangles, guitars, double basses, saxophones, trumpets, trombones, and whatever else seemed musically appropriate.[22]

However, the music of black Holiness-Pentecostal churches, unlike the slave spirituals which concentrated on the Old Testament, focused on the New Testament and the key role Jesus played in salvation. This was illustrated in Bishop Garfield Thomas Haywood's "Jesus the Son of God," written in 1915:

God gave Him a ransom, Our souls to recover, Jesus the
Son of God. His blood made us worthy His Spirit to hover;
Jesus the Son of God.[23]

The message of black Holiness-Pentecostal music was also therapeutic, relieving the hardships of the poor in the secular world by promising them a better life if they put their trust in the Lord. The saved did not have to worry about the lack of material wealth, as illustrated by Charles Price Jones's 1900 composition, "I'm Happy with Jesus Alone":

There's nothing so precious as Jesus to me;
Let earth with its treasures be gone;
I'm rich as can be when my Saviour I see;
I'm happy with Jesus alone. I'm happy with Jesus alone,
I'm happy with Jesus alone; Tho poor and deserted,
    thank God,
I can say I'm happy with Jesus alone.[24]

Songwriters of the early Holiness-Pentecostal church wrote in a style of personal testimony, sometimes using the first person to describe the power and goodness of Jesus. Titles such as Theodore Harris's "I Owe My All to Jesus," Charles W. Williams's "I Feel

Like Going On," Charles Price Jones's "Jesus Has Made It All Right," R. C. Lawson's "God Is Great in My Soul," and Mrs. S. K. Grimes's "Since the Comforter Came" all reveal the testimonial nature of these songs. Mary Tyler's study of 104 gospel songs of Charles Henry Pace, an early pioneer of Pentecostalism, claimed that many of the songs were personal testimonies as well as personal counsel to listeners.[25]

The lyrics of Mrs. S. K. Grimes's "Jesus" illustrate the bond believers had with their Christ:

> When I was bow'd by distress and grief, Jesus, the Joy of my soul came to my heart and brought sweet relief, Jesus, the Joy of my soul.[26]

In another shared practice, Holiness-Pentecostal sermons also involved the participation of the congregation. Pastors of Holiness-Pentecostal churches attempt to evoke a response from the congregation by using numerous methods such as shouting, raising their voices, singing and dancing for the Lord, and the repetition of key phrases. In his study of black metropolitan religious forms, Arthur Fauset describes one such sermon at the Mount Sinai Holy Church of America, Inc., in Philadelphia:

> If the preacher senses that her words are not getting over, or that there is a lassitude creeping over the congregation, she will cry out, "Help me!" or she will plead, "Holy Ghost, speak through me!" At various times during the sermon a single member or a group of members will rise suddenly and speak in tongues and perhaps dance about either in place or through the hall.[27]

However, like music, sermons represented more than a form of collective worship. Holiness-Pentecostal sermons were testimonies revealing a personal relationship between the believer and God. In some cases, the person was on the brink of death and God was said to have stepped in to demonstrate his powers and love by rescuing the individual. R. C. Lawson contended that after living a sinful life and developing a deadly case of tuberculosis, he turned to God and was healed. The founder of the Church of Our Lord Jesus Christ (COOLJC) testified to his congregation that God had taken him through a special journey. "God had a way of bringing me. He had to strip me first, He had to bring me out of the crowd and into the Church, He had to pull me out of the world, He had a way of doing it." As a teenage preacher, Bishop Smallwood Williams wrote that "other times I introduced my evangelistic sermons with a personal testimony of my preteen experience of salvation by saying `After spending twelve long years in sin, God saved me.'"[28]

Along with music and sermons, testimonials are common in Holiness-Pentecostal churches as a means of reinforcing beliefs. During the testimonial period, members take turns speaking to the congregation of the blessings they have received from God and how He has worked miracles. Testimony is also antiphonal, involving a response from the congregation as a member "gives testimony."[29]

Black Holiness-Pentecostal Churches in Brooklyn

As blacks migrated to the North they attempted to create a viable community life, building institutions that expressed their customs and traditions. These included the Holiness-Pentecostal churches. In *Black Chicago*, Allan Spear notes: "Of all aspects of community life, religious activities were most profoundly changed by the migration." According to Spear, migrants established a large number of Holiness-Pentecostal churches: "The migration, however, brought into the city thousands of Negroes accustomed to the informal, demonstrative, preacher-oriented churches of the rural South. Alienated by the formality of the middle-class churches, many of the newcomers organized small congregations that met in stores and houses and that maintained the old-time shouting religion."[30]

Like Chicago and other urban areas with a large influx of black migrants, Brooklyn, New York, became the site of many black Holiness-Pentecostal churches. It is difficult to determine when Holiness-Pentecostal churches began to appear in Brooklyn, since many located in apartments and storefronts went unrecorded. Also these institutions did not leave records. A study published by the Protestant Council of Churches in 1931 noted that the Holiness-Pentecostal churches represented a small segment of Brooklyn's black population in the early 1930s. According to the study, there were at least fifty-four mainline Protestant churches in Brooklyn, with a combined membership of 28,260. The council listed only three Churches of God in Christ, with an estimated population of 354; three "Pentecostal" churches, also estimated at 354; two Church of God institutions, with a population of 236; and three Church of the Nazarene (a Holiness sect established in 1908), with a combined membership of 242. The number of members belonging to another twenty-six unidentified churches was estimated at a little over two thousand.[31]

When compared to other groups, the number of Holiness-Pentecostal churches was small. By 1952 there were at least thirty-seven black Baptist churches in Brooklyn. Of the thirty-seven, sixteen reported a combined membership of 34,125. The second largest Protestant group among blacks was the African Methodist Episcopal and the African Methodist Episcopal Zion churches. Of the six AME churches, five reported a combined membership of 5,358 while two of the three AME Zion reported a total membership of 4,456.

However, throughout the 1940s and 1950s the number of Holiness-Pentecostal churches and their membership grew dramatically. Many were located in Bedford-Stuyvesant, including the Life and Time of Jesus Pentecostal Church, St. Mark's Holy Church, St. Paul's Church of Christ Disciples, the Elect Church, Mount Hope United Holy Church of America, the Church of God and Saints on Gates Avenue, the Faith Tabernacle Church of God at 573 Gates Avenue, House of Prayer for All People on Sumpter Street, Jesus Christ's Triumphant Church of the Apostolic Faith on Quincy Street, Glorious Pentecostal True Holiness on Fulton Street, True Holiness on Fulton Street, and the Pentecostal Church of All Nations on Gates Avenue. According to the *Amsterdam News*, by the 1950s Pentecostal churches were the "fastest-growing churches" in Brooklyn.[32]

The Church of God in Christ (COGIC) became the largest Holiness-Pentecostal sect in Brooklyn. In 1952 the Protestant Council of Greater New York listed twelve COGIC institutions, three with a combined membership of 1,250. The first group was established in 1925 by Frank Clemmons, a native of Washington, North Carolina, who had converted to the Church of God in Christ in 1914. Forced to leave school to help support his family, Clemmons soon began preaching. In 1918, after a few months in the army, he moved to Brooklyn and began worshiping with Peter J. F. Bridges, a minister of the Pentecostal group Church of Our Lord

Jesus Christ of the Apostolic Faith (COOLJC) and a close friend of Clemmons. However, Clemmons was unsatisfied with the doctrine of COOLJC and decided to establish a COGIC church in Brooklyn.[33]

Clemmons and his wife Polly began holding prayer services in their apartment, attracting a loyal following. As the prayer group grew, they moved to Rochester and Dean streets in Bedford-Stuyvesant, renting a storefront. By 1939 the group had raised enough money to purchase a church at 1745 Pacific Street, in the rapidly growing black community of Bed-Stuy.[34]

Three years after the first COGIC, a second COGIC was established. No early records exist for the church, making it difficult to reconstruct its early history. The church was located in a storefront at 29 Lafayette Street. Ulysses Corbett, one of the church's earliest members, recalls a storefront seating only a few dozen. Taffie Brannon, another founding member of the church, recalls that the church was on the ground floor of a walk-up. The founder and pastor of the church, a Reverend Cartwright, lived with his family above the church.[35]

By the early 1930s, under the leadership of John E. Bryant, the congregation had organized numerous auxiliaries including a music department, a Home and Foreign Mission, a Bible band, a Young People's Society, and a gospel choir. Throughout the 1930s the church grew, forcing the congregation to move to other storefronts, first on Fulton and then on Marion Street. Eventually, in 1936, the church purchased its first and only building at 137 Buffalo Avenue.[36]

Throughout the 1940s and 1950s more COGIC congregations were organized in Brooklyn, including at least two in East New York, one in Brownsville, and another in the Coney Island section. But the majority—nine of the twelve reported by the Protestant Directory of Metropolitan New York—were found in Bedford-Stuyvesant.[37]

The best-known COGIC established in Brooklyn in the 1950s was Frederick D. Washington's Washington Temple. Washington was born in Hot Springs, Arkansas, in 1903, the son of a minister in the Church of God in Christ. Following in his father's footsteps, Washington began preaching in Arkansas before his teens and became a minister in the COGIC before adulthood. He eventually settled in Montclair, New Jersey, where he became pastor of the

Trinity Temple COGIC from 1933 to 1951. Claiming a divine order to go to Brooklyn, he left Montclair after eighteen years of service and in July 1951 established a canvas cloth tent service on Fulton Street in a vacant lot at the corner of Grand Avenue. Accompanied by his wife Ernestine, a well-known gospel singer, and Alfred Miller, an organist and choral master, Washington held nightly revivals delivering fiery sermons and prayers, "healing" the sick, and baptizing by water those who converted to the faith. Washington's tent, known as the "Sawdust Trail" because of the sawdust covering the floor, grew rapidly. Between July and October 1951 many volunteered to serve as ushers, choir singers, deacons, ministers, and nurses. During its first public baptism, eighty converts appeared, and crowds overflowed into the streets. Eventually, the nightly tent services were filled to capacity, forcing Washington to move first to a storefront at 26 Reid Avenue, and then to another storefront at 1142 Herkimer Street, where Washington paid $110 a week in rent. Through members' efforts, in 1952 Washington was able to buy the Loews Theater on Bedford Avenue and convert it to a house of worship.[38]

Besides the Church of God in Christ, other sanctified groups were established in Brooklyn before World War II. A Jesus Christ's Triumphant Church of the Apostolic Faith at 289 Quincy Street was founded in 1938, a Glorious Pentecostal True Holiness Church in 1932, the Elect Church in 1936, several Churches of God in the late 1920s and early 1930s, a United Holy Church of America, two Daddy Grace's Houses of Prayer for All People in 1932 and 1937, a True Holiness Church, and a Pentecostal church of All Nations, Inc., at 402 Gates Avenue.[39]

One of Brooklyn's most popular Pentecostal groups was the Church of Our Lord Jesus Christ of the Apostolic Faith, Inc. The first group was formed by Peter J. F. Bridges, born in Washington, North Carolina, in 1890, into a Methodist home. Introduced to a Holiness church at an early age, he became fascinated with the charismatic preaching style. As a child, he would kill chickens and preach their funerals.

Unable to finish school, Bridges went to work as a laborer; he married and left the South seeking better economic opportunities. He became involved with R. C. Lawson and the Church of Our Lord Jesus Christ of the Apostolic Faith, although it is unclear when he first joined. Under Lawson he was ordained and established his first church in his Bed-Stuy apartment in the late 1930s. Through tithes, special offerings, and money contributed by Bridges from his salary, the members purchased a church on Marcy Avenue, selecting the name Beulah COOLJC. From this branch other ministers were trained who established churches in Brooklyn.[40]

By the end of World War II, black Holiness-Pentecostal churches in Brooklyn had multiplied. There were several churches of the Apostolic Faith, at least three Apostolic Overcoming Holiness Churches of God, a Church of God and Saints, and a United Holy Church of America, Inc. By the mid-1960s there were four COOLJC and at least a dozen Churches of God. In addition, the number of COGIC institutions had dramatically increased to thirty-one, with twenty-eight located in Bedford-Stuyvesant. There were also new organizations such as the Deliverance Evangelistic Center and the Tabernacle Prayer for All People. Most of these black Holiness-Pentecostals practiced conversion, sanctification, baptism of the Holy Spirit, and speaking in tongues.[41]

Probably the most dynamic Pentecostal minister in Brooklyn during the post–World War II period was Arturo Skinner (1924–1975), who was born in Brooklyn and educated in the New York Public School system. As a young man, he felt trapped in a life of despair and turned to drugs. Skinner claims that while he was walking in the streets of New York and contemplating suicide, God spoke to him, convincing him to dedicate his life to God. Skinner began attending Pentecostal churches, including Mother Rosa Artimus Horn's Pentecostal church on Lenox Avenue in Harlem, but moved to New Jersey. Adopting the style and structure of Pentecostal churches, Skinner established by the late 1940s a Pentecostal church in a Newark apartment. As his congregation grew, Skinner moved to larger quarters, renting storefronts and eventually buying a place of worship in the 1950s and naming it the Deliverance Evangelistic Center. Skinner soon opened another center on Dekalb Avenue in downtown Brooklyn.[42]

Although not affiliated with any major Holiness-Pentecostal groups, Skinner's Deliverance Evangelistic Center borrowed liberally from them. This group advocated sanctification, speaking in tongues, washing of the saints' feet, divine healing, and the Trinity. Prayer services, a testimony period, and gospel singing continued to be a part of every service. Despite the similarities between Deliverance Evangelistic and other Holiness-Pentecostal groups, the major emphasis and attraction of Skinner's group was divine healing. According to Skinner and his followers, God had given him the special gift of healing. The healer was said to be in direct communication with God, practiced the laying on of hands (the healer has the power to heal by touching the inflicted area), and called on God in an assertive voice to heal the invalid. As proof of his power, Skinner decorated the walls of his church with the wheelchairs, canes, and crutches of the people he claimed to have healed. In his *Nine Gifts of the Spirit*, Skinner asserted, "We do not attempt to negate the ethics of the medical profession. If you don't have faith in God, you had better get a good doctor. We simply believe in God's Word." For Skinner, healing meant that

life triumphs over death. God bless doctors! but they do not have the final say. They cannot command sight into blinded eyes. Through the means of surgery, cripples have been made to walk; but when God heals, he leaves no scars! Psychiatrists with all their logic, cannot restore minds, or speak peace to a troubled and tormented soul. Nor is there a psychiatrist who can renew a right spirit within man. The Gift of healing is a supernatural expression of the HEALTH OF GOD.[43]

Besides services at Deliverance Evangelistic Centers in Newark, Brooklyn, and later Philadelphia, Skinner occasionally held "Deliverance Crusades" at Madison Square Garden and Rockland Palace in Harlem, attracting large crowds. There was singing by the 500-voice Deliverance Choir and "Holy Ghost Rallies" with praying and healing of the sick.[44]

Similar in doctrine and rituals to Skinner's group was Johnnie Washington's Tabernacle. Born in Mississippi in 1929, Washington grew up in poverty and left school to help support his family. Raised as a Baptist, he was exposed to a Church of God in Christ at an early age. The religious service had a great impact on him, according to Washington, especially the emotional singing and preaching and the personal relationship the saints had with God. As a teenager, he became a gospel singer performing in many Holiness-Pentecostal churches. Washington moved to Brooklyn and briefly joined a Disciple of Christ church where he conducted prayer meetings and revivals. After gaining experience, Washington began a street ministry on Franklin and Nostrand Avenues in Bedford-Stuyvesant. In 1967 Washington broke away from the Disciples and established his own group in Red Hook, Brooklyn. He later moved to Rockaway Avenue in Brownsville and called his new church the Tabernacle Prayer for All People.[45]

Although similar to Skinner's Deliverance Evangelistic Center, Tabernacle Prayer was not part of any organized group. It adopted practices from other Holiness-Pentecostal groups, including speaking in tongues, testimonies, long prayer services, and divine healing. Music included congregational participation and tambourines, scrub boards, guitars, and drums. Strict codes of behavior were adopted by the body, prohibiting parties, dancing, and smoking. The congregants referred to themselves as saints, noting their special status with God and distinguishing themselves from the sinful.[46]

Huie Rogers's Greater Bibleway Temple of Brooklyn was another important Holiness-Pentecostal church. Born in Georgia, Rogers was converted to the Holiness faith at an early age and became a preacher at fourteen. Migrating to Brooklyn, he joined the newly established Bible Way Church. An ambitious man, Rogers rose through the ranks of the organization and in 1959 was appointed president of the Bibleway General Young People's Congress, winning fame as a hard worker. In 1967 Rogers became pastor of the Bibleway Temple on Gates Avenue, which soon became one of the largest Pentecostal churches in Brooklyn.[47]

The Significance of Holiness-Pentecostal Churches in the Black Community

According to interviews, the early members of Holiness-Pentecostal churches were poor. Taffie Brannon, who joined COGIC in the late 1920s, asserted that the early members of her church were poor and had "nowhere to go." Maritcha Harvey, a member of Beulah Church of Our Lord Jesus Christ of the Apostolic Faith and daughter of its founder, Peter J. F. Bridges, noted that the first members of her father's church were working-class poor people. "Many did domestic work" and there were "no professional" people in the early church. On many occasions when members of Beulah could not meet the financial obligations of the church, Pastor Bridges would have to assist. According to his daughter, "The church did not take care of him, he took care of the church."[48] Similarly, Frank Clemmons, founder of the First COGIC, had to work at various jobs in order to meet the expenses of his church because the congregation was unable to provide the money. Morry Bryant McGuire, a member of Church of God and Christ on the Hill and daughter of Rev. John Bryant, notes that when she was a young child growing up in the church, many people were poor and suffered greatly during the Depression. She recalled that many members of the church turned to Reverend Bryant for financial assistance, and "he did all that he could in order to help." Many people joining Holiness-Pentecostal churches were poor southern migrants.[49]

Nettie Kennedy was one of those poor migrants joining a Holiness-Pentecostal church in Brooklyn. Born in North Carolina in 1903, Kennedy stopped attending school at the age of nine in order to "go to work on a farm" picking cotton to help support her family. Like many blacks working in the cotton fields, she received less than a dollar a day. Kennedy married in North Carolina and had four children. However, the relationship with her husband deteriorated and she decided to end her marriage. Left alone with four children and little opportunity to advance economically, Kennedy decided to move North. She had relatives living in Philadelphia and New York and had corresponded with them. They had informed her that opportunities were great in the North and race relations were better. Moreover, Kennedy read a rural southern magazine called the *Grit* that informed her of the great opportunities in northern urban centers. Convinced that she could improve her economic condition and get a better education for her four children, Kennedy became part of the large wave of migrants who set out for the North, and she headed for Philadelphia in 1929.[50] Despite her optimism, life was rough in Philadelphia during the Depression. Although she stayed with her aunt, Kennedy found it difficult to make ends meet. She was unable to find a job and soon decided to leave Philadelphia and move to Brooklyn. Kennedy stayed with a cousin on Herkimer Street in Brooklyn and soon found work as a domestic servant. "I was sleeping in white folk's houses and working." Kennedy also joined a small Pentecostal church. "This church was like a family," according to Kennedy. Many members had migrated from the South and were poor. But they banded together for worship and social events. The members met on Sunday for services and during the week for prayer meetings, choir rehearsal, and club meetings. For Kennedy, the church was an important institution in her life. "I watched children grow up in the church and have children. It means so much."[51]

Brooklyn's black residents, like blacks in other urban areas, had few economic and political choices. Although social and economic conditions handicapped blacks, their plight did not stop them from seeking ways to improve their lives. The creation of the Holiness-Pentecostal churches illustrates a conscious effort by blacks to establish an identity and self-worth. Through these religious institutions, people of African descent created an identity by defining Christianity, asserting important theological issues and doctrine, and expressing a unique view of God, heaven, and earth.

Many contended that they were uncomfortable in the large churches and were unable to express themselves as they did in Southern churches. Their style of worship differed from the mainline churches that many found boring and too formal. U. L. Corbett, born in North Carolina in 1894, migrated to Brooklyn in the 1920s. Corbett, who joined a COGIC on Fulton Street in 1928, asserted that "there is but one Church, the Church of God and Christ. People use the word churches when talking about the other churches but these churches are not real."[52]

Holiness-Pentecostalism was used as a means to adjust to an urban environment. For Pentecostals the world was seen as an evil and hostile place. It was in the camp of Satan, and all secular pleasures were counterproductive to spiritual development. Consequently, the believers contended that they must separate from the world. As black Pentecostal scholar Leonard Lovett notes:

> The world for Black holiness-pentecostals is viewed as human society without Christ, or may refer to human behavior which reflects fallen man and does not conform to the image of Christ as revealed in the presence and power of the Holy Spirit. 1 John 2:15 is the bedrock for the belief concerning the world. Members of the movement are constantly exhorted to "love not the world, neither the things that are in the world, and if any man love the world, the love of

the Father is not in him." Within Black holiness-pentecostalism the individual is exhorted to "give up worldliness" as a part of the sanctifying process.[53]

For the most part, black Holiness-Pentecostals in Brooklyn, like Holiness-Pentecostals in other communities, cut themselves off from the outside world by rejecting many aspects of urban life including mass culture. They established a strict code of behavior that included aspects of dress, language, and proper etiquette in and outside of church. Holiness-Pentecostals condemned contemporary secular fashion and popular entertainment and were puritanical about speech and behavior. They insisted that at all times members must live a clean life. Samuel Gibson, who joined Arturo Skinner's Deliverance Evangelistic Center in the early 1950s, notes that dancing, gambling, drinking, smoking, and other "pleasures of the World" were rejected by the "saints." According to Gibson, the only dancing allowed in church was dancing to "praise the Lord." Maritcha Harvey lamented over the modern ways of today's members. During the early period of the church, people were faithful to holiness; they did not participate in secular social affairs. "The Apostolic church today is not as strict as it was fifty and sixty years ago. When I got saved, I promised the Lord I would not go to the movies anymore. So I don't go to the movies. Today, there is a change. Some are on the fence. I don't want to be on the fence."[54]

Not all were able to conform to this strict code of behavior. Evelyn Smith, an early Beulah member whose parents were founding members, notes:

> I had lots of friends and they were of various denominations. And I went to all their churches. Beulah was very hard. I dropped out for a while. The reason I stopped going to church, I'll tell you in plain English. One day I had a middrif on and someone in church made a remark and it was blown out of proportion and at that time I was twenty-two. I decided that this is it for me.

Smith could not conform to the strict code of the church.

> Anyone who knows Pentecostal-Apostolic know that there are rigid formalities. You can't wear makeup, you can't

wear this or that and the other. In my house you could not wear short dresses and you better not go to church without a hat over your head. It didn't bother me about the makeup but it was that things were so rigid. At twenty-two I had a 12:30 curfew. If I came in later I could not get in my house. I would have to stay at a friend's house. The way I came up was pure pain living.[55]

This strict code of behavior among black Holiness-Pentecostals revealed a theory of human value, a doctrine that attempted to restore the dignity, self-worth, and humanity of African Americans. In order to gain self-esteem and a sense of humanity, Holiness-Pentecostals attacked a society that measured success by the rational accumulation of goods, education, and job status. In a racist society in which African Americans were unable to meet the demands for success because they were closed out of the avenues to upward social and economic mobility, black Holiness-Pentecostals in Brooklyn, as elsewhere, labeled these criteria demonic. Sinners were attempting to be successful in Satan's camp but failed because they did not put God first. According to black Holiness-Pentecostals, the criteria for success in the larger society was a diversion from true salvation because people were in the world but not of the world. They asserted that by living a sanctified life one could become a saint and part of God's kingdom, the highest achievement for any person.

Moreover, Holiness-Pentecostals stressed virtues that offered a solution to alienation in an urban society. They advocated egalitarianism by asserting that all were equal before God and reached salvation in the same manner, and by stressing a sense of community and belonging, of mutual obligation and commonality.

By rejecting aspects of the dominant culture, Brooklyn's black Pentecostals were attempting to make sense of the world. By not accepting the values of the hegemonic culture, they limited their involvement with the larger community and created their own community. Thus, they helped each other cope with their environment. It helped bring order to their disordered world and provided them with a support system. They gained solidarity with each other.

Mother Taffie Brannon of COGIC on the Hill recalled coming to Brooklyn from the South in the late 1920s with her daughter.

She came upon a Church of God in Christ located in a storefront on Lafayette Avenue led by a Pastor Cartwright. Brannon began attending services and became part of the church community. The pastor and his wife invited Brannon and her daughter to stay with them in the storefront. "The Cartwrights treated me like a daughter," Brannon said.

Brannon noted that the services were always special events. They lifted her out of the humdrum and brought her closer to God and the members of the congregation. Brannon asserts that many people were attracted to the church because they were allowed to participate. Many were poor and had nowhere to go. The church was a home where people could gather, laugh, and have a good time.[57]

Services were held every Sunday morning and during weekdays in the evening. The Sunday service began at 11:00 A.M. and lasted till 3:00 in the afternoon, while the evening services began around 7:30 or 8:00 and sometimes would last until early in the morning. The services included gospel singing, prayer and testimony period, the sermon, and devotional. According to Brannon, the services were lively events involving the participation of the congregation in every aspect of worship. The services helped people escape their problems by joining members in "fellowship."[58]

Because the members of the Beulah Church of Our Lord Jesus Christ of the Apostolic Faith met several times a week for services, Maritcha Harvey asserted that the congregation was like a family.[59]

Myra Lovell, a member of the Lafayette Church of God, recalled:

> I remember what good times a few saints used to have, old and young. The age didn't mean anything to the young ones, as long as we were saved. That's what was important. We worked together and had a good time in the Lord. At Herkimer Street I remember in the contests we used to have with the Red and Blue teams. What a time on Thanksgiving night when we had the program. When the team raising the most money was announced we would shout for joy in sweet fellowship. No fuss! What we raised helped to purchase 404 Lafayette Avenue in a sweet spirit.[60]

Bessie Smalls, also a member of Lafayette Church of God since 1944, remembered "coming to Lafayette in 1944. I found some beautiful young people consisting of the Yearwoods, Boyces, McConnells, Coulthursts, Turpins, the Marshalls and their children. We had some wonderful times in the Lord. I am still at Lafayette enjoying the Lord."[61]

Some members lived above the churches in crowded quarters, thus helping create additionally close bonds. Darlington Coulthurst recalled living as a child in the same building in which her church was located.

> I remember that Rev. Marshall used to keep his bicycle chained to the radiator on the first floor at 426 Herkimer Street. I used to pass it every day when I came home from school to have my lunch. The Marshall Family lived in the apartment above the church and we lived on the floor above them. My father used to take care of the house. In the winter time Pop would bank the fire at night and in the morning, around 6 a.m., it was my job to fix the fire and close the furnace door so that the heat would come up. I had to go downstairs two flights, pass the door at the back of the church and then go down into the cellar.
>
> I can remember going downstairs on the mornings following a funeral in the church. The body would remain in the church overnight. The open casket was placed near the door that I had to pass on the way to the cellar. I had to go downstairs, but I was scared to go past the open door, scared to be down in the cellar by myself, scared to come back up past the door again, but I was more scared not to take care of the fire because I'd have to answer to my father.[62]

Adding to the view that the Pentecostal churches helped members cope with their environment by rejecting the values of the dominant society was the belief in healing. Healing was the best illustration of God taking care of believers. It took place among the community of saints and was proof that no believer needs to turn to the world, for God took care of every need.

The story of Penny Hooks is just one of many examples that Holiness-Pentecostals used to prove how faith in God delivered them from worldly tribulations. It also illustrates their personal relationship with God. As a young woman living in Harlem in 1962, Hooks was stricken with multiple sclerosis, which left her unable to walk. Her family took Hooks to several doctors, and she was eventually admitted to hospitals for treatment. However, Hooks's condition grew worse. She lost control of her body, and her mental state deteriorated. She had screaming fits and threatened family members with bodily harm. After a brief stay at home, Hooks became deranged and violent and was finally admitted to the Psychiatric Ward at Harlem Hospital.[63]

One Sunday Hooks's mother met an old friend who told her about Arturo Skinner and how God worked through him to heal people. Mildred Hooks traveled to Brooklyn and spoke to Reverend Skinner, who assured her that everything would be all right and then went to the hospital to meet Penny Hooks. On February 21, 1963, Hooks was released from Harlem Hospital, and the Hooks family began attending Sunday services at Deliverance Evangelistic Center in Brooklyn. Eventually Hooks's family began accepting the notion that her suffering was due to spiritual not medical reasons. According to her sister Esther Hooks, "Penny was demon possessed." Skinner used prayer and anointed her with oil. Gradually Hooks began to improve. By October 1963 her mental faculties were restored. She regained her speech and the violent outbursts stopped. By the fall of 1964, Hooks began to walk.[64]

The Penny Hooks story, like other Pentecostal stories of supernatural healing, reveals both an individual and a communal relationship with God. The roots of all human problems are said to be spiritual; therefore, if a person accepts God and attempts to live a sanctified life, God will personally take care of the needs of his saints. At the same time, healing confirms for the community of saints that their doctrine and practices are legitimate. It is a paradigmatic act, confirming that the world described in the Bible is authentic. For Pentecostals there is only good and evil. If one has faith, no matter what the circumstances are, God will deliver. There was no need to turn to the practices of a society that rejected their humanity. As Maritcha Harvey contends, "Healing makes the Bible real."[65]

As noted earlier, Holiness-Pentecostalism stressed an otherworldly doctrine, rejecting many values of the larger community. However, despite Holiness-Pentecostalism's counter hegemonic features, black Holiness-Pentecostals shared many values with the larger society, including moral orientation, seeing the world in terms of right and wrong, and progress, and a belief that things in the future will improve. Sociologists assert that these are core values shared by the majority of Americans.[66]

Scholars argue that adherence to a strict code of behavior "motivates individuals to work hard and spend their limited resources prudently." The economic success of some Holiness-Pentecostal members suggests that elements of Holiness-Pentecostal beliefs equipped them with values (such as seeking economic independence) that helped them adapt to a capitalist society, thus keeping them from being part of the growing urban underclass. So while sanctified churches rejected "the world," they attempted to instill virtues that were helpful in the dominant society. When Peter J. F. Bridges migrated from Washington, North Carolina, he had only an elementary school education and was relegated to manual labor. However, according to his daughter, he believed that "you could not get rich working for anyone." He saved and invested his money in real estate. Near the end of his life, Bridges owned five houses.[67]

Samuel Gibson of Deliverance Evangelistic Center, although working as an unskilled laborer and as caretaker of the church, managed to save some money and, with a loan from the church, purchased a home in Bedford-Stuyvesant.[68]

Ruby Richards's life also demonstrates this drive for economic independence. Born in 1928, Richards came to New York at an early age with her parents and moved to Bedford-Stuyvesant. Richards grew up in a religious home. Both her parents were ministers and operated a storefront church on Marcy Avenue. However, they lost the church when the city decided to build a public high school in the place where the church stood. Her parents were so discouraged they decided to join another Pentecostal church instead of operating their own. They joined St. Mark's Holy Pentecostal Church founded by Eva Lambert. Richards loved the church and developed a close relationship with Bishop Lambert. She remembers the bishop referring to her as "my little girl."[69]

In 1944 Richards graduated from Girl's High School and soon married Alva Richards, second assistant pastor of Concord Baptist Church. Alva Richards met Ruby at St. Mark's when he began working with that church's choir. Despite the fact that Alva was a Baptist, Richards refused to give up the Pentecostal church. Ruby and Alva reached a compromise. They decided they would not interfere in each other's religious practices. Each would attend the church of his or her choice.

Richards began working as a practical nurse soon after graduation and continued working after her marriage. However, after a few months of working in a hospital, she was assigned to work with syphilis patients. She also learned that she was pregnant. Fearful of contracting a venereal disease, and with her husband urging her to quit, Richards left nursing and became a "homemaker." In 1945 Richards's first child, Rudy, was born. It would not be until eight years later that her second child, Debra, was born. In 1955 Richards gave birth to her third child, Janet. The children attended St. Mark's Holy Church.

Because Alva Richards did not earn much as an assistant pastor, he applied for public housing. The application was accepted, and the family moved to a housing project in Brownsville, Brooklyn. But tragedy soon struck the Richards household. In 1960 Alva developed prostate cancer and died less than a year later. Ruby Richards suddenly found herself alone with three children and no income. She decided to look for work. Although her oldest was sixteen, the two girls, eight and six, needed supervision; therefore, she could only take part-time work. In her search for employment, she passed George Gershwin Junior High School on Van Siclin Avenue and Linden Boulevard in Brooklyn and decided to apply for any available position. She was hired as a school aide for four hours a day. It was a hard struggle, but she managed on her small income. While working at Gershwin as a school aide in the late 1970s, Richards learned about a career ladder program for paraprofessionals. Paraprofessionals earning college credits would be promoted and receive a raise. Richards decided that this was a great opportunity. Her children were getting older and were able to take care of each other. Richards first applied for a paraprofessional position and was accepted. She worked during the day and attended Brooklyn College in the evening. Eventually Richards earned enough credits and moved from educational assistant to educational associate, the highest level of a paraprofessional.

Richards believes that her decision to involve her children in the Pentecostal church may have set them on the right track. The structure and discipline demanded by the church and the number of church social activities that the children were involved in helped keep them out of trouble and "focused on positive things." Rudy became a butcher and eventually moved into a supervisory position for the Atlantic and Pacific Company. Debra became a traffic violation patrol officer, and Janet is employed by the Traffic Department as a computer programmer.[70]

The collective effort of members of several congregations to economically improve their churches also reflects the desire among Holiness-Pentecostals to achieve economic independence. In 1931 the Protestant Church Council reported that neither of two Church of God congregations nor the three COGIC churches owned property. However, by 1939 the second COGIC established in Brooklyn was able to purchase a building valued at $20,000. Although the first COGIC did not report property throughout the 1940s, by 1952 the church reported having $25,000 in property. Jesus Christ's Triumphant Church of the Apostolic Faith had had humble beginnings in 1938, but by 1947 it reported having $17,000, and by 1952 it had $35,000 in property. St. Paul's Church of Christ Disciples had also had "humble beginnings," starting out as a storefront operation; but due to the fund-raising efforts and savings of its members, it purchased a theater on Gates Avenue for more than $100,000 and converted it into a church. Between 1938 and 1944 Beulah's pastor, Peter J. F. Bridges, used money from tithes and offerings from his congregation and put a down payment on a church building on Marcy Avenue. The congregation of St. Mark's Holy Church managed to raise $7,000 in four weeks in order to pay off the remainder of its mortgage.[71]

These illustrations of individual and collective efforts, avoidance of worldly pleasures, and stress on discipline suggest that Holiness-Pentecostals developed an appreciation for hard work, a desire for economic independence, and respect for ownership. This in turn created a culture that helped black Holiness-Pentecostals adjust to the demands of the larger society and to avoid becoming members of a socioeconomic underclass increasingly identified by its involvement in violent crime and a cycle of unwed pregnancies and welfare dependency.

The search for economic independence among black Holiness-Pentecostal church members was not in contradiction to the notion of human value. The search for economic independence never interfered with the goals of being saved and maintaining the good of the larger church community. In fact, it complemented them. When church members acted collectively to become independent, it was in order to be able to be in complete control of a place of worship. The ownership of a church removed the dependency on others outside of their community who could decide their fate. In addition, individual efforts to be personally independent were not primary objectives of Holiness-Pentecostals. They saw it as part of their obligation to remain morally upright and protected from temptation. If one is dependent, it leaves the person vulnerable to the temptations of the world. According to Pentecostals, when people put luxury and extravagance before God and use it to measure success, they are committing sin.

In his study of an urban Pentecostal church, Melvin Williams notes that it "serves as a place where members take refuge from the world among familiar faces. It is a source of identity and a matrix of interaction for the members it recruits. It is a subculture that creates and transmits symbols and enforces standards of belief and behavior." Williams goes on to note that, besides conferring social status, the Pentecostal church gives "meaning, order and style to its members' lives, and provides for social mobility and social rewards within its confines."[72]

What Williams found is also true of the black Holiness-Pentecostal churches of Brooklyn. These institutions should not be seen as inconsequential, evidence of social disorder, or as Joseph Washington asserts, " exhibit little or no ability to contribute to the religious dimension of the Negro."[73] Like the black mainline churches, black Holiness-Pentecostal churches were used by both black men and women to define their lives and the world despite the attempt by the larger society to depict people of African origins as savages or brutes, incapable of improving their lives. Black people of Brooklyn, like African Americans in other urban areas, used black Holiness-Pentecostal churches to express their humanity and protect themselves against racism. They see the world as a hostile place, in Satan's camp. This worldview is a shield against the harsh realities of the larger society. In addition, people who are denied the social and economic mobility valued by the larger society seek alternative ways of improving themselves. People in the Pentecostal churches of Brooklyn have gathered together for support, making their environment meaningful and stable. These churches provide what Williams contends is a meaningful human interaction. Holiness-Pentecostal churches established "new forms of community life relevant to the residents' present social and economic plight. Responding to the threat of a fraudulent, remote, or incomprehensible social order which is beyond real hope or desire and invites apathy, boredom, and even hostility, these Blacks are creating bounded groups which give them a stake in a social order."[74] Thus, black Holiness-Pentecostal culture opposed the racist images and oppressive practices of the dominant order that hedged in so many working-class blacks.

CHAPTER THREE

Brooklyn's Black Churches and the Growth

of Mass Culture

In September 1941 the Willing Workers Club of the Newman Memorial Methodist Church, an African American church located on Herkimer Street in Bedford-Stuyvesant, Brooklyn, held a "successful fashion show." The *Amsterdam News* reported, "The fashion show given by the Willing Workers Club of Newman Memorial Church on Friday evening proved to be one of the season's most colorful events." Women and teenage girls, who were members of Newman, walked in front of a large crowd modeling white and black gowns, and colorful dresses. After the "elaborate show which featured the latest in milady's fashions, an entertaining program was presented and refreshments were served."[1]

The significance of the Newman fashion show was its shift from the high cultural activities practiced by most of Brooklyn's mainline black churches in the late nineteenth and early twentieth centuries. Numerous black churches, including Newman during that earlier period, sponsored elocution contests, recitals, classical music concerts, literary events, and lectures as a means of moral and intellectual uplift.

The fashion show at Newman suggests that a dramatic change in consciousness had taken place among church members by the fourth decade of the twentieth century. People attending this show revealed their admiration for mass consumption and popular entertainment. Newman was not unique. By the 1930s, as mass culture took on greater significance in Brooklyn's black communities, numerous black churches began sponsoring mass cultural entertainment. This is not to say that black churches stopped sponsoring high cultural activities. Recitals, organ concerts, lectures, and other elite cultural events remained important activities of the churches. However, mass cultural events became popular activities attracting large audiences.

Mass culture continues to have an enormous impact on blacks in Brooklyn. For the most part, African Americans embraced mass cultural forms with little resistance. Yet they were not just passive recipients who swallowed mass culture whole. They molded it to suit their needs as African Americans in an urban environment. They made choices in music, clothing, products, movies, and other forms of recreation. Lawrence Levine correctly notes that popular culture is not just a matter of what entrepreneurs present. Nor is it just an attempt on the part of entrepreneurs to exploit the masses. It is an arena that people are actively involved in shaping. This trend to mass culture cannot simply be described as assimilation. It was both creativity and resistance to the dominant society. Although blacks adopted mass cultural forms that were popular in the larger white society, the trend toward mass culture was part of the larger struggle led by African Americans that challenged the racist view of blacks as lazy and incapable of succeeding. African Americans used mass culture to become economically independent and make black communities viable. In her study on Chicago during the Depression, historian Lizabeth Cohen argues that "blacks came to feel more independent and influential as a race, not more integrated into white middle class society. Mass culture—chain stores, brand goods, popular music—offered blacks the ingredients from which to construct a new, urban black culture."[2]

Black churches were pivotal in this reworking of mass culture. By the 1930s, Brooklyn's black churches had begun incorporating aspects of popular culture, including dance, fashion shows, drama, popular music, and recreation, thereby blending the sacred with the secular and making the churches responsive to the desires of African American communities. They brought their own meaning and style to popular culture. They decided what was acceptable entertainment, practicing some forms of entertainment and forbidding others. Black churches also used these popular cultural forms to remain economically stable and socially independent from the white society. Mass culture offered them a means of both raising money and allowing blacks to turn inward for social gratification within a Christian context. Thus, black churches struggled to be institutions that were the cohesive factor in the black community. This chapter examines the impact mass culture had on the black community and on Brooklyn's black churches and how both community forces and the churches manipulated various mass cultural forms.

Popular Entertainment

By the turn of the century, new forms of popular entertainment emerged in America. Cabarets, dance halls, amusement parks, and nickelodeons sprang up in major Northern cities in the early part of the twentieth century. These forms of popular entertainment not only attracted the middle classes but also the growing urban working classes because they offered them new forms of amusement at affordable prices.[3]

In addition, modern technology brought entertainment into millions of American homes. By the 1920s the radio had introduced Americans to African American music (ragtime, blues, jazz), to prizefighting, baseball (the World Series), and other competitive sports, and to weekly series such as "Amos 'n' Andy" and "Gang Busters."[4]

The motion picture industry was perhaps the most powerful of the forms of entertainment shaping Brooklyn in the twentieth century. By the early part of the century, numerous theaters had been established in storefronts. Proprietors set up rows of benches and used a projector to show reels of film that flickered on a screen. The five-cent admission fee attracted crowds. On Pitkin Avenue in the Brownsville section of Brooklyn, more than twenty "five-cent variety theaters" were operating in 1910.[5]

Many were alarmed at the movies because this new form of entertainment seemed contrary to many conventional values such as hard work, self control, sober earnestness, and industriousness. Opponents of movies argued that the motion pictures stressed senseless entertainment, uninhibited fun, and contributed to immoral behavior. Many felt that leisure time should be spent productively: reading, writing, hard work, and other activities that help develop the moral character of the individual.[6]

Along with being a threat to individual morality, movie opponents argued that movies were a threat to the community at large. Opponents feared that neighborhoods would be destroyed by the undesirables attracted by this form of entertainment. They noted that children were especially vulnerable to the new form of entertainment. According to the *Brooklyn Daily Eagle*:

> It is said that since the establishment of these places the majority of the children who were in the habit of spending their winter evenings in the reading rooms have evinced a liking for the moving picture shows. There has been a noticeable decrease in the number of child readers in the libraries. The manual training classes cannot boast of the

good attendance that they had formerly. It is claimed that this is largely due to the moving picture shows.[7]

The community's leading citizens, among them Alexander S. Drescher, director of the Brownsville Board of Trades, went "on record as unalterably opposed" to these businesses. Dr. Abraham Silverstein, the rabbi of a large Brownsville congregation, lashed out against the moving picture theaters, asserting that they were a menace to the public morals. Several attorneys representing citizens of Brownsville threatened to seek an injunction against the theaters.[8]

Movie theaters met resistance not only in Brownsville but also in other areas of Brooklyn. In May 1910 a group known as the Children's Society obtained evidence showing that Jacob Prisland, a doorkeeper at a theater on Myrtle Avenue and Skillman Street, had allowed minors to enter. The Court of Special Sessions fined him twenty-five dollars.[9] Two days later, the *Brooklyn Daily Eagle* reported, Deputy Chief John B. Braken of the Bureau of Licenses met with prominent Brooklynites, including attorneys, clergy, and people "owning more than a million dollars' worth of property." The meeting, at Borough Hall, protested the granting of a license to the Albany Parkway Amusement Company for a movie theater at Eastern Parkway and Albany Avenue. A lawyer for the group, Manasseh Miller, objected because

> the issuance of a license for a common show on Eastern Parkway was contrary to the law regulating the parkway. Second, before the license is granted the permission of the park commissioner would first have to be obtained. Third, it was contrary to public policy. Fourth, it was contrary to the will of the individuals immediately affected by the proposed show.[10]

A member of the Twenty-fourth Ward's Board of Trades asserted that he had been instructed by his organization to oppose the granting of the license because "it was something out of place in the section." He stated emphatically that "the people did not want it." Some even challenged the artistic value of movies. Adolph Rosenfeldt, an attorney representing property owners in the area, disputed the Albany Parkway Amusement

Company's assertion that there were redeeming qualities in the picture show.

They will tell you, the lawyer contended, that they are

> educational institutions and that they give people a chance to enjoy music and art. If there is any music in the class of songs that are sung in such houses, I don't know what their idea of music must be. And where is the art in the pictures? They will throw any kind of picture on the screen to draw the people, pictures that are often broad and suggestive.[11]

Some people worried that the moving pictures posed a threat to the community because they attracted working-class people. One man, who testified that Eastern Parkway "was unquestionably the handsomest street in Brooklyn," protested in behalf of St. Paul's Chapel and the children. A movie theater on Eastern Parkway would "bring an undesirable class of people from other sections of the city that were not wanted." Mrs. E. Smith, a property owner, pleaded with Braken not to issue a license "for the sake of the children." As a mother, she did not want her children "to come in contact with the element that was drawn by moving picture houses." Father John I. Smith, assistant rector of St. Gregory's Church on Brooklyn Avenue, spoke for his congregation in opposing a place of amusement in their neighborhood, which had an "orderly, and quiet atmosphere." The cleric called movie theaters "hell-holes."[12] These privileged members of Brooklyn feared that their communities would be under siege by working-class people who would destroy their way of life.

Despite the protest, movies attracted a wide audience. Many enjoyed the excitement of screen action. It offered consumers of entertainment an inexpensive, fun activity during their free time. Because of the popularity of motion pictures, movie stars became more popular and more well known than national political leaders. People admired actors and actresses on the screen and adored their extravagant lifestyles. Newspaper gossip columns reported on the latest rumors about their lives, and mass circulation magazines such as *Daily Variety* were created solely to report on Hollywood.

Entrepreneurs rushed to take advantage of the growing popularity of movies. Recognizing that there were great profits in the movie-making industry, they began building movie palaces able to seat thousands. In Bedford-Stuyvesant numerous movie houses were built, including the Brevoort theater on Brevoort Place and Bedford Avenue, with a seating capacity of 2,500, one of the largest theaters in New York. According to the *Brooklyn Daily Eagle*, "The structure, both outside and in, is pleasing." The exterior was made of tapestry and brick. The lobby was well-lighted and had polished marble, plate mirrors, and tiled floors. The spacious auditorium had 1,800 chairs on the main floor and 700 in the balcony. The theater contained "massive pilasters of classic design, a painted domed ceiling, ornamental cornices and richly paneled walls." According to the *Eagle*, "There is a promenade foyer on the mezzanine floor. On this same floor are homelike waiting and lounging rooms, with open fireplaces, seats, reading tables and writing desks and all things needed for comfort. There are also well-appointed retiring rooms for women and children. Men will find a smoking room at their disposal."[13]

Besides the Brevoort, other Bed-Stuy theaters included the Apollo, Howard, Comet, Sumner, Tompkins, and Regent. Located in the major commercial areas of Bed-Stuy, they were geographically as well as economically accessible to working-class people. On weekday evenings double features were offered at special bargain prices. On Saturdays, children attended matinees with a double feature of comedy, adventure, or horror films, preceded by several cartoons.[14]

As blacks migrated to Northern urban centers, they did not go unnoticed by entrepreneurs of commercial entertainment. By the late 1930s and early 1940s, the owners and managers of the Bed-Stuy movie theaters were attempting to appeal to the taste of African Americans, with ads in the black press offering double and triple features, late shows, matinees, and movies with black casts. The Regent, Howard, Sumner, and other theaters advertised such films as the black filmmaker Oscar Micheaux's *God's Stepchildren* (1937), and Edgar G. Ulmer's *Moon Over Harlem* (1939), as well as *Tales of Manhattan* (1942), featuring Paul Robeson and Ethel Waters, and *Song of Freedom* (1937), starring Paul Robeson.[15]

In October 1939 the *New York Age* reported that Benjamin Resnick, manager of the Regent, had brought "bigger and better screen attractions starring Negroes" to the Bed-Stuy audience. The movie *Moon Over Harlem*, a "powerful drama ripped from the

William Augustus Jones (Bethany Baptist Church, 1962) (*Bethany Baptist Church Centennial Celebration*, 1983)

Mount Pisgah Baptist Church (founded by Salina Perry in 1931)

Berean Missionary Baptist Church (built in 1894) (*Weeksville Then and Now*, 1983)

St. Phillip's Protestant
Episcopal Church (1914)
(*Weeksville Then and Now*,
1983)

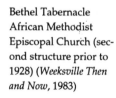

Bethel Tabernacle
African Methodist
Episcopal Church (sec-
ond structure prior to
1928) (*Weeksville Then
and Now*, 1983)

Mount Lebanon Baptist Church (building purchased in 1911) (*Mount Lebanon Baptist Church
Jubilee Year Book*)

Apostle Arturo Skinner, founder and pastor of Deliverance Evangelistic Center, at a healing service in the 1970s (*Deliverance Voice* 9, no. 1, January–February 1975)

Mortgage-burning ceremony at Mount Lebanon Baptist Church in 1955 (*bottom row, far right:* C. L. Franklin, pastor; *top row, far left:* Gardner C. Taylor, pastor of Concord Baptist Church) (*Mount Lebanon Baptist Church Jubilee Year Book*)

Church of God in Christ on the Hill

Milton A. Galamison (1923–1988), pastor of Siloam Presbyterian Church from 1948 to 1988 (photo property of author)

First Boy Scout Troop, no. 498 (Mount Lebanon Baptist Church, circa 1954)
(*Mount Lebanon Baptist Church Jubilee Year Book*)

Sunday service at Mount Lebanon Baptist Church on Howard Avenue (*Mount Lebanon Baptist Church Jubilee Year Book*)

Sunday school teachers and officers, First African Methodist Episcopal Zion Church (circa 1922) (*First AME Zion Centennial Celebration Book, 1885–1985*)

Board of Trustees, First African Methodist Episcopal Zion Church, circa 1950
(*First AME Zion Centennial Celebration Book, 1885–1985*)

Rev. William Orlando Carrington greets First Lady Eleanor Roosevelt, First African Methodist Episcopal Zion Church, circa 1940 (*First AME Zion Centennial Celebration Book, 1885–1985*)

heart of Harlem" with an all-black cast, promised to be a fine film, "not because it is a sepia picture [movies with black casts targeted at black audiences] rather because it is a good one." The Howard Theater sensationalized the film *God's Stepchildren* with the following ad in the *Amsterdam News*: "THE UNFORGETTABLE STORY OF A BEAUTIFUL MULATTO GIRL WHO DIDN'T WANT TO BE COLORED AND THE STRANGE AND UNUSUAL CIRCUMSTANCES THAT WAS THE RESULT OF IT—AN AMAZING PARALLEL TO 'IMITATION OF LIFE.'" In November 1942 the Brevoort began featuring the first all-black newsreel. Current information on African American celebrities, including actors, singers, and sports figures, were major features of the newsreel.

The showing of black films revealed the impact that the black community had on Bed-Stuy theaters. Blacks' eagerness to see and spend money on films with black casts demonstrated their taste and motivated more companies to produce them and more theater owners and managers to show them. The *New York Age* noted that the Regent Theater, under the management of Benjamin Resnick, rushed to the forefront to present "sepia" films. "When bigger and better screen attractions starring Negroes are brought to this town of ours, Manager Benjamin F. Resnick will bring them. He always has and first."[16]

Bedford-Stuyvesant, especially the area on and around Fulton Street, was known in this period not only for its movies but also for its sparkling nightlife. As the black community grew, entertainment entrepreneurs rushed to establish bars and grills, lounges, cafes, and nightclubs. By the late 1930s Bedford-Stuyvesant had begun to rival Harlem, offering the best in entertainment.

Blacks were part of the evening entertainment world, not just as consumers but also as employers and workers. Although white entrepreneurs owned many of these establishments, African Americans began opening such centers during and after World War II. Cain Young's Kingston Lounge, Alex and Sylvia Harry's Bedford Lounge, and Henry and Edna Gantt's Pleasant Lounge were among the notable establishments operated by blacks. The bar and grill industry also offered blacks employment opportunities as bartenders, barmaids, chefs, waiters, floor managers, and hosts and hostesses.[17]

Bartenders and barmaids were important employees in the new nightlife establishments, in some instances a major drawing card of bars and grills. Elmo's Lounge at 243 Reid Avenue advertised that it had a "Cozy cocktail Bar & Restaurant," and the Turbo Village on the corner of Reid Avenue and Halsey Street had an "unusual Cocktail Lounge." Cafe Verona on 1330 Fulton Street featured "Mel Williams, chief bartender of the Cafe Verona along with Tony, mixing too, and barmaid Jeanette Britt . . . the center of attraction at this spot. This trio possesses a large following and, thereby, keeps the Verona in the Limelight." Dotty Moore of the Decatur Bar and Grill "has one of the finest personalities and her style of serving drinks is far above par." Described as a mecca of tavern seekers, the Arlington Inn featured barmaid Catherine Williams, who was "one of the most well-liked barmaids in Brooklyn" and "brought new life to this place."[18]

Unlike local pubs, which served a predominantly male clientele, the large bars and grills were portrayed as nice places to bring a date, thus becoming centers for heterosexual mixing. Women patronized them as much as men, thus challenging the notion that night entertainment establishments were only for men. Of the forty-one people attending the grand opening of the Kingston Lounge in 1944, twenty-one were women. Dozens of married couples were on hand to celebrate the Kingston Lounge's first and second anniversaries in 1945 and 1946.[19] One element prompting both men and women to patronize the lounges and clubs of Bedford-Stuyvesant was their fine cuisine. Many of these places were sophisticated entertainment centers serving full course dinners.

In order to accommodate people for dinner, lounges, cafes, and bars and grills built spacious dining rooms. Frank's Caravan on Hancock Street and Throop Avenue advertised "Excellent Food in 'The Arabian Room,' the Finest Dining Room in the Area." The owners of Wellworth Cafe prided themselves on a spacious dining room.[20]

Moreover, food represented a form of syncretism. As African Americans came into contact with various ethnic and racial groups in the urban centers, they gained a taste for new cuisines, which they integrated and adopted along with their traditional African American favorites. The variety of foods adopted can be found in the night entertainment establishments in the black community. Many bars and grills, lounges, and taverns served the finest in Chinese cuisine. Smitty's Corner offered both Chinese and American dishes. Both the Wellworth Cafe and Travelers Inn hired "famous" Chinese chefs. The Arlington Inn on Fulton Street offered an open seafood bar including the "freshest Crabs, Lobsters, Fish obtainable" and specialized in "Chinese-American Foods prepared by our Two Chinese Chefs." Fong Chong "heads the Kitchen" at the Baby Grand and specializes in Chinese-American dishes. The Traffic Lounge at Bedford and Lafayette Avenues served buffet dinners and featured Italian cuisine.[21]

Yet Bed-Stuy nightclubs were more than places of acculturation. They became places offering traditional African American cuisine, thus appealing to a more traditional African American taste. Many of these places continued offering "southern cooking." The Ten-Twelve Bar and Grill at 1012 Myrtle Avenue in downtown Brooklyn boasted that its "Southern cooking is supreme." "Fried Chicken and Chops" were the specialty of the Kingston Lounge, established in 1944. Jack Man's Corporation Bar and Grill advertised its chef Charles Higgins as the "barbecue King," while the Flying Horse Bar and Grill located on Gates Avenue specialized in steaks, chops, and seafood.[22]

Bars and grills also offered the best in entertainment that appealed to an African American audience. Not surprisingly, jazz and blues were the music most frequently heard at the clubs. Famous jazz celebrities appeared at Brooklyn's nightspots. Jazz greats like King Curtis, Dinah Washington, and Carmen McRae appeared at nightclubs in Bedford-Stuyvesant. However, more often Bed-Stuy nightclubs offered less well-known talent an opportunity to perform. Many musicians, comedians, and other entertainers got their start at these establishments. At Cafe Verona, Tuesdays were "Audition Nights" offering amateurs the opportunity to win an appearance in the cafe's floor show. The Baby Grand at Fulton Street featured Melvin Smith, "King of the Blues," Janie Mickins, "Song Stylist," and Betty Brisbane, "Queen of the Exotic Dancers." The Eddie Coombs Quartet played at the Baby Grand. Cafe Verona at 1330 Fulton Street offered comedians, jazz bands, trios, and pianists a place to perform. Snooky Marsh, well-known in Brooklyn circles, teamed up with Manhattan Paul, the "dynamic emcee" at the Cafe Verona "leaving the audience in the aisles."[23]

In his weekly column in the *Amsterdam News*, "Brooklyn Tavern Jottings," Ike McFowler reported on activities at Brooklyn's bars and grills in the 1940s:

Shows at the Cafe Verona have become the talk of the town. Each week there is a fine performance headlining some of the top-notch entertainers of the day. Highlights of the current bits of entertainment the Verona has to offer you is the piano playing of Robert Harvell. This young man has a playing style similar to that of The Nat King Cole Trio. Keep your eye on this young artist, for he is destined to be one of our stars in the near future. Ray Simmons and his trio have gained a bevy of friends and well-wishers via their fine style. They will satisfy your own dancing desires.[24]

These venues offered many blacks an opportunity to perform that was otherwise denied them in the larger society. Among the many entertainers were Rector Baily, featured on the Hammond organ at the Kingston Lounge, Johnny Guitar Sanders, appearing weekends at Quincy, and the Eddie Coombs Quartet, performing nightly at Manhattan Paul's.[25]

Nightlife in Bedford-Stuyvesant reflected the African American community's assimilation into an urban culture and consumer society. But for them it meant more than just accepting the values of the larger society. These places became centers of an African American culture that focused on cuisine, dance, and music. While adapting to elements of the dominant culture, it was also an urban black culture that stressed both economic and social independence from the white community. Movie theaters that showed "sepia films" and bars and grills became a source of pride, demonstrating that blacks were capable human beings able to participate on any level. It was a turn inward for services and entertainment. Nightclubs also provided opportunities for blacks to socialize and enjoy each other's company. This adaptation increasingly transformed and enriched the dominant culture as well, with that culture coming more and more to include elements of the black urban culture.

African Americans and the Impact of Mass Consumption

As in other black urban communities, blacks in Brooklyn owned few businesses. By late 1929, although more than 68,900 blacks lived in Brooklyn, there were only ninety-four black-owned retail stores, including thirty-one candy stores, twenty meat markets, sixteen restaurants (only seven with table service), and thirteen car garage and repair shops. Although the total number of black entrepreneurs increased by 1940, only 4.7 percent of Brooklyn's 107,263 blacks were classified by the census as employers or self-employed. The dearth of black-owned businesses in Bedford-Stuyvesant meant that blacks were relegated to purchase goods and services from chain stores and local merchant stores owned by whites that operated in the community.[26]

Companies advertised in the black press, indicating they had a market in the black community. Clothing stores, car dealerships, food markets, wine and liquor stores, and numerous other businesses attempted to appeal to blacks as well as whites. However, certain products advertised in the black press appealed only to a black clientele. Nowhere is this more clear than in beauty products. Beginning in the early part of the twentieth century and accelerating in the 1930s, beauty products—including hot combs or "straightening combs," soaps, pomade for men, hair products for women pledging to make hair longer, brighter and wavier, and skin lightening or "bleaching" creams—were advertised in the black weeklies and sold in local pharmacies and other businesses in black neighborhoods. For example, in 1905 Crane's "Wonderful Face Bleach and Hair Tonic," advertised in the *New York Age*, promised to make the skin of a "black or brown person four or five shades lighter and a mulatto person perfectly white . . . and make anyone's hair grow long and straight." Charles Ford's Hair Pomade promised to straighten kinky or curly hair. "Dr. Fred Palmer's Skin Whitener" advertised in the 1930s and 1940s to give the user "lovelier, lighter skin in just a few days . . . lightens too dark, tanned weather-beaten skin to new loveliness."

Thanks to Madam C. J. Walker, who established the first successful black-owned business making and selling hair and skin preparation products for African Americans, some blacks established businesses producing and selling these products. For example, Anthony George, well known in Bedford-Stuyvesant in the 1940s for selling religious articles such as candles, crosses, Bibles, and oils, also sold "Anthony's Pressing Oil, Anthony's Lipstick, Anthony's Love Me Perfume, Anthony's Menthol Bleach, Anthony's Cream Scalp, Anthony's Cold Cream," and loads of other beauty products.[27]

It has been argued that African Americans' indulgence in these products suggests a "cultural colonialism." Advocates of this view contend that because black physical features had been portrayed as ugly by the larger white society, many blacks were ashamed of their African features and adopted the beauty standards of white America. They believe that the use of skin lighteners and hair-straightening products was an attempt to hide their African features and look white. This view gained prominence during the black aesthetic movement ("Black Is Beautiful") of the 1960s. Unlike an earlier view that criticized the producers of these products for manipulating the poor and ignorant, critics in the 1960s aimed their attack at the users of these beauty commodities.[28]

Without a doubt this view has merit. To a large degree, blacks who bought these products were attempting to alter their natural features. However, the cultural colonialism view ignores the fact that African Americans were also actively involved in applying their own standards of beauty. African Americans knew they could not be white nor, for the most part, did they desire to be anything other than black. The use of lightening creams and products that would help make hair wavy is no more of an attempt on the part of blacks to become white than the use of suntan lotion by whites is an attempt to become black. The use of lightening creams and hair products indicates that black consumers had particular beauty standards in their community. Black men and women did not just desire lighter skin but wanted even skin tone and unblemished skin, or hair that was long and wavy with an African American texture; hair styles for black women included curling, braiding, and weaving that was familiar to the black community. Black women used ribbons and flowers on the top or sides of their heads with curls extending on the foreheads adhered to the skin and other rare hair designs. They took the standards of beauty used by the larger white society and manipulated them to suit their own taste.

This attempt at "beautifying" also demonstrates that African Americans challenged the popular view that they were unattractive. They clearly demonstrated black men and women were exquisite. The desire for beauty products also strongly suggests the influence blacks had on the beauty industry. It was an attempt on the industry's part to satisfy the taste of African Americans by providing such products. Black people in Brooklyn were not only shaping mass culture as consumers operating in the free market system and making their demands for certain products known; they were also involved in attempting to win respect and economic independence by waging campaigns for better treatment and jobs in businesses of mass consumption. By the early 1930s African Americans had formed numerous organizations that launched demonstrations against local merchant clothing stores, chain grocery stores, movie theaters, and other mass consumption institutions, demanding employment and better services. One such organization was Post no. 2, founded in 1932 as part of the National War Veterans Association, which was established by white war veterans complaining that the traditional veterans' organizations did not address the political, social, and economic needs of veterans.[29]

Thanks to an aggressive membership drive led by its president, Elvia I. Sullinger, within a few years Post no. 2 claimed it grew from a small number to 8,500 members. Most members of the National War Veterans Association were not veterans or men. Of the 8,500 members reported, 6,000 were women. One reason accounting for the attraction of a large number of nonveterans was the group's insistence on fighting all forms of discrimination. The group held numerous rallies and led boycotts against stores in Bedford-Stuyvesant that were disrespectful to African Americans or refused to hire them. In 1933 the veterans' association collected a large number of signatures from area residents who accused the manager of the Bohack supermarket on Buffalo Avenue in Brooklyn of sexual harassment. The association launched a boycott when Bohack's general manager's office refused to fire the manager. The veterans responded by holding demonstrations in front of the store and attempting to record the names of blacks defying the boycott. The group threatened to publish the names of the boycott offenders in local black weeklies. In July, E. I. Sullinger, who also held the post of "commander" of the National Colored War Veterans League, expanded the protest by leading a demonstration against a Bohack supermarket on Sumner and Jefferson Avenues. Sullinger and others wore signs reading "This Bohack Store does not Employ Colored Clerks."[30]

Other community organizations demanded that businesses grant African Americans fair treatment. In 1937 the African

Nationalist Movement, a group associated with Marcus Garvey and the Universal Negro Improvement Association, announced that by picketing it had forced the Square Deal Drugstore on Fulton Street to hire two blacks. Soon after its victory, the African Nationalist Movement launched a boycott against the Woolworth store at Nostrand Avenue and Fulton Street.[31]

In 1940 the Amalgamated Labor Association (the Brooklyn branch of the Harlem Labor Union), along with the Brooklyn Branch of the Greater New York Coordinating Committee and the local Affairs Committee of the Kings County Young Republican League, accused the Fulton Civic Association, a group of two hundred Fulton Street merchants, of stalling on their promise to hire blacks. The three organizations decided to picket Fulton Street stores that refused to hire blacks. According to the groups:

> Fulton street merchants in the Bedford-Stuyvesant area are notoriously unfair to Negroes who patronize their business heavily. We are endeavoring to make some impression upon the Negro people of this area to induce them to realize that as long as they patronize these ungrateful merchants, so long will the merchants remain ungrateful.[32]

Movie theaters were also seen as businesses that were obligated to provide not only quality entertainment but fair treatment to black patrons. Major movie houses of Bed-Stuy experienced demonstrations by blacks demanding the right to work where they spent their dollars. In September 1937, for example, the African Nationalist Movement picketed the Sumner Theatre on Sumner Avenue and Quincy Street in Bed-Stuy, demanding that the owners hire blacks. Demonstrators carried signs that read, "This theater is unfair to Negroes. It does not give employment to the race that patronizes it." The theater manager declared that 75 percent of the patrons were white. "I fail to see the justice in forcing others to give up their jobs on the grounds of representation when the representation isn't sufficient." Yet even by the manager's own estimate, business had fallen off considerably due to the picketing.[33]

The Brooklyn African American community's encounter with mass culture, represented in these conditions, resulted in a politicized consumer consciousness stressing the belief that, as consumers spending money and making entrepreneurs wealthy, blacks were entitled to fair treatment. African Americans defined fair treatment as better services, respect as customers, and the right to work where they spent their money. Businesses were seen by many African Americans as agencies that should be responsible for the social and economic well-being of the community. Any businesses failing to provide jobs or respect to consumers should be held accountable to the community. Borrowing from the Chicago and Harlem "Don't Buy Where You Can't Work" campaigns of the late 1920s and early 1930s, that urged blacks not to buy in stores that did not hire them, Brooklyn blacks launched similar crusades.

In her book on the New Deal era in Chicago, Lizabeth Cohen notes that a "spirited movement to achieve black economic independence through employment rather than entrepreneurship occurred on many fronts."[34] This was also the case in Brooklyn. People constantly searched for ways to improve the quality of their lives. The lack of financial institutions in Bedford-Stuyvesant and discrimination against blacks practiced by banks compounded the exclusion of many from establishing businesses. Yet they attempted to search for ways to gain economic integrity. African Americans in Brooklyn developed a consumer ideology that demanded hiring from businesses of mass consumption and entertainment that operated in the black community. Although the various struggles that erupted met with limited early success, they noted a determination for economic independence among African Americans and provided experience for the struggles and successes yet to come.

Brooklyn's Black Churches and Amusement

Some black mainline church leaders abhorred the growth of mass culture. They saw it as corrupting the moral values of their communities.[35] For example, in 1930 the Reverend Henry Hugh Proctor, pastor of Nazarene Congregational Church, continued that tradition by lashing out against immoral nightlife in Brooklyn's black sections. Proctor claimed that Harlem's better class of blacks were leaving for Brooklyn to escape the unhealthy effects of Harlem's nightlife, and he warned that Brooklyn might suffer the same moral deterioration if it continued to indulge in night entertainment.[36]

Not only were taverns, bars, and nightclubs under attack, Christian institutions promoting popular activities also came under criticism. For example, at a meeting of the Interdenominational Ministers Conference of New York, Rev. F. A. Cullen of Salem Methodist Episcopal attacked the YMCA for "fostering unchristian ideals." Rev. Manual Bolden of the First Emmanuel Church in New York reiterated the dangers of the YMCA, warning that this modern age of "materialism and lawlessness" must be challenged.

> The modern idea of the gospel as a social cult for a few pretended intellects or demoralizing social uplift agency, such as is seen in some Young Men's and Young Women's Christian Associations and some religious denominations who stress all kinds of attractions, paraphernalia, festivals, demoralizing activities and degenerating dances, is misleading, erroneous and unrighteous. There may be certain values, but I am sure that they do not represent the Ideal Man, Jesus Christ our Lord; nor his Apostles. The Minister of our Lord should not compromise with evil factors in the nation, in his city, in his community, in his established church, in his home and in his private life. The spirit of lawlessness self-expression and apostasy is rampant throughout the world, and its effects are felt in our immediate local environment. The compromising attitude of professed followers of our Lord strengthens and encourages such conditions as bootlegging, bold prostitution, gambling, cabarets, dens of vice, pool rooms, dance halls and places of degeneracy.[37]

Despite the warnings from a few such ministers, by the 1930s the members of Brooklyn's black mainline churches had begun to incorporate aspects of popular entertainment into their regular activities. Responding to growing demand in the black community, parishioners of black churches offered gala recitals, musicales, beauty contests, popularity contests, banquets, sporting events, and other forms of popular entertainment. Usually described as "pure fun," these events blurred the boundaries between sacred and secular and demonstrated a growing tolerance for popular amusement. Heterosexual social activities and recreation were not only sanctioned but encouraged by churches.

By the 1930s the black mainline churches of Brooklyn had adopted many mass cultural forms. Like the larger black community, black churches used mass culture to maintain their economic and social integrity and to foster community spirit. The black churches acted as cohesive entities in the African American community. By using mass culture, the people in these mainline religious institutions continued to challenge persistent popular images of blacks as nonthinking and socially dysfunctional beings, incapable of succeeding in American society. Instead they adopted a form of nationalism that stressed pride in the capabilities of African Americans in economic as well as social affairs. Like the late nineteenth and early twentieth centuries, black churches appropriated the dominant culture and molded it to serve blacks.

For the most part, members of the black Holiness-Pentecostal churches rejected these mass cultural forms. They held firm to the notion that believers were "in the world but not of the world." Their opposition to individualist values of the market meant that mass consumption, movies, and other commercial forms of enjoyment were contrary to their beliefs. However, even some Holiness-Pentecostal churches felt obligated to incorporate mass cultural forms as part of the church's activities, although the majority continued to resist. Baer and Singer suggest that the movement toward accommodating the cultural hegemony of the larger society may be due to a process of "embourgeoisement" (a growing number of members becoming affluent and influencing the church) of members of some black Holiness-Pentecostal churches.[38]

Church Auxiliaries and Clubs

The expansion of church auxiliaries and clubs are examples of how black church members used forms of mass culture to gain both economic and social independence and build a cohesive black community. Auxiliaries had always been an important feature of church structure, serving the members, assisting pastors, and improving the quality of worship. A good example was the missionary society, which cared for the sick, disabled, young, old, and poor of the church. Other clubs included floral societies, usher boards, and choirs, which also raised funds.[39]

By the late 1920s and early 1930s and continuing through the 1950s, the number of organizations in Brooklyn's large mainline churches increased dramatically. For example, between 1925 and 1940 Brown Memorial Baptist added thirteen auxiliaries; between 1928 and 1948 Mount Sinai Baptist Church increased from a handful of clubs to twenty-five auxiliaries. Bridge Street had fifteen auxiliaries in 1917; by the late 1950s it had established twenty-seven more. By the mid-1950s Concord Baptist Church had forty-five auxiliaries functioning regularly, making it one of the largest in the nation.[40]

The large influx of blacks into Brooklyn's churches in the 1920s and the acceleration during the post–World War II period, along with a changing consciousness about entertainment, help explain the increase in clubs and auxiliaries. Between 1920 and 1931 the number of mainline churches increased from twenty to forty-nine, with the largest growth among the Baptists (from nine to thirty-six). Even more compelling is the increase in Brooklyn's black church congregations. Between 1920 and 1931, Bridge Street grew from 1,300 to 2,800 members; Fleet Street AME Zion from 986 to 2,400; Berean Baptist from 545 to 1,500; Bethany from 700 to 1,600; Concord from 900 to 2,800; and Holy Trinity from 500 to 3,100.[41] Although Berean experienced a decline from 1931 to 1952 (from 1,500 to 1,300), both Bethany and Concord increased to 3,666 and 8,674, respectively. Cornerstone Baptist went from a storefront operation in the 1920s to a church of 1,500 in 1943. First Baptist Church in Brownsville, Brooklyn, increased from fifty members in 1940 to four hundred by 1952. Mount Lebanon Baptist soared from 350 members in 1940 to 4,500 in 1952. Zion Baptist (established in 1917; not to be confused with Mount Zion Baptist, organized in 1923) increased from 856 to 2,526 between 1940 and 1952.[42]

The Baptists and African Methodists were not the only mainline black churches to experience rapid growth. The white-affiliated denominations also increased in membership, although far less dramatically. Siloam Presbyterian grew between 1920 and 1931 from 215 to 580 members; St. Augustine from 390 to 651; St. Phillip's from 220 to 460; and Nazarene Congregational from 135 to 800. Although Nazarene's population had decreased to 380 by 1952, St. Phillip's increased to 1,250 and Siloam to 1,020.[43]

Again, the growth of these major denominations was due, in large part, to the influx of migrants into Brooklyn. Many older established black churches left the downtown area and followed the stream of blacks moving to Bedford-Stuyvesant in the 1930s and 1940s. The first of these older churches to relocate was Bridge Street AME Church, which purchased the White Grace Presbyterian Church building in 1938. The Concord Baptist Church soon followed, purchasing the Marcy Baptist Church in the early 1940s. First AME Zion, Siloam, and St. Phillip's Protestant Episcopal all moved to Bed-Stuy in the 1940s.[44] Owing to relocation and the establishment of new churches, by the late 1950s there were more than eighty black congregations, including thirty-nine Baptist, and eleven African Methodist in Bed-Stuy.[45]

Ministers, church officials, and parishioners established clubs, among other reasons, because of their revenue. Both members and ministers led in the creation of these clubs, although it is often easiest to trace the founding of those started by ministers. Rev. Sandy Ray, pastor of Cornerstone Baptist Church from 1944 until 1979, established numerous clubs, including the Friendship Club in 1948, the Bench Members in 1956, the South Carolina Club in 1938, and the Superior and Victory clubs in 1947. All the state clubs of Brown Memorial were organized by its pastor, George Thomas, in 1940, including the South Carolina, North Carolina, Virginia, and Georgia clubs.[46]

One major function of clubs was to raise funds by sponsoring social events, such as anniversaries, dinners, and pledges. Nazarene clubs helped pay off the church's mortgage. The Concord organizations raised money for the building campaign. In some cases, ministers relied on clubs to supplement the budgetary needs of the church. As was noted in the weekly bulletin of Bridge Street AWME: To "All presidents, groups, all monies being held in your club treasury must be turned in by Sunday October 28 *Budget Sunday*. . . . We must meet our Budget." Clubs became economically indispensable to their churches.[47]

The migration of blacks to Brooklyn and into the churches probably made many within the churches attentive to the wants and desires of the newcomers. Unlike the late nineteenth and early twentieth centuries, in which black churches stressed moral and intellectual uplift, the 1930s forced churches to examine additional concerns. As mass culture took on greater significance, churches decided to adopt it, in part, to attract and hold on to members. Many churches made a decision that they could reconcile mass cultural activities with Christian principles. They accepted certain types of activities that were not socially offensive, or seemed less in opposition to the scriptures. This, however, varied from church to church. No church condoned drinking alcoholic beverages, but some allowed dancing and beauty contests. Church leaders were also attempting to challenge the growing preoccupation with secular mass culture by offering their own brand of popular entertainment, remaining moral leaders of the community as they attempted to adopt mass forms within the boundaries of Christian principles.

The social activities planned by auxiliaries demonstrate the growing role of mass culture. Their names alone suggest a growing interest in entertainment. Siloam's Dance Committee, Stitch and Chatter, Currents Events, Talent Guild, and Fortnight clubs; Cornerstone Baptist's Bench Members, Recreation group, social action committee, and Superior clubs; and the First AME Zion Intercultural Club were all established between 1929 and the middle 1940s. Bridge Street AWME Church organized the Silver Spray Social, Mary McLeod Bethune Dramatic, the Rainbow, and the Eureka clubs, while the Nazarene Congregational Church established the Progressive Art and the Epicurean clubs. Mount Sinai Baptist Church organized the Paul Earl Jones Friendly Circle; the Brown Memorial Baptist Church's Men's Energetic Club and St. Martin's Art Guild were others. Many of Nazarene Congregational Church's affairs were organized by the Epicurean Club.

Siloam's events were planned by a variety of auxiliaries, including the Dance Committee, Current Events Club, Stitch and Chatter Club, the Talent Guild, and the Fortnight club. Even some Pentecostal churches, which stressed fundamentalism, associating entertainment with worldly evil and forbidding recreational and leisure activities, had established social clubs by the 1930s and 1940s. The Church of God in Christ (COGIC) on the Hill had sewing, Mothers, and Young People's Willing Workers clubs. The Church of God on Lafayette Avenue had a Men's Progressive League and a Youth Fellowship. The Neighborhood Mission of the COGIC on Fulton Street had a youth organization, the Victory Temple of COGIC had a Women's Circle, and the First COGIC organized a Sunshine Band.[48]

By the 1930s popular music had taken on greater significance in Brooklyn's black churches, supplementing the traditional programs of spirituals, recitals, and classical concerts. Musical programs in many cases provided both entertainment and fund-raising for the church. The Intercultural Club of the First AME Zion Church sponsored a talent show called "The Stars of Tomorrow," featuring promising young vocalists, instrumentalists, and dramatic performers. Noted stars appearing included the "father of the St. Louis Blues," W. C. Handy, and popular radio host Joe Bostic. The Talent Guild of Siloam Presbyterian presented a show entitled "The Stairway to Stardom," presenting romantic songs such as "Don't Even Say Goodby," "I Wonder Can It Be Love," and "Say You Love Me Too." Mount Sinai Baptist set aside one Sunday a month for "cultural activities, particularly musicales." At the annual Spring Concert of Concord Baptist Church a 300-voice choir, the combined Gospel and Youth choirs of the church, mixed classical with popular music. Besides performing Beethoven's "Mount of Olives," "Oh Rejoice, in the Lord," and Leisring's "Let the Nations Rejoice," the chorus sang folk tunes including "Erie Canal" and the "Savage Warrior."[49]

The Reverend James Adams of Concord Baptist organized a youth band, with boys twelve to eighteen, which played at church functions and "for recreational purposes outside and apart from the church." The Women's Auxiliary of St. Phillip's sponsored a musical and "tea" for its congregation. The Auxiliary of the Men's Club of St. Augustine Episcopal presented a "Night in Brooklyn" described as "real fun," featuring a "master magician" as well as popular music. In some religious circles, dancing became a legitimate form of entertainment. In 1942 St. Phillip's Protestant Episcopal Church sponsored a "gala fall dance" at Webster Hall in Manhattan, arranged by the church's dance committee, with music by Don Wilson and "his Blue Ribbon orchestra." The Dance Committee of Siloam Presbyterian gave a Coronation Ball presenting a Calypso singer, the "Great MacBeth and his Orchestra," as well as a contest crowning the Queen of the Ball.[50]

Gospel Music

The emergence of gospel music is one of the most significant events in black religious culture in the twentieth century. The

89

content and performance style of gospel, which had its origins in the Holiness-Pentecostal churches, altered the nature of worship, recapturing a traditional African American Christianity that emphasized the immediate presence of God and guaranteed deliverance by faith. Gospel gave the congregation in mainline churches a greater participatory role. Moreover, no other cultural form revealed the blurring of the boundaries between the sacred and the secular better than gospel music. Gospel demonstrated how blacks had shaped mass culture for their own taste and needs. Gospel music events in and outside the churches became not just religious ceremonies but entertainment and fund-raising events.[51]

Like African American Christianity during the antebellum period, gospel music required the participation of the congregants as well as the leader. Thus, the call-and-response format in gospel music altered worship in many black churches. Trained professionals and church officials conducted services, but ordinary parishioners were also given a voice and helped set the emotional atmosphere through their responses. The members would participate in the performance by clapping, shouting, saying amen, and joining in the singing. The audience response, usually elicited by gospel singers, made worship more democratic by allowing all members the opportunity to actively take part in the service.[52]

Although the message of gospel music rejected the secular, the performance style promoted acculturation to a secular consciousness. To be sure, by the 1930s gospel itself had become an element of popular entertainment. Gospel performers, including Mahalia Jackson and Thomas A. Dorsey, made records and gained wide popularity. Exciting, emotional, usually accompanied by shouting, hand-clapping, and dancing in the aisles, gospel music was sometimes labeled by some as jazz and blues with a religious message because it borrowed instruments, rhythms, and performance styles from popular African American music. Writers Paul Oliver, Max Harrison, and William Bolcom point out that by the 1930s:

It is likely that the contrasts of falsetto and bass on the recordings of the Ink Spots and the vocal imitations of instruments and strong rhythmic emphasis of the Mills

Brothers were influences on gospel groups. The Alphabetical Four used a guitar for additional rhythmic support, and jazz technique was clearly evident in the comb-and-paper muted 'trumpet' accompaniment of their first recording. Dorsey's "Precious Lord Hold My Hand," and many others. Most recording quartets of the 1930s appear to have been Baptist, but the Golden Eagle Gospel Singers led by Thelma Byrd was probably Sanctified. Their "Tome the Bell" is a driving performance, with congregational singing behind the lead, and piano, guitar, harmonica and tambourine accompaniment. In "He's My Rock" the blues harmonica player Hammie Nixon not only played the accompaniment but took a blues-style solo over a humming chorus.[53]

The Growth of Gospel Music in Brooklyn

Many migrants joined the numerous Holiness-Pentecostal churches with their emphasis on ecstatic participatory style of worship, but others joined the Baptist and Methodists, bringing this style of music with them.[54] In Brooklyn, Siloam Presbyterian, Nazarene Congregational, and the two Protestant Episcopal churches did not establish gospel choruses; they adhered to the liturgical models of their white counterparts, adopting refined European music. Although it was easier to establish gospel choirs in Baptist and Methodist churches because of their individual autonomy (as opposed to the hierarchical control in Episcopal, Presbyterian, and Catholic denominations), before the Depression few had such musical groups. Class consciousness played a major role in the elite churches' decision not to create gospel choruses before the 1930s. Many in these churches were consciously middle class and saw this music, which originated in the religious institutions of the working class, as a threat to their status and image. Myra M. Gregory, a member of Berean Baptist Church since 1912, recalled that during the pastorships of Rev. Matthews and Rev. Eldridge, from the 1920s through the middle 1940s, such "primitive" music was not heard in the church. Instead of gospel groups, these churches had large cathedral choirs.[55]

However, as Brooklyn entered the Depression, gospel choruses were established despite strong opposition from both leaders and congregants. Some of the first mainline churches to establish gospel groups were Cornerstone Baptist (1932), Bridge Street AWME (1935), and Bethany Baptist (1937). By the mid-1940s some twenty-four Brooklyn mainline churches, mostly Baptist and African Methodist, had gospel choruses.[56]

Gospel choruses may have been established in the churches because of their message of uplift. During the Depression years, gospel songs offered a message of hope to millions afflicted by economic hardship. As Mahalia Jackson noted: "Blues are the songs of despair, but gospel songs are songs of hope. When you sing them you are delivered of your burden. You have a feeling that here is a cure for what's wrong. It always gives me joy to sing gospel songs. I get to sing and feel better right away."[57]

In Brooklyn as elsewhere, gospel became not only religious but also popular entertainment, thus representing the blurring of sacred and secular. Gospel songs could be heard in record stores in Bedford-Stuyvesant as often as the most popular rhythm and blues hits. Moreover, gospel concerts were inexpensive entertainment. A gospel concert held at Convention Hall in Brooklyn featured the Coleman Brothers, the Sensational Harmonaires, the Jubilee Stars, and Mrs. Ernestine Washington, the renowned gospel singer and the wife of the pastor of Brooklyn's Washington Temple COGIC, F. D. Washington. Admission was $1.50 at the door or seventy-five cents in advance. In November 1943 the Brooklyn Palace on Rockaway Avenue and Fulton Street featured the famed gospel group, the Clouds of Joy, at an admission price of eighty-five cents.[58] Gospel music had crossed the line into the realm of popular entertainment at an affordable price for working-class people. This musical form was now part of the entertainment business, in competition for the leisure dollar of consumers.

Brooklyn's black churches also became arenas for inexpensive entertainment. By using gospel music they were able to entertain people in a Christian context and raise money. Both Concord and Cornerstone Baptist gave annual gospel concerts as fund-raisers. To prepare for its concerts, the Brown Memorial Baptist Church Gospel Choir created the offices of traveling secretary, traveling treasurer, and program and refreshment chairmen (although the posts were typically held by women). In 1958 Varick Memorial AME Church hosted a special gospel program featuring Thomas

A. Dorsey and various Brooklyn gospel groups that attracted hundreds. In 1941 some two thousand people attended a national convention of gospel choral groups at Bridge Street AWME. More than five thousand people attended the fifth annual WWRL radio station's Gospel Singing Contest at Washington Temple COGIC. The Lunenberg Travelers of Brooklyn took first prize, winning a one-week engagement at the Apollo Theatre in Harlem and a recording contract with Vee Jay Records.[59]

At the *Amsterdam News's* Welfare Fund–sponsored "City-Wide Jubilee and Gospel Festival" in 1945, forty-five church gospel choirs performed, including twenty-four from Brooklyn. The popularity of gospel as entertainment was demonstrated by ticket sales. The first concert at Holy Trinity Baptist Church drew a crowd of one thousand people. Choir directors and presidents of gospel choirs purchased two thousand tickets for their friends and church members, leaving none for the performers to give to their families. In addition, hundreds of audience members requested the choirs to perform particular gospel songs.[60] Consequently, black churches played a major role in helping gospel music to cross over into the arena of popular entertainment. By doing so, they appealed to the taste of African Americans and remained an important cultural force in the community.

Church Fashion Shows and Banquets

Besides music and dances, churches sponsored fashion shows, outings, and bazaars. In 1933 the Young Men's Club of St. Phillip's Protestant Episcopal Church sponsored a three-day carnival, featuring "a popularity contest participated in by Brooklyn's most beautiful girls," amusement booths, and "dancing to the music of a three-piece novelty orchestra." Club president Edward DeGrant hoped to prove that "church-going girls are just as pretty, fashionable and peppy as those found in other wholesome places." That same year, a revue was presented by the combined organizations of St. Phillip's at the Brooklyn Labor Lyceum, featuring scenes from *The Emperor Jones*. In 1944 the *Amsterdam News* reported that the fifteenth annual Spring Bazaar of Berean Baptist Church, running from April 25 to the first of May, had attracted a "throng" of people and raised $2,000 for the church. In 1951 Siloam held a dance at the Chateau Gardens, featuring "the jumping sounds of Jimmie Simmons' Orchestra," and a fashion show, in which "some of this town's most delectable models undulated across the floor." Elsewhere, the Epicurean Club of Nazarene Congregational Church presented a "Fashion Extravaganza" featuring the wife of film and dance entertainer Bill (Bojangles) Robinson, to "entertain and inform our folk in the art of appropriate styles from head to foot." Mrs. Robinson displayed "fashions around the clock." Another fashion show, for women and men held at the Tabernacle Baptist Church at 388 Chester Street in Brownsville, was described by the press as an "evening of wonderful entertainment."[61] The Willing Workers Club of Newman Memorial Methodist sponsored a fashion show featuring "popular lassies" modeling the latest fashions. And the choir of Bethany Baptist sponsored a fashion exhibit of spring and summer styles in its lecture room. Beauty became such an important value that Brown Memorial Baptist gave classes in dermatology and cosmetics in the 1930s.[62]

Guests attending the seventh annual National Sunday School Convention at Washington Temple COGIC were treated to a boat ride around the Hudson. These church-sponsored rides could be social as well as leisurely excursions. By 1938 the annual St. Phillip's Protestant Episcopal Church boat ride became popular enough to be worth a mention in Tommy Watkins's famous gossip column in the *Amsterdam News*:

> The St. Phillips boat ride was a humdinger . . . never saw so many pretty sepia maids in my life . . . and the gossip. . . . Guess I'd better commence spilling it. . . . A certain young thing was rampaging after Walter King—and she should have not been. . . . Eric Lane was tripping like a kitten over a barbed wired fence in the company of pretty Barbara [of the Ronrica Girls]. . . . Dorothy Jenkins sighed slightly as she lulled about without her current heart beat. . . . Bernice Degard and Warren Hodges portrayed love in all its glory. . . . Ray Pease was romeoing about in terrific frenzy while endeavoring to captivate the hearts of all the young girlies.[63]

Another popular social event sponsored by churches was the banquet. Unlike dancing, which in some religious circles was viewed as morally offensive, banquets, testimonial dinners, and other meals gave people the opportunity to socialize without violating the scriptures. Like taverns, and bars and grills, church banquets brought people together, but in this case it offered them a chance to combine worship with conspicuous consumption and showing off their formal wear.[64]

Many banquets and dinners were elaborate affairs in which participants could display their affluence through formal attire. At least two receptions and banquets were held for Rev. Kimball Warren of Bethany Baptist Church, sponsored by the auxiliaries of the church, with a master of ceremonies, entertainment, and prominent guests. In 1938 the First AME Zion Church held a formal banquet in the church; prominent guests sat on a dais, men wore fine tuxedos, and women were elegantly dressed. The walls were hung with flowers, adding to the ambience. Both Cornerstone Baptist Church and Bridge Street AWME Church held banquets in the luxurious St. George Hotel.[65]

Banquets required planning, so committees were established to provide fine food and entertainment. For Bridge Street AWME's 187th anniversary celebration in 1953, several planning committees were established, including a banquet committee, program committee, decoration committee, a hostess committee, an ice cream committee, cake committee, three kitchen committees, a purchasing committee, and a person to handle the special guests on banquet night.[66]

Although the black Pentecostal churches of Brooklyn tended to downplay amusements, by the late 1950s even some of these institutions held formal banquets offering elaborate cuisine. In 1955 the Victory Temple COGIC highlighted its twenty-third anniversary celebration with a reception. In November 1957 a testimonial banquet was held at a Church of God in Christ in Manhattan. Guests included Wilber Chandler of the COGIC on the Hill and F. D. Washington of Washington Temple COGIC. A banquet was held at the Waldorf Astoria for Rev. Samuel A. White, pastor of the COGIC on the Hill, with a menu featuring quiche lorraine, breast of chicken à l'orange, continental rice, brussels sprouts with chestnuts, bibescot glacé, golden rhum sabayo, and petits fours. Committees organizing the affair included banquet, arrangement, ticket and finance, program, seating, floral, and music committees.[67]

Church banquets, like other church-sponsored leisure events, were unifying elements in the black community. They gave blacks the opportunity to network, build church and community organizations, raise money, discuss politics, and simply socialize. At the same time, they emerged as a source of black pride, demonstrating that African Americans were able to organize and carry out sophisticated affairs.

Scholars have noted the growing impact of secularism on the black churches. Some have concluded that black churches have moved away from the sacred aspect of religious life and toward a greater concern with worldly matters. E. Franklin Frazier's *The Negro Church In America* suggests that "by secularization . . . the Negro churches lost their predominately other-worldly outlook and began to focus attention upon the Negro's condition in this world. . . . The churches have been forced to tolerate card playing and dancing and theater-going."[68]

Frazier did not take into account the capacity of African American religion to expand, incorporate, alter the secular while maintaining the sacred. Brooklyn's black churches in the twentieth century did not exclude the sacred as they incorporated various secular forms of amusement. On the contrary, church-sponsored social and cultural events usually incorporated the sacred by including religious rituals in these affairs, never losing sight of the church's mission. Invocation, reading of the scripture, singing religious songs, and giving the benediction became important parts of church-sponsored social functions.

Various social events demonstrate the blending of the sacred and the secular. The annual Bridge Street AWME Senior Choir Tea not only included entertainment and refreshments but an invocation by a minister, recitation of the Lord's Prayer by the congregation, readings of the scripture, and a benediction. The Twenty-fifth Anniversary celebration of the Bridge Street Boy Scouts included a doxology, an invocation, a scripture lesson, a sermon by the pastor, and an "Invitation to Christian Discipline." At the fourth annual vespers services of the Brooklyn chapter of the National Association of Business and Professional Women's Club, Rev. Archie Hargraves, pastor of the Nazarene Congregational Church was the principal speaker.[69]

These and other events mark a transformation in Brooklyn's black church culture. As blacks were exposed to commercial forms of entertainment, they began to incorporate many of its aspects into a religious life. They did not forsake the sacred for the secular, as has been suggested. For the black churches a world-view emerged that was less restrictive in its cultural patterns. It became heterogeneous, blurring the boundaries between accept-able cultural forms. This is not to argue that the churches were blindly accommodationist. As noted, they used mass cultural forms to remain economically and socially independent. The churches demonstrated that they were able to be a cohesive force in the community, incorporating forms of entertainment that appealed to the masses of blacks without abandoning their reli-gious mission.

Evidence suggests that the relationship between the sacred and the secular was not one way. The secular did not just influ-ence the sacred, rather the secular and sacred were naturally transforming. It was not unusual for religious rituals such as invocations, benedictions, and hymns to appear at popular events outside of the church. The Carlton YMCA's gala reception, "Stars on Parade" featured the Striders (an all-male quartet seen in New York nightclubs), "Melody Matt and his five piece ensemble," who performed "several popular numbers which brought the house down," and Maine Sullivan from the Kingston Lounge. An invocation was delivered by Rev. Milton Galamison of Siloam Presbyterian Church. On another occasion, Rev. Garrison Waters, pastor of Newman's Memorial Methodist Church, even spoke at the opening of the Allure Beauty Salon on Fulton Street. In 1942 the Dormitory Club of the Carlton YMCA held a Mother's Day Breakfast. Included in the program was a "brief religious cere-mony led by Jacob Marr, Chaplain of the Club."[70]

By the mid-twentieth century, Brooklyn's black churches had responded to a growing community that emphasized secular val-ues, including commercial recreation, and embraced popular cul-ture. Simultaneously, as the secular penetrated the sacred, the sacred spread beyond the boundaries of the church and began to influence popular entertainment. The result was a form of syn-cretism, creating a cohesive new cultural practice. Accommodat-ing these changes and embracing the secular, while at the same time holding on to their sacred heritage, black churches served the community in a broader social and cultural sphere.

Brooklyn's black churches have always struggled to be an inte-gral part of the black community. As the black population of

Brooklyn grew from the 1930s through the 1950s, and popular culture preoccupied more of its time, black churches molded religious principles and popular leisure entertainment. They reshaped urban America by becoming institutions that offered more cultural choices to blacks. In addition, they redefined popular entertainment by incorporating religious rituals, thus maintaining their positions as moral leaders in their community. Instead of putting people in a position where they were forced to select between sacred and secular, they attempted to provide the best of both worlds. More than any other institution, the church became an organization that linked the secular and religious worlds. It became an important cultural institution by giving people across class lines in the community a means of enjoying pop entertainment and maintaining their religious values. As the community changed, so did the churches. No institution in the black community responded as the churches did, thus making Brooklyn's black churches unique in the community. In a real sense, they were the pulse of the community.

CHAPTER FOUR

The Failure to Make Things Better: Brooklyn's Black Ministers and the Deterioration of Bedford-Stuyvesant

By the 1930s Bedford-Stuyvesant, Brooklyn's largest black community, was becoming one of the city's worst slums. The story of the ghettoization of Bedford-Stuyvesant (popularly, Bed-Stuy) is the story of official government neglect. While housing, employment, education, health care, and other social and economic conditions in Bed-Stuy worsened, little action was taken by government officials to remedy the situation.

Bed-Stuy had also become the home of numerous black churches of various denominations. In fact, many had become the largest institutions in the borough. Many black churches had thousands of members, and the pastors of these institutions were in a position to launch a movement to challenge the forces that were making Bed-Stuy into a ghetto. By the early 1930s black churches had responded to the growth of mass culture by using mass cultural forms to maintain their cultural and economic independence. Yet how did the churches and the men who led them directly respond to the rapid deterioration of Brooklyn's largest black community?

Black Holiness-Pentecostal pastors opposed the dominant political system, urging members to focus on saving their souls by divorcing themselves from secular affairs and concentrating on God. With the exception of a few Church of God in Christ (COGIC) institutions, black Holiness-Pentecostal ministers were not politically active or involved in the social issues of the community. They usually did not back candidates for political office, use their churches for political rallies, participate in demonstrations, form alliances with left and independent forces, or run for political office. Despite their oppositional message, they were not a significant threat to the dominant white society.[1]

However, many ministers of the black mainline churches were active in politics and community affairs. Nevertheless, many were political moderates who were not involved in any independent movements or militant activities to fight the ghettoization of Bed-Stuy. Moreover, before the 1960s there were few individual or combined attempts on the part of Brooklyn's black clergy to wage a significant campaign to force city, state, and federal officials to help better the lives of the ghetto poor. For the most part, ministers viewed the two-party system as the only legitimate political domain. They played the role of insiders, limiting their allegiance to the Democratic or Republican parties. Hence, they also failed to challenge the forces that were making Bed-Stuy into a slum.

However, the church is more than its ministers. Parishioners of mainline and some Holiness-Pentecostal churches did not divorce themselves from the community's crucial concerns. Besides offering religious services and leisurely entertainment, several people in the churches offered a variety of programs for social and moral uplift, especially for children. Scouting and religious education became two major means people in the churches used to save children from the impact of ghetto life.

Unlike the earlier pages of this work, which primarily examined Brooklyn's black church culture, this chapter now moves into the realm of politics. The deterioration of Bed-Stuy and the response to that deterioration were essentially political decisions made by people with power. In part, this chapter looks at why Brooklyn's largest black community became a ghetto and assesses the political performance of some of the most powerful and active black ministers in Bed-Stuy during that neighborhood's decay. However, it would be unfair to ignore the response of ordinary members of Brooklyn's black churches to the ghettoization of Bed-Stuy. During Bed-Stuy's transformation from a viable community to a ghetto, countless numbers of parishioners struggled to improve conditions in that community. Their performance is also an important part of this period and is therefore examined in this chapter.[2]

Bed-Stuy is located in north central Brooklyn. Its northern boundary runs across Clinton Avenue across to Flushing Avenue, dividing it from the community of Williamsburg. Its eastern boundary is at Broadway and Saratoga Avenue, separating that community from the community of Bushwick. Classon Avenue, running from Flushing Avenue to Atlantic Avenue, makes up Bed-Stuy's western border. Atlantic Avenue extending from Classon Avenue to Broadway is its southern border.[3]

By the 1930s the black population of Bed-Stuy grew dramatically. The community became an attractive alternative to the already overcrowded black neighborhood of Fort Greene and an increasingly overcrowded Harlem. The opening of the Independent subway line (the IND) made it convenient for individuals to travel from other parts of the city to Bed-Stuy. Finally, by the 1940s the area became a magnet for Southern black migrants because of the already established black community.[4]

According to the Community Council of Greater New York, in 1930 Bedford-Stuyvesant's black population was a little over 31,000, or 12 percent of the total number of residents. By 1940 the number of blacks residing in the area had grown to 65,000, or 25 percent of the total population. By 1957 the 166,213 blacks in Bed-Stuy accounted for 66 percent of the total population.

At the same time that the black population was growing, whites were leaving Bed-Stuy in large numbers. This population shift was part of a national trend of whites moving from urban areas to the suburbs. Between 1935 and 1960 the white population of Bed-Stuy decreased by more than 40 percent, leaving the area to be inhabited mostly by working-class blacks.[5]

Housing

Coinciding with the growth of the black population of Bed-Stuy was the rapid deterioration of the community. The most obvious sign of Bed-Stuy's transformation from a viable community to a slum was the rapid deterioration of housing. By the 1930s, as blacks came into the area, realtors saw an opportunity to make profits and bought brownstones and homes, converting them into apartments and charging high rents. Many were absentee landlords who rented to large numbers but provided few services and failed to keep up their property, thus causing overcrowding and inadequate living conditions.[6]

Despite the effort of community groups to convince federal authorities to take action against banks who made loans to these speculators, nothing was done. As sociologist Ernest Quimby notes, this process continued in Bed-Stuy throughout the 1930s and 1940s with no government interference.

More and more private homes were subdivided into apartments and single rooms. Overcrowding became commonplace. An increase in absentee landlords resulted in decreased services to tenants. From 1930 to 1940 there was minimal construction. Two neighborhood locales were known by the police and non-residents for prostitution and vice, Myrtle Avenue, between Nostrand Avenue and Broadway, and the vicinity of Franklin Avenue and Fulton Street. Despite protests from churches, black and white, home owners and other groups, the city did nothing.[7]

In 1938 Albert Clark, representing the Brooklyn Federation for Better Housing, a community group struggling for better housing conditions for blacks, reported the results of a study on the living conditions of blacks. Examining a twenty-two block area in Bed-Stuy, Clark reported that "4,807 families were forced to live in 3,421 dwelling units in the heart of the slum area covering twenty-two city blocks." A staggering 91 percent of the apartments were in old buildings without central heating; 85 percent were without hot water, 26 percent were without tubs or showers, 4 percent were without electricity or gas cooking, while 16.1 percent lacked private toilets; 80 percent of the dwellings were owned by absentee landlords. Moreover, 84 percent of the housing was between forty and fifty years old.[8]

The early construction of public housing did little to relieve the poor housing conditions. The first housing projects in Brooklyn were built in Williamsburg and Red Hook, where few blacks lived. For the most part blacks were excluded from these projects.[9]

As Bed-Stuy approached the 1950s, housing did not improve. In 1949 a representative for five families living in a tenement on Sumpter Street in Bed-Stuy noted the horrible conditions of their dwelling. Hot water was only available for a few hours a day, rodents were rampant in the building, there were big holes in the walls, and the building and halls were filthy. Despite a formal complaint by the tenants to the Board of Health, the absentee landlord was not forced to make changes.[10]

During the postwar boom, the Community Council of Greater New York reported that the number of dwellings in Bed-Stuy decreased from 74,849 units in 1950 to 74,095 in 1957. The decrease was partly blamed on demolition, which accounted for the loss of more than six hundred units. The building of public housing projects in the 1950s did little to relieve the situation. Most people lived in privately owned two-family and multidwellings. By the late 1950s, Bed-Stuy had the second highest rate of overcrowding in Brooklyn. In addition, 19 percent of the housing was considered substandard, the highest percentage in Brooklyn.[11]

Employment and Health Care

The World War I demand for industrial labor allowed blacks in Brooklyn to enter the manufacturing industries in unprecedented numbers. Harold X. Connolly notes that by 1920 a quarter of Brooklyn women in the labor force were employed in manufacturing establishments. The largest number of women were in clothing and textiles, while the men were heavily employed as semiskilled operatives and longshoremen.[12]

Yet despite these gains made by African Americans in employment in the 1920s, the Brooklyn Urban League reported that unemployment among Brooklyn's black population had reached its highest level in six years, a fact the league attributed to the "closing of opportunities which brought them here in large numbers during the war." A 1928 Brooklyn Urban League survey of 106 Brooklyn firms revealed that only fifty-eight hired blacks; of the 1,534 black workers hired by the fifty-eight firms, 80 percent were classified as unskilled. A public hearing conducted by the State Temporary Commission on the Condition of Urban Colored Population reported that the public utilities companies in Brooklyn discriminated widely against blacks. The New York Telephone Company refused to hire black operators on any level; the Consolidated Edison Electric Company refused to hire blacks as meter readers, and the Brooklyn-Manhattan Transit Company barred blacks from any position higher than conductor.[13]

The Depression brought hardships to many Americans. However, this period was especially rough on African Americans. In Brooklyn unemployment among blacks was high, despite the effort of the Brooklyn Urban League to find employment for black men, an effort that for the most part was unsuccessful. In 1931 the league noted that only "emergency work" was available for black men. Although many black women were employed, of the 13,825 in the work force in 1930, some 11,664 were in domestic and personal service.[14]

By World War II, employment conditions for Brooklyn's black population improved. Although opportunities opened up for blacks in the defense sector of the economy, the greatest number were employed in nondefense jobs. Firms that had locked out blacks began to hire them in large numbers. This change was due to a labor shortage created by the war.[15]

Although the employment picture for Brooklyn's black population improved during the postwar period, employment conditions for black residents of Bed-Stuy did not get better. The 1950 median income of community residents was well below the borough's median income of $3,447. According to the Community Council of Greater New York, the southwestern part of Bedford-Stuyvesant had a median income of $2,228, the lowest in Brooklyn. The range in other areas of Bed-Stuy was $2,426 to $3,120. By 1957 Bed-Stuy's 9,825 welfare cases accounted for 23 percent of the borough's public assistance cases.[16]

Closely connected with growing poverty in Bed-Stuy was the lack of health care facilities servicing the community. In 1957 the infant mortality rate was 38.3 per 1,000, compared with the borough's rate of 25.2 per 1,000. In some parts of Bed-Stuy the rate was over 40 per 1,000 (in one section it was 52.5).

Venereal disease in Bed-Stuy was the highest in Brooklyn. And although there was a slight improvement in the tuberculosis rate between 1956 and 1958 (from 2.88 to 2.30), it was still well above the 1958 borough rate of 0.98.[17]

Despite these grim statistics, city officials failed to provide adequate health care to Bed-Stuy residents. In a 1953 report, the Hospital Council of the City of New York reversed its 1949 opinion, which had called for the city to allocate funds for a hospital in Bed-Stuy. The council acknowledged the horrible conditions in Bed-Stuy but rationalized that the causes were environmental. "As long as persons in need of hospital care receive it, the location of hospital beds within the area is not of itself a means for reducing the incidence of tuberculosis, venereal disease, infant mortality or maternal mortality. . . . Of major consequence for the incidence of the above conditions are environmental factors, such as sanitation, housing, nutrition, and health education." This was a clear case of blaming the victim.

Acknowledging that residents of Bed-Stuy must go outside their community for health care, the Hospital Council justified not building a hospital by asserting that it was no real burden for people to travel thirty or forty-five minutes on public transportation to reach other facilities. Moreover, it concluded that a new hospital in Bed-Stuy would be detrimental because it would reduce occupancy of neighboring hospitals and "thereby increase their operating costs per patient day and impair their present level of efficiency." According to the council, the solution to Bed-Stuy's health problems was to add 125 beds to Cumberland Hospital, almost thirty minutes away by public transportation.[18]

The Bedford-Stuyvesant Health Congress, a coalition made up of community activists and other local groups, protested the city's reluctance to provide a hospital. Requesting that the mayor release funds from the capital budget to build a hospital in Bed-Stuy, the congress noted:

> The people of the Bedford-Stuyvesant area of Brooklyn, especially the Negro people, have paid and continue to pay a terrible toll in death and suffering because of their residence, race, creed, color and economic status. Year after year twice as many babies die. Dr. Kogel, Former Commissioner of Hospitals, characterized Bedford-Stuyvesant as an area rich in tuberculosis and poor in hospital facilities. The toll of death and suffering increases with the years. . . . Our community is acutely aware of its needs, and experiences mounting resentment over the continued inaction of City authorities to date.[19]

Despite the protest of the Bedford-Stuyvesant Health Congress and its insistence that Cumberland was obsolete and too far away for Bed-Stuy residents, the Board of Estimate (which had decided, in 1951, to set aside $1,250,000 for construction of a hospital in Bed-Stuy) chose, in 1956, to expand Cumberland Hospital, leaving Bed-Stuy without proper health care.[20]

Despite the health crisis in Bed-Stuy and the high rates of infant mortality, tuberculosis, and venereal disease, city officials did nothing. This failure to act, and the view that the health care problems in Bed-Stuy were purely "environmental," demonstrated that city officials had little concern for black people and that black life was of little consequence.

Education

More than any other institution in America, public schools were seen as a means of upward social and economic mobility. It was a means by which poor children climbed out of poverty and became successful. However, despite the fact that education was an important means of gaining success, racism and discrimination led to segregated inferior education for black children throughout the nation. Brooklyn was no exception. As early as 1940, when Bed-Stuy's black population was increasing, community and civic leaders complained about overcrowding and segregation in many public schools that serviced the community.

The School Council of Bed-Stuy and Williamsburg, a community group consisting of parents and teachers, asserted that children were receiving an inadequate education in those communities. The group pointed out that twenty of the fifty-six classes at P.S. 3 on Hancock Street and Bedford Avenue received the normal six hours of daily instruction, while all other classes received only four hours because of a teacher shortage. The school was considered the worst in the city. It was called a fire trap with only one hallway for 1,700 children. Classes were overcrowded with forty children assigned to a room; and shop classes were located near the school's boiler, creating a situation in which children could be burned.

P.S. 3 was not unique; other schools in Bed-Stuy limited daily instruction for children to four hours, and classes were overcrowded as well. At P.S. 35, all classes received four hours of instruction. Because of a teacher shortage at both P.S. 44 on Throop Avenue and Madison Street and at P.S. 129 on Gates and Lewis Avenues, overcrowded and oversized classes were the norm. In addition, children were denied hot lunches because of inadequate kitchen facilities. The School Council also complained that children graduating from junior high schools in Bed-Stuy were zoned to older high schools that lacked modern facilities, including swimming pools and industrial shops.[21]

Despite numerous complaints, the Board of Education did little to change these conditions. In the 1950s, community groups reported that the New York school system was essentially segregated and that black and Hispanic children received an inferior education. In 1954 at a symposium of the National Urban League, Kenneth Clark, an associate professor of psychology at City College, asserted that the New York City public school system was segregated and black children were receiving an inferior education. In addition, segregated schools according to Clark left black

108

children with a sense of inferiority and hindered their educational progress.[22]

The Parents' Workshop for Equality in New York City Schools, a community group that struggled for school integration and was led by the Reverend Milton Galamison of Siloam Presbyterian Church, examined the racial makeup of students in ten junior high schools located in Bed-Stuy. It reported that seven ranged from 70 to 88 percent black and Puerto Rican, while three were between 90 and 100 percent black and Puerto Rican. Although the expected reading level for eighth graders should have been 8.6, the average reading level for eighth graders in these schools ranged from 5.4 to 6.2. Students reading on a third grade level or lower in these ten schools ranged from 44 to 63 percent.[23]

The Parents' Workshop noted that thirty elementary schools in Bed-Stuy and Brownsville were almost totally segregated. According to the Parents' Workshop, in the late 1950s nine ranged from 86 to 89 percent black and Puerto Rican, while twenty-one schools were from 92 to 100 percent black and Puerto Rican. Although the reading level for sixth graders should have been 6.3, it ranged from 3.9 to 5.2.[24] Although the Superintendent and other officials of the Board of Education stated that the board was opposed to "racially homogeneous schools," and that it would integrate segregated schools as soon as possible, little concrete action was taken. The controversy over Junior High School 258 was a good example of the board's inaction. In the early part of 1955, JHS 258 on Marcy Avenue and Halsey Street in Bed-Stuy opened with a student body that was 99 percent black and Puerto Rican. Community groups advocating that the school be integrated claimed that children were not receiving the same instruction as children in predominantly white schools. In addition, few teachers were regularly appointed and thirty-three of the forty-five teachers had requested transfers due to poor working conditions.[25] However, despite protests from the Brooklyn branch of the National Association for the Advancement of Colored People (NAACP), the Brooklyn Urban League, and other community groups, members of the board argued that the school was located in the heart of the black community; therefore, it was not practical to integrate it. Moreover, Superintendent William Jansen asserted that he was in favor of the neighborhood school concept, the belief that children should attend schools in their own neighborhood. In reality, he supported segregation. In March 1957 Jansen assured a group of white parents in Queens who feared that their children were going to be bused to predominantly black schools in Bed-Stuy, "We have no intention whatsoever of long distance bussing or bussing of children simply because of their color. If we bus children, it will be because there is room in one school and not in another, as we do now. We believe in the neighborhood school."[26]

To add insult to injury, few blacks were hired as teachers. In 1949 blacks accounted for only 2.5 percent of the teaching staff and 1.5 percent were regularly appointed. Of the 64,130 teachers in 1955, 544 were black, 312 had regular appointments, while 232 were substitutes. When the Teachers Union requested that the Board of Education hire more black teachers and integrate its schools, it was ignored. Instead the board argued that it hired teachers based on ability and not race. In 1952 Jack Greenberg, Associate Superintendent of schools, responded to the charge that the board was practicing racism in its hiring practices. "Anyone who can present evidence of discrimination in the appointment of teachers and fails to do so is guilty of racial discrimination. Anyone who charges discrimination where none exists is equally guilty of racial discrimination." Neither Jansen nor the board took serious steps to integrate the teaching staff of segregated schools in the mid-1950s. The board only adopted a voluntary transfer plan for teachers and received very few responses. Board officials did not recognize the impact that a predominantly white teaching staff had on children. By not making an effort to hire blacks and Hispanics as teachers, they denied children good role models and contributed to the notion that people of color were intellectually inferior. [27]

The board took little action to turn schools in Bed-Stuy into viable learning centers for children. For the most part, education became a narrow avenue to success for black children residing in Bed-Stuy.

Juvenile Delinquency

As Brooklyn's black communities grew in the 1930s and 1940s, juvenile delinquency became one of the most devastating phenomena in the black community. Many young people, "turned off" by school and alienated from their community, committed unlawful acts including robbery, fighting, and other types of violence. It should be noted that juvenile delinquency was not a social problem unique to the black community. Nationally, juvenile crime was on the increase. This was largely due to the Depression, which had led to massive unemployment and the breakup of many families. In addition, fathers were drafted into the military during the war, and mothers entered the work force. The lack of child-care facilities left many children without adult supervision.[28]

Juvenile delinquency became such a major problem in Bed-Stuy that in 1936 the editor of the *Bedford Home Owners News* urged Mayor LaGuardia to sponsor boys clubs as a means of prevention. "We believe that such clubs, properly supervised, would do much in giving our youth a healthy outlook on life and at the same time would inculcate a true spirit of Americanism."[29] Similarly, in 1943 the editors of the *Amsterdam News* launched a campaign to get community activists, churches, and civic organizations involved in the fight against juvenile delinquency. The *Amsterdam News* called for programs that would "keep the children off the streets and away from temptation. Supervised dances should be planned. . . . Athletic leagues should be brought to the attention of children in the community."[30]

The alarm over juvenile violence was not without its racial overtones. In August 1943 a Kings County grand jury noted the "alarming incidence" of juvenile crime. The all-white grand jury interviewed very few blacks, thus giving credence to the charge that the report was biased. Recalling an earlier period when Bed-Stuy was "one of the finest residential sections of Brooklyn," the jury asserted that a "state of lawlessness" existed in the area:

> Groups of young boys armed with penknives of all sizes and other weapons roam the streets at will and threaten and assault passersby and commit mugging and holdups with increasing frequency. Gangs of hoodlums armed with such knives and weapons commit holdups, stabbing, homicides and serious crimes.[31]

Claiming that most crimes in Bed-Stuy were committed by young people below the age of twenty-one, the grand jury asserted, "These children form into little groups, run into stores, steal merchandise and run away. They break windows; they snatch pocketbooks; they commit mugging, holdups and assaults."

Although the grand jury stated that "this is in no sense a race problem," it was clear that African Americans were blamed for the dramatic increase of crime in Bed-Stuy. In order to appear nonbiased, the jury argued that African Americans were also fed up with the increase in crime and wanted something done.

> The foregoing conditions have been testified to by the many eminent, responsible and trustworthy Colored citizens of this area. They strongly deplore these conditions and have asked and appealed to this Grand jury to do something about them. . . . The desirable elements of this area, negro and white, and of all faiths, are all begging and pleading for relief from these deplorable and shameful conditions.

Despite attempts to appear nonbiased, the jury's racism was blatantly evident. "A great influx of people from out of the State and other areas into this district require more stringent supervision by the public authorities." The jury called for an investigation of the "relief rolls,"and a longer waiting period for relief "in order to eliminate the tendency to live off relief." Moreover, the jury advised that the Colored State Guard in Brooklyn could be enlarged and given an armory with recreational facilities to help take care of three thousand boys. It implied that Guard members could be good role models for black youth.[32]

Although the grand jury was correct to point out that juvenile delinquency was a growing problem in Bed-Stuy, it inferred that the sole reason for the problem was because more blacks were moving into the area. It made no attempt to examine the causes of juvenile crime.

Police reports indicate that, during the first ten months of 1943, there had been a 53.4 percent increase in juvenile arrests, compared to the first ten months of 1942. In eight police precincts serving Bed-Stuy, there were 356 juvenile arrests in 1941. In the first ten months of 1943, there had been 565 juvenile arrests. By the 1950s juvenile crime had reached epidemic proportions in Bed-Stuy. While in 1957 the overall borough rate was 33.4 per 1,000, in some areas of Bed-Stuy the rate ranged from 46.4 to 89.9 per 1,000. In 1958 the rates in Bed-Stuy ranged from 65.8 to 119.0 per 1,000.[33]

One explanation for the increase of juvenile crime in Bed-Stuy was the growth of the "under thirty" population. By 1957 half the area's population was under thirty. Bed-Stuy had more children under the age of fourteen than any other section of Brooklyn (11.4 percent of a total of 606,564). From 1950 to 1957 the number of children between the ages of six and thirteen increased by 19 percent. As the Police Commissioner notes in his report to Mayor LaGuardia in 1943, "The greater the number of children, the greater is the number of possible delinquents." By 1957 Bed-Stuy had more children between the ages of fourteen and nineteen than any other section of Brooklyn.[34]

Yet the increase in the youth population alone cannot explain the dramatic growth in juvenile arrests. Three other sections had a greater proportion of children overall than Bed-Stuy, yet their juvenile crime figures were lower. Other factors played a significant role, including more accurate reporting on juvenile crime by police and greater police presence in the area. Poverty and despair were also factors. As noted earlier, by 1949 Bed-Stuy's population earned well below the boroughwide median income and by 1959 had one-quarter of the borough's home relief cases. In addition, the area had the worst housing in the borough. These conditions helped create despair and a sense of hopelessness, important factors motivating antisocial behavior.

Institutional racism was also an important factor in the number of arrests of black children. There were very few black police officers in New York, and the vast majority of white officers were from outside of Bed-Stuy and had little understanding of African Americans. They held the same racist beliefs toward blacks as the larger society. This lack of understanding led innocent people to suffer unwarranted arrest and physical assault at the hands of the police; many of these victims were teenagers.[35]

From the 1930s to the 1950s, the Bed-Stuy branch of the American Communist Party, the American Labor Party, and the Brooklyn branch of the NAACP all waged campaigns against police abuse. The American Communist Party carried numerous articles in its paper, *The Daily Worker*, reporting on acts of police brutality in Bed-Stuy and other parts of the city. In 1936 the Bed-Stuy branch of the American Communist Party sent a letter to Mayor LaGuardia protesting acts of police brutality against children.[36] In the 1940s the American Labor Party, a leftist political party, demanded that Gov. Thomas Dewey name a special prosecutor to investigate allegations of police brutality in the city. Again in 1952, the American Labor Party publicly joined with the NAACP and other groups in Brownsville to win the conviction of a police officer who had shot and killed a twenty-seven-year-old black man. The Brooklyn branch of the NAACP conducted numerous campaigns against police abuse. In May 1959, for example, the NAACP held a rally protesting "This New Wave of Police Brutality in Brooklyn," the death of yet another black man (Al Garret) at the hands of the police, and the beating of a fourteen-year-old girl by police.[37] However, despite numerous cases of police brutality and protests from political and civil rights groups, no action was taken by city officials to stop police assaults. This lack of effort was just another indication of the lack of concern and respect that government officials had for people of African origins.

By the late 1940s and the 1950s, and probably due to the rapid increase in juvenile crime and pressure from various community groups, the city launched an accelerated program of building both playgrounds and recreational centers in Bed-Stuy. City officials asserted that a variety of sporting and recreational activities was an effective means of stopping juvenile crime because they built character, sportsmanship, and discipline. Proponents of using sports and recreation as a way of fighting juvenile delinquency also asserted that organized physical activity in parks, playgrounds, and recreational centers took children and teenagers off the streets, thus decreasing their chances of breaking the law. Referring to the city's efforts to open playgrounds in Bed-Stuy, Parks Commissioner Robert Moses noted:

> The playground is a powerful weapon in the war on "so called" juvenile delinquency. To quote City Council President [Abe] Stark, "only supervised recreational centers, playground activities and healthy athletic competition can provide our city's boys and girls with a healthy environment. How much better it is to fight juvenile delinquency in this manner than to let young people congregate in bars, cellar clubs, and disreputable honky tonks.[38]

Consequently, parks, playgrounds, and recreational centers became a means of social control. According to Moses, the objective of the parks and playgrounds was not only to provide "healthy exercise for millions of juveniles, but to create a calming as well as a stabilizing effect on large numbers of people who have experienced ill effects of urbanization."[39]

By 1944, a year after the Kings County grand jury's report, Brooklyn's borough president John Cashmore persuaded the Board of Education to open fourteen school gymnasiums in Bed-Stuy during the summer. By the 1950s the city operated twenty-two playgrounds in Bed-Stuy, with various recreational facilities, including wading pools, sand pits, and a comfort station. The parks provided teens and older people with softball, basketball, and handball courts, shuffle board, tennis, horse shoe pitching, volley-ball, roller skating, and ice skating areas for "healthy exercise."[40]

In addition to the playgrounds, the city established at least five evening, two afternoon, and seven afternoon and evening centers in Bed-Stuy in the 1950s in order to fight juvenile crime. Most operated in elementary and junior high schools, offering young people basketball, table games, and arts and crafts.[41]

The Saint John's Recreation Center, located at Saint John's Park in Bed-Stuy was specifically aimed at curbing juvenile delinquency in that community. Opened in 1956, it offered a gymnasium for basketball, boxing, and other sports; a huge swimming pool for recreational and competitive swimming; a senior game room with ping pong tables, a pool table, table hockey sets, and lounge chairs; a junior game room with checker sets, table hockey sets, and ping pong tables; and a woodwork shop. Operating seven days a week from ten in the morning to ten in the evening, the center was staffed by fifty-one people, including specialists in swimming, arts and crafts, cooking, and physical education.[42]

However, despite the effort of city government to halt juvenile crime, it failed to address the larger issues which helped produce delinquency, such as poverty, dysfunctional family life, unemployment, powerlessness, and alienation. By providing recreational facilities as the sole solution to juvenile delinquency, government officials and many outside of government demonstrated, at best, a lack of vision and at worst a lack of concern for the urban poor. City officials assumed that the major solution to juvenile delinquency in Bed-Stuy was to keep the children in that community off the streets. There was no attempt on the part of the city to understand the problems facing migrants new to urban living. Little assistance was given to people living in dilapidated housing or to children attending schools that were understaffed, had oversized classes, and received few funds for improvement. Bed-Stuy was a community in crisis. There was a need for a financial commitment on the part of the federal, state, and city governments along with private sources to help improve housing, employment opportunities, and health care and education. Instead of meeting the challenge, government at the city, state, and federal levels limited its involvement.

Black Ministers and Political Leaders

As noted in chapter 3, there was a dramatic increase in Brooklyn's black congregations. The growth was due in large part to the influx of migrants into Brooklyn. Many older established black churches left the downtown area and, in the 1930s and 1940s, followed the stream of blacks moving into Bedford-Stuyvesant, Brooklyn's largest black community. Bridge Street AWME, Concord Baptist, First AME Zion, Siloam Presbyterian, and St. Phillip's Protestant Episcopal were just a few of the churches that relocated from the downtown area of Brooklyn to Bedford-Stuyvesant.[43]

This dramatic increase in overall membership in the black churches made black ministers increasingly important figures in the community, giving them an enormous potential for waging a significant war against the ghettoization of Bed-Stuy. Unlike other community organizations which had limited resources and members, the black churches were in a position to organize large numbers of people, raise large sums of money, act as an independent political bloc, hold rallies and demonstrations, speak out against government inaction without fear of retaliation, and take other independent measures to make Bed-Stuy a viable community.

The middle-class ideology of moral uplift and individualism which had been stressed in the late nineteenth and early twentieth centuries by African Americans was still a major theme of black churches. Nevertheless, the realities of ghettoization and the Depression called for more drastic solutions and a greater role for the institutionalized church in the lives of its members and in the community.

However, for the most part the churches and the men who led them during Bed-Stuy's decline did not live up to their potential.

Most ministers did not champion belligerent tactics or provide independent leadership. Some were well connected with the major political parties and were unwilling to take aggressive action to force government officials to address the harsh conditions of the ghetto's poor. This is not to say that the ministers did not believe that the government should play a greater role in assisting the urban poor. Many publicly argued that the government must take an active role in ending poverty and racism. However, these ministers did little to force government to take an active role.

A closer examination of several active black ministers during Bed-Stuy's decline reveals that they had strong connections with the major parties. They limited their political activities to working for the election of prominent Republican or Democratic candidates, received political appointments, and ran for political office.

Several Brooklyn black ministers were well-known Republicans, including William Orlando Carrington, pastor of First AME Zion Church from 1936 to 1964; George Shippen Stark, pastor of Siloam from 1920 to 1947; and Schuyler Thomas Eldridge, pastor of Berean Missionary Baptist Church from 1928 to 1946. James Adams, pastor of Concord from 1921 to 1936 was an active member of the Kings County Colored Republicans and often spoke at their functions. In 1936 Adams was the guest speaker at a celebration the Kings County Colored Republicans held at First AME Zion Church. Again in 1936, Adams endorsed the Republican candidate for President, Alfred M. Landon, along with W. O. Carrington; Rev. Mansfield F. Jackson, pastor of Bridge Street AWME Church; and C. P. Cole, pastor of Bethel AME Church. Adams's close connection with the Republican Party and his endorsement of Landon prompted one militant Brooklyn black minister to attack the Concord pastor by calling him a "no account."[44]

Boise Dent was known as a "staunch Republican." Dent, who was born in Virginia in 1895, came to Brownsville and became pastor of Tabernacle Baptist Church. In 1949 Dent was selected to head Republican politician Abe Stark's campaign for borough president. Benjamin Lowery, who became pastor of Zion Baptist Church in 1921, headed a ministers and citizens committee to reelect New York Republican Gov. Thomas Dewey in 1950. George Thomas, who became pastor of Brown Memorial Baptist Church in 1938, was selected by the Republican Party to run for Congress in a Brooklyn district.[45]

Sandy F. Ray, pastor of Cornerstone Baptist Church from 1944 until his death in 1980, was probably the most influential Brooklyn black minister in the Republican Party. Ray, who received his B.A. from Morehouse College, was known as a "stalwart" of the Republican Party. Before starting his tenure at Cornerstone, he had been a member of the Ohio State Legislature. In Brooklyn he developed close ties with Republican top brass and worked for the reelection of Governor Dewey in 1950. Ray would later develop a close relationship with Nelson Rockefeller, who served as governor of New York from 1958 to 1973. Rockefeller was a frequent visitor to Cornerstone. Ray worked for other Republican candidates and even considered running for a congressional seat.[46]

Gardner C. Taylor noted that he was one of the few Democrats among the active black clergy in Brooklyn. Taylor became the most noted black minister in the Democratic Party. Born in Baton Rouge, Louisiana, he received his B.A. from Leland College and his B.D. from Oberlin. He came to Concord in 1948. After serving only eleven months at Concord, the thirty-year-old minister was appointed to a local school board by Brooklyn Borough President John Cashmore. Taylor later developed close ties with Mayor Robert Wagner, who in 1954 named Taylor to an advisory group to improve city services. In 1958 Taylor was selected by Mayor Wagner to serve on the Board of Education, and in January 1962 the Brooklyn pastor was one of three men selected by Wagner to replace Joseph T. Sharkey as Democratic leader of Brooklyn.[47]

Because pastors of several black Brooklyn churches could potentially influence a large number of people, leaders of the Republican and Democratic parties turned to them for support. Consequently, these black ministers gained a certain political leverage within the mainline parties. However, such close political ties probably made these Brooklyn black ministers less likely to seek alliances with the left or to use tactics that would jeopardize their political positions.

At least two Brooklyn ministers even joined the Cold War crusade and attacked the left. Oliver Wendell Jones, pastor of Newman Memorial Methodist Church, accused Communists of attempting to "stamp out Christianity." He asserted, "We have a large group of people in the Kremlin . . . who are in effort to put out the fires of Christianity, close the doors of the church and imprison the ministers."[48]

Although Sandy F. Ray, who was head of the National Baptist Social Commission, testified before Congress calling for the repeal of the Smith Act of 1940 (which made it a crime to advocate the forcible overthrow of the United States government), he joined the anti-Communist crusade and even expressed faith that the democratic system during the Jim Crow era would work for blacks. In 1947 Ray spoke before a Senate committee declaring that the United States was a free and democratic country whose task was to help make the world safe for democracy. The prominent Brooklyn pastor argued, "Our approach is from the Christian point of view. We have not, and shall not commit our convention to any Foreign or subversive ideology.[49]

Ray also told a crowd of fifteen hundred at a National Baptist Convention meeting, "We are going to work within the framework of the United States Constitution and not be fooled by any foreign group or foreign philosophy, for we have in our Constitution provision for equal rights." Again in 1953, Ray defended Protestant clergy from McCarthyism by declaring, "Neither the Negro Protestant clergy nor laymen have given any support to communism."[50] Historian Manning Marable notes that during the McCarthy period, when black intellectuals such as W. E. B. Du Bois and Paul Robeson were defamed, the black clergy were silent. On the whole, this was certainly true of the black ministers of Brooklyn. Despite their position as prominent men in the community, few ever used their clout to condemn the attacks on left of center forces.[51] For most black clergy of Brooklyn, theology did not serve as a radical ideology calling for concrete action against oppression.

Despite their association with the two mainstream parties, their moderate views, and disassociation from the left and grassroots groups, most black clergy did not join conservative forces that called for the least amount of government involvement in domestic affairs. From their pulpits and in newspaper interviews, the black ministers of Bed-Stuy called on government to take action against racial injustice. In addition, many Brooklyn black ministers were involved in community and civil rights organizations. Many were active members of the NAACP and the Urban League. Hilton L. James of Berean Missionary Baptist, Sandy F. Ray (Cornerstone Baptist), Benjamin Lowery (Zion Baptist), John Coleman (rector of St. Phillip's Protestant Episcopal Church from

1932 to 1962), Richard Saunders (Stuyvesant Heights), Archie Hargraves (pastor of Nazarene Congregational Church), C. L. Franklin (pastor of Mount Lebanon Baptist Church from 1938 to 1950), and Thomas Goodall of Bethany Baptist Church were all executive board members of the NAACP and participated in the group's annual membership drives. In addition, these ministers helped recruit members for the civil rights organization from among their parishioners.[52]

Gardner C. Taylor was an active member of the executive board of the Urban League. In fact, Taylor testified on behalf of the Brooklyn Urban League at public hearings held by the Board of Education. At one such hearing Taylor told Board of Education officials that "the way to integrate is to integrate." In June 1959 Taylor sent the members of the board a copy of a newspaper article that compared New York City to Little Rock, Arkansas. In a cover letter, Taylor suggested that the comparison between Little Rock, Arkansas, and New York was frightening. Taylor warned board members, "I am confident that you will see this as one more instance of the forthrightness with which we must move, in the matter of full and complete integration of New York schools. We condemn the assault on our democracy which came in the infamous attacks on nine little Negro children, and rightly—but Little Rock will never be right until New York is right; and New York will never be right until Little Rock is right."[53]

Besides individual church and ministerial efforts, there was some collective action on the part of Brooklyn's black clergy to provide assistance to African Americans. One of the most active ministerial organizations in Brooklyn was the Interdenominational Ministers Alliance. Founded in the 1920s in order to promote interfaith cooperation, the group sponsored Emancipation Day celebrations commemorating the destruction of slavery. The group conducted annual services in January by reading the Emancipation Proclamation and commenting on its significance. In the 1930s the Alliance provided food and aid for black families suffering from the impact of the Depression. In the 1940s the Alliance worked with City Councilman J. Daniel Diggs to improve bus service in Bedford-Stuyvesant. In addition, the ministerial group met with city hospital officials and was able to persuade the hospital commissioner to order voluntary hospitals to improve ambulance service in Bedford-Stuyvesant. The group also convinced the commissioner to lift a ban that barred city hospitals from issuing contraceptive devices. This action was in response to the demand by black leaders for city officials to take action against the growing problem of teenage pregnancies in Bed-Stuy. In 1950 members of the Interdenominational Ministers Alliance, including C. L. Franklin, W. O. Carrington, and John E. Bryant from the First Church of God in Christ, were selected as delegates to a national civil rights conference sponsored by the NAACP. Benjamin Lowery, Thomas Goodall, and Hilton L. James also attended the conference as representatives of a Baptist organization.[54]

The Interdenominational Ministers Alliance also addressed the issue of education. It sponsored a meeting at Siloam Presbyterian to protest the Board of Education's lack of effort to integrate schools and to seek ways of organizing a campaign for integration. Besides attempting to organize people, the meeting also gave parents and others an opportunity to express their views and to offer suggestions for the struggle for school integration.[55]

Many ministers of the community also joined the struggle for a hospital for Bed-Stuy. In 1950 a community meeting was held at First AME Zion to protest the health conditions of the community. Three years later a community drive was launched in order to get the City of New York to allocate funds for a hospital under a select committee of ministers and civic leaders. The drive was headed by Benjamin Lowery of Zion Baptist Church and was supported by the ministers of Bedford-Stuyvesant. The group, which met at First AME Zion Church, named itself the Citizens Committee for a Bedford-Stuyvesant Hospital Site. Besides many political figures such as the borough presidential candidate Abe Stark and Municipal Court Judge Lewis S. Flag, noted ministers attended, such as Rev. George Thomas of Brown Memorial Baptist, Rev. Charles England of St. Augustine, and John Coleman of St. Phillip's. The *Amsterdam News* reported that many in Bedford-Stuyvesant held special prayer services for the hospital site. The prayer services give evidence that the ministers were keeping their congregations informed on this vital issue. Prayer was a means to raise the issue and, therefore, to make people conscious of the importance of the struggle.[56]

However, when the city decided not to use funds first allocated to build a hospital in Bed-Stuy, the committee had no followup plan. Lowery and others made complaints but to no avail.

There were no protests, no organized street demonstrations, no attempt to organize ordinary people in the community. The strategy used by the committee was to win support among prominent politicians in order to influence city officials. When this effort failed, the committee disbanded. The same shortfall was also true of the efforts taken by black ministers of Brooklyn to improve employment conditions for African Americans. Little direct action was taken by ministers to address the employment conditions of blacks. Although they grabbed headlines for various activities, there was no attempt to launch a campaign to challenge government inaction.

It should be noted that there were exceptional ministers, starting from the early part of the twentieth century, who attempted to provide a political voice for the community and addressed crucial issues that had an impact on blacks. The Reverends George Frazier Miller, Thomas Harten, and Theophilus Alcantara were some of the most outspoken clergy in Brooklyn.

Rev. George Frazier Miller was one of the most noted early twentieth-century politically active ministers. Born in South Carolina in 1864, Miller attended Howard University and earned a B.A. in 1888. He served as rector of an Episcopal church in Charleston and soon after as rector of an Episcopal church in North Carolina. He moved to Brooklyn in 1896 to become the rector of St. Augustine Protestant Episcopal Church.[57]

Miller used his pulpit as a political forum. For example, in 1917 when seventeen black soldiers were executed for allegedly inciting a riot in San Antonio, Texas, Miller accused the commanding officer of carrying out a "military lynching" done for the purpose of appeasing the racists in the South. "I ask if this is calculated to increase our patriotism? There are many of us who are not bound by ties of blood to these men who consider that a deep wrong was done to them. They were offered as a sacrifice upon the altar of infamous Southern prejudice." [58]

Miller became a socialist, arguing that Christ was a "revolutionary" who addressed the social needs of the poor. He wrote for A. Philip Randolph's socialist magazine, the *Messenger*, and in 1918 Miller ran for a congressional seat on the Socialist ticket. By ideologically connecting socialism and Christianity, he attempted to put the black church in the vanguard of addressing economic concerns of blacks.[59] Thus, Miller became an independent voice in the black community. Nevertheless, Miller did not manage to establish a strong link with working-class African Americans. Despite Miller's concern for the economic plight of blacks, very few were members of the Socialist Party, partly because the party did little to attract African Americans. Miller was never a part of any significant effort to organize blacks for political action.

Another well-known minister publicly addressing the political and social conditions of African Americans in Brooklyn was Rev. Thomas Harten. Harten became pastor of Holy Trinity Baptist Church in 1922. By the late 1920s, Reverend Harten had become one of the most dynamic pastors in New York City. He had gained a reputation as a fiery preacher who was able to excite audiences, bringing men and women to a frenzy. Moreover, Harten gained a reputation as a protest leader. In 1925 he became head of the Brooklyn chapter of the National Equal Rights League, which was organized by William Monroe Trotter. Harten later organized another protest group named the Afro-Protective League. Both groups protested lynchings in the South and combated police brutality and racial discrimination in New York City.[60]

In July 1925 nearly two thousand people jammed Holy Trinity in response to a plea by the National Equal Rights League, protesting the "apparent propaganda of racial prejudice and oppression carried on by the police force in Brooklyn." Several black men had been picked up and brought in for questioning in regard to the murder of a white woman. The crowd at Holy Trinity selected a committee to call upon the office of the District Attorney of Brooklyn and demand an end to police harassment of black men and the prosecution of all offending officers. The delegation included Harten, Rev. George Frazier Miller of St. Augustine Protestant Episcopal, and Rev. Henry Hugh Proctor of Nazarene Congregational Church.

Several months later, more than one thousand people attended a rally called by the National Equal Rights League at Holy Trinity to protest the brutal police assault on a black woman. A few days after the rally, Harten led a crowd of three hundred protesters to Brooklyn Borough Hall to demand that officials take action against the police officer who had attacked the woman.[61]

In 1926 Harten led a crowd of five hundred to Brooklyn's Borough Hall demanding "justice and a fair deal" for two black women who claimed to have been beaten by a white police officer. The demonstration was an attempt to put pressure on District Attorney Charles J. Dodd and a grand jury investigating the alleged beating. Harten, who was joined by William Monroe Trotter, attacked the grand jury for its delay in action. Demonstrators carried banners and marched around Borough Hall.[62]

In 1928 Harten was arrested when he protested in front of the Court of Special Sessions on Atlantic Avenue in Brooklyn for its mishandling of a case where a black woman was allegedly beaten up by police. After Harten's release, the National Equal Rights League held a mass rally at Holy Trinity Church to protest the pastor's arrest.[63]

Although Harten asserted that he would stay out of politics and concentrate only on his church after the Democratic Party passed him over in 1932 for an elected office, he continued his activities for civil rights and trying to improve the conditions of blacks. In 1936 the militant minister announced he would organize an annual conference of members of several political parties, including Democrats, Republicans, Socialists, and Communists, to discuss "labor problems, lynching, discrimination, jim-crowism, and other evils of the present day social system." He asserted that the conference would motivate these parties to take constructive action to eliminate such problems.[64]

In 1937 he became involved in the defense committee for the Scottsboro Boys. Risking his reputation as a distinguished pastor and criticism from black leaders, he teamed up with the religious cult leader Father Divine in the fall of 1937 and held a mass rally in Manhattan for the defense of the Scottsboro Boys. They attracted thousands to the rally, where Harten declared:

> I never thought I'd be on the same platform with Father Divine. . . . I never wanted to meet him—to tell you the truth. But God had to go down to the darkness of an Alabama cell and bring these four lads to Brooklyn to get Harten and Divine on the same rostrum. There are a lot of people who are here and a lot who aren't who are going to talk about me for appearing here. But that doesn't matter. They talk about you wherever you go. That doesn't worry me. I want you to know however, . . . that Father Divine will not convert to me tonight nor I to him. . . . I want you to know that we're not here to do battle. But we are here for a com-

mon cause. For the cause of justice, liberty and righteousness.[65]

In 1938 Harten hosted a meeting of the United Beauty Culturists Association of America at Holy Trinity. At the meeting Harten addressed the plight of domestic workers and promised ways to improve their lot.[66]

In 1942 the *Amsterdam News* reported that two thousand people attended a meeting at Holy Trinity to hear Harten attack lynching and "Jim Crow" tactics throughout the country. The people attending the meeting voted to forward a resolution to President Roosevelt urging him to "use his high office to make the democracy for which we are fighting for abroad a reality for the 15 million Colored Americans." Harten later told the crowd that it was time for an African American to be elected to Brooklyn's 17th Assembly District. "We must endorse our own man. That will prevent the political leaders from endorsing one of us who would be a Negro handkerchief head Uncle Tom, political stool pigeon."[67]

Despite all of the publicity that Harten received, he accomplished little. There was no follow-up in his campaigns, nor did he actively seek to forge any long-term alliance with his fellow clergy. Hence, he gained headlines but little in the way of solutions. Nevertheless, he used his church to organize people for numerous campaigns. In addition, he gained a great deal of news coverage and brought some of the problems African Americans faced to the attention of many New Yorkers. His greatest achievement was in becoming a militant voice for blacks and bringing to the fore the issue of police brutality and lack of black empowerment.

Theophilus Joseph Alcantara was another celebrated black minister of Brooklyn. Born in Guyana in the early part of the century, Alcantara came to the United States in 1921. He soon became a member of the newly formed African Orthodox Church (AOC). The AOC was organized by George Alexander McGuire, a follower of Marcus Garvey, who believed that blacks should reject the whiteness in Christianity and see God in their own likeness. McGuire was a former Episcopalian priest who left the priesthood in order to become a chaplain in Garvey's Universal Negro Improvement Association. He contended that a black religious hierarchy and liturgy should be created for people of African origins. AOC adheres to the Niceo-Constantinopolitan Creed. McGuire became the AOC's first bishop. As bishop he headed a diocese and was president of the diocesan synod.[68]

In 1928 St. Simon, located at 300 Putnam Avenue in Bedford-Stuyvesant, became the first AOC in Brooklyn. Soon after the establishment of St. Simon, other African Orthodox churches were formed in Bed-Stuy, including St. Michael's, St. Leonard's, St. Paul's, St. Mary the Virgin, and St. Ambrose. In 1935 Alcantara became rector of St. Ambrose.

Alcantara became a central figure in the fight for better housing in Bed-Stuy. He became the cochair of the Brooklyn Federation for Better Housing, a community group that fought for the abolition of slums and for a housing project. The group attempted to make government officials aware of the poor housing conditions for blacks in Bed-Stuy by conducting surveys and making them public. Moreover, the group lobbied government officials for support. When $25 million was set aside by the federal government for slum clearance in New York City in the 1930s, Alcantara contacted Nathan Straus, administrator of the U.S. Housing Authority and Alfred Rheinstein, chair of the New York Housing Authority in order to lobby for part of the funds to go to Brooklyn. Eventually, the Kingsboro housing project was built in the early 1940s, no doubt in part due to the persistence of Alcantara.[69]

Alcantara also became involved in leftist politics. He ran for the state assembly seat during the 1930s and 1940s on the American Labor Party ticket, a leftist political party that had ties with the Communist Party. In addition, Alcantara was part of a group of prominent Bed-Stuy residents who publicly called for the release of American Communist Party leader Earl Browder, who was jailed in the 1940s.[70] Like Miller and Harten, Alcantara was an important and militant voice in the black community.

Despite his efforts, Alcantara noted that he could not rally the support of his fellow clergy in his bid to develop a militant voice. Expressing surprise at his failure to win the seat for the 17th assembly district, he lashed out at his fellow black ministers, accusing them of supporting the incumbent Fred G. Moritt. Attempting to figure out what went wrong, the fiery minister told reporters:

I looked back over the innumerable happenings—the speeches, the requests by the opposition to back down from the assembly race in favor of Mr. Moritt, for which a $6,000 patronage job would be my payment, the endorsements of honest white and outstanding Negro organizations. Looking back over all those things and sifting them with thorough investigations I can come to no other conclusion than that the Negro ministers of Brooklyn, the very same who publicly disdain politics, politicians and patronage, are in it up to their heads.

"'Look around you. Name any minister . . .'" After naming a few ministers who were exceptions, Alcantara went on to condemn the borough's black ministers for not supporting him.[71]

The individual and collective endeavors by ministers were noble at best but fell short of having a real impact on the deteriorating conditions of the ghetto. Although they could point to a few achievements, there were no important gains, largely due to the fact that there was no long-range effort to battle the ghetto's problems. Despite individual efforts on the part of a few of the black pastors of Brooklyn, these could not alleviate the dreadful living conditions in Bedford-Stuyvesant, Brownsville, and the borough's other growing black communities. Ministers needed to collectively build a movement to address the lack of effort on the part of government officials to provide needed financial support to the community. People needed a collective voice from the black clergy to find solutions to the crises in housing, education, health care, and employment. The black clergy of Brooklyn did not attempt to organize and lead a campaign for financial assistance from the government in order to provide vital health facilities and other services to the children of Bed-Stuy. They did not become a force challenging the hegemonic power of the state. The ministers of Bed-Stuy lacked a class analysis. They did not speak of blacks as part of the economically exploited working class in a capitalist society. Nor was their talk of the detrimental impact of capitalism on the working poor. Instead, they held a view that they could help solve the problems of the ghetto poor through a policy of constructive engagement with government officials. Through a dialogue with people in power, pastors presumed they could win needed services for people in Bed-Stuy.

An important exception was Milton A. Galamison, pastor of Siloam Presbyterian Church. More than any minister in Brooklyn, he attempted to build a movement specifically for school integration that consisted of parents, ministers, and community activists and civil rights organizations. Besides forging alliances, Galamison was willing to use aggressive action to win integration.

Galamison, born in Philadelphia in 1923, received his undergraduate degree from Lincoln and a master's degree from Princeton Theological Seminary in 1947. Galamison was a "political independent." He embraced socialism and even praised the Communist leader Fidel Castro. Shortly after the Cuban Revolution, Galamison visited the island and was amazed at the feeling of enthusiasm and the love for Castro. He noted that "everywhere there was a feeling of enthusiasm and a sense of newfound freedom. The experience helped me to understand more than ever before what Moses meant to the Jewish people, what Chou En Lai meant to the Chinese people, what George Washington meant to the American people—this is what Fidel Castro meant to the Cuban people." Although not publicly endorsing communism, Galamison condemned capitalism for its failure to end hunger, for not giving "spiritual and moral drink to the thirsty," and for failing to abolish race and class divisions.[72]

Coming to Siloam in 1948 at the age of twenty-five, Galamison soon asserted his opposition to segregation by refusing to pay a tax to the Brooklyn-Nassau Presbytery, which was attempting to build a Presbyterian church in Long Island where the Levittown private homes were being built. Noting that blacks could not buy the new homes, Galamison told the *Amsterdam News*, "We want to see the extension of the Presbyterian Church . . . but we cannot support movements into areas where we are not certain Negroes would be welcome."[73]

In the late 1950s Annie Stein, Claire Cumberbatch, and Winston Craig, community activists and militant members of the Brooklyn branch of the NAACP, approached Galamison complaining that the organization was not doing enough to fight for school integration. They asked Galamison to join the fight to integrate the new junior high school on Marcy Avenue and Halsey Street. Galamison agreed and ran successfully for the position of chairperson of the Education Committee of the Brooklyn branch of the NAACP. He later won the presidency of the organization, hoping to influence the group to take a strong position against the Board of Education's policy. During his tenure, Galamison attempted to force the board to come up with an integration plan and a date of implementation. He launched a campaign to force the resignation of Superintendent William Jansen, whom Galamison accused of not being in favor of school integration.[74]

Unable to persuade the branch, Galamison left in 1959 and formed the Parents' Workshop for Equality in New York City Schools. Consisting of parents and community activists, the group held regular meetings and rallies at Siloam Presbyterian Church and published a newsletter to keep people informed of the its work, such as meetings with Board of Education officials and other activities and events.[75]

In addition, the new organization took militant action, including a number of boycotts of schools, in order to force the board to integrate its schools. In one such boycott, more than one thousand parents kept their children out of schools in Bedford-Stuyvesant, Williamsburg, and Harlem and demanded that the board allow parents to send their children to schools of their choice. Another favorite tactic of the Parents' Workshop was to have parents show up at the school of their choice and attempt to register their children. The board responded to the movement for integration by offering a number of voluntary plans, including an open enrollment plan that offered black and Hispanic students the option of transferring to predominantly white schools.[76]

However, Galamison's and the Parents' Workshop's most extensive effort for school integration came in the winter of 1964 when the group organized two citywide boycotts of schools. This effort began in 1963 when the Parents' Workshop joined forces with the Brooklyn branches of the NAACP and the Congress of Racial Equality (CORE), and the Harlem Parents Committee and formed a new organization called the City-Wide Committee for School Integration. Milton Galamison was named president of the organization. He announced that the coalition would launch a one-day boycott in protest of the Board of Education's refusal to take concrete steps to integrate its schools.[77]

A number of rallies were held at Siloam and other churches in order to organize parents; ministers urged parents to keep their children out of school, and the Parents' Workshop's newsletters called for support of the boycott. In addition, the large press coverage before the boycott made many aware of the event. Some parents were frightened and thought there would be trouble the day of the boycott and decided not to send their children to school. Besides receiving support from parents and civil rights groups, ministers threw their support behind the efforts of the Parents' Workshop. Many churches throughout the city announced that their buildings would be used as "freedom schools," giving children instruction in math, reading, and black history.

In addition, some ministers were involved in attempting to organize clergy throughout the city for support of the boycott. In July 1963 William Jones, Benjamin Lowery, Sandy F. Ray, and Milton Galamison sent the following letter to the ministers throughout the city:

> The times in which we live demand the Ministers of New York City help resolve the crisis in our public school system. To this end, the undersigned ministers, in conjunction with the Parents' Workshop for Equality in New York City Schools and other agencies, have agreed on a plan of action. . . . If you consent to have your church used as a "freedom school" to accommodate children who refuse to attend the public schools, please return the enclosed reply card.[78]

On February 3, 1964, the anticipated boycott took place. Close to half a million children stayed out of schools. They stayed home, joined one of the three hundred picket lines, or attended one of the "freedom schools." Galamison threatened to launch a second boycott if the board refused to integrate the schools. Many who supported the first boycott withdrew from the second one, including the NAACP and the Urban League. They were angry that Galamison had called for the second boycott without their consent. Many also feared that a second boycott threatened their leverage to bargain with the board and would cost the support of white liberals. Despite this lack of support, a second boycott was carried out on March 15, 1964.[79]

Although it was half the size of the first one, Galamison proved that he was able to mobilize thousands of people without the support of the traditional civil rights organizations. The boycotts gained Galamison a reputation as one of the most militant civil rights leaders in Brooklyn and catapulted him to the head of the school integration movement in New York.

Parishioners and Their Struggle to Make Bedford-Stuyvesant a Viable Community

As noted earlier, the black churches were more than just the pastors and ministers. Ordinary people in the churches actively sought ways to address the problems plaguing their community. In order to have a better picture of the churches, one must go beyond the pulpit and examine the activities of the parishioners. Through individual and collective action countless numbers of parishioners were responsible for making their churches into social welfare agencies. They contributed to their church and community by establishing programs, committees, and clubs and organizations that were involved not only in leisure activities but also social and welfare endeavors.

Combating juvenile delinquency became one of the major goals of the members of black churches. Many saw their religious institutions with the imperative mission of helping to protect children from crime, drugs, and other social evils that lead juveniles down a destructive path. By organizing programs for children and teenagers, parishioners attempted to present healthy alternatives to street life. By the 1930s several church members helped keep the church doors open past the usual service hours in order to offer social, recreational, and sporting events for black children. Accordingly, they made their churches into social service centers stressing moral uplift.

Women played a crucial role in the mission to save children. It is mainly through their efforts that the churches were able to offer a variety of services for young people. They were in the fore of attempting to mold the minds of children so they would remain on a straight and narrow course to success. There was nothing oppositional in their approach. Ordinary people in the black churches did not challenge the dominant political order. Instead, they found ways of objecting to the persistent notion of the larger society that black people were incapable of succeeding. As Evelyn Brooks Higgenbotham notes for black Baptist women, "Their efforts represented not dramatic protest but everyday forms of resistance to oppression and demoralization."[80]

One of the most popular programs promoting moral uplift was scouting. For many, scouting represented "clean speech, clean sport, clean habits, and travels with a clean crowd."[81] Many in the church and community contended that scouting was a means of saving kids from the mean streets and instilling values such as discipline, hard work, gentility, respect for human life, and concern for others.

Scouting programs in Brooklyn's black churches were established in the first half of the twentieth century. Sometime between 1910 and 1925, Nazarene Congregational Church organized a scouting program. Both the girl and boy scouts were involved in recreational and "Christian endeavors." The boy scouts also had a musical program, including a band that played in annual school parades and for community organizations, thus connecting the children to their community.[82]

Other churches followed suit, and between 1925 and 1945 St. Augustine Protestant Episcopal, St. Phillip's Protestant Episcopal, First AME Zion, Mount Lebanon Baptist, and Cornerstone Baptist all established scouting programs. Herbert V. King organized the First AME Zion boy scout troop in 1933 and became its first scout master. Although the Reverend George Thomas was given credit for creating a boy scout unit at Brown Memorial Baptist, several parishioners, including Alexander Jones (the first scout master at Brown Memorial), dedicated their time and effort to recruit boys from the church and community and to meet with them on a regular basis and train them. It was through their efforts that the scouting group at Brown Memorial grew and became a viable unit, winning several scouting awards.[83]

A group of dedicated members of Bridge Street AWME whose major task was to provide children with a "wholesome atmosphere" created several scouting units. Lawrence Fields, nicknamed "Pap" Fields by church members, organized a boy scout unit in December 1932. Pauline Fields, also a devoted member and wife of Lawrence, created a girl scout unit in 1935. Both Lawrence and Pauline created the Drum and Bugle Corps. The Fields trained both boys and girls corps members to play field, tenor, and bass drums, as well as the bugle. In 1939 Spencer Burton, who was assistant boy scout master to Lawrence Fields, organized a cub scout division. By the early 1940s, several people were involved in operating a Brownie, intermediate, and senior troop units.[84]

The various scouting units at Bridge Street AWME met on certain days of the week in the basement of the church and sponsored several events. The adult leaders attempted to instill in the children religious values and a sense of humanitarianism. During scouting events, children were given a scripture lesson, sang religious songs, and recited a scouting pledge that emphasized trust in Jesus and striving to "make this old world better." Bridge Street claimed that its scouting program was successful, reaching a large number of children. Church officials claimed that between 1932 and 1957 more than five hundred boys had been trained as scouts and had advanced to higher ranks within the scouting units.[85]

Thanks to three members of Concord Baptist Church—Paul Stewart, Miss. H. Smith, and Frances Phillips—by the 1930s the church's scouting program was one of the most active in Brooklyn. Stewart supervised the boy scout units, and both Smith and Phillips directed the girl scout division of the church. The scouts had a fife and drum group, a library, and facilities for arts and crafts. Both the girl and boy scouts of Concord used the local YMCAs throughout the year for sports. Additionally, the scouts left the city for sleep-away camp during the summer months, thus exposing children to the outdoors and nature.[86]

Scouting also offered many parents the opportunity to become involved in activities that would help foster better relationships between them and their children. Parents became not just scout masters, cub masters, and other leaders but also den mothers and advisers on committees as well as participants in numerous scouting events. In 1945 the First AME Zion Church hosted the "Scout Parents Organization's Annual Honor Night Celebration." More than five hundred people attended. "Among the events of the evening were eight parent patrols contesting for the most beautifully-dressed table." This and similar activities helped promote a strong bond between parent and child.[87]

Women played a significant role as den mothers. Den mothers served as positive role models for children. Their actions, including financial support for scouting, clearly demonstrated to children that they were caring adults who supported their children's efforts. They presented an image of concerned and reliable parents whose job was to bolster the positive activities of their children. Most importantly, they saw themselves as guardians of children, assisting in their religious development. Moreover, through their actions they espoused a theory of self help, as black people who were capable of providing for the needs of their children. For example, the girl scout Parents Guild of Concord Baptist Church (which was formed in 1947 and later changed its name to the Mothers' Club) provided financial and moral support to the youth of the church. The club provided food for camping, drums, bugles, flags, and sports equipment. The group hosted a number of "mother and daughter" dinners, cake and pie sales, and fashion shows as means of raising money for the girl scout units. The group asserted that its major objective was to provide children with the opportunity to "grow up with an increasing spiritual enlightenment."[88]

Along with scouting programs, members of churches established recreational and athletic programs. Members of Bethany Baptist established a basketball team. Paul Stewart of Concord organized and supervised baseball and basketball teams. Concord's boy scout unit, basketball team, and baseball teams serviced two hundred boys in the community. As members of the Brooklyn and Queens Athletic Association, Bethany and Concord teams competed with other teams in the city. H. Smith supervised a tennis team for girls while other members of Concord organized a dramatics club and choral groups that were open to both church members and nonmembers.[89]

Besides recreation, several churches offered educational activities. Bridge Street AWME, Mount Lebanon Baptist, Berean Missionary Baptist, and Concord Baptist churches all had summer vacation schools that also offered children a host of activities. Black women were crucial in the creation and operation of vacation Bible schools, Bible classes, and Sunday school departments (see chapter 6).

Women saw their churches as institutions whose major mission was to help provide children with a proper education. It was to nurture them and motivate them to learn. People in the black churches were aware of the failure of the educational system to serve black children adequately and that intervention was needed to save them from delinquency. Through their religious activities, women were taking a prominent role in the fight to save black children.

By the 1930s several of Brooklyn's black churches, including Pentecostal churches, were attempting to involve children in their activities by creating junior usher boards, children's youth choirs, sunshine bands, and youth day committees. Youth committees were particularly active in sponsoring numerous events for young people, including outings, musical and literary programs, and youth day services. Both Washington Temple Church of God in Christ and Cornerstone Baptist Church illustrate this point. To entertain the young people of the congregation, Washington Temple occasionally showed religious motion pictures. In addition, the young people of the Pentecostal church operated snack bars after Sunday services. The Youth Committee of Cornerstone Baptist Church showed religious movies, made sound movies, and presented dramatic performances.[90] It should be noted that women played a principal role in the youth committees of Brooklyn's black churches. For example, between 1930 and 1950 the vast majority of the presidents of the young people's auxiliaries were women. Thus, women were in the forefront of fighting juvenile crime by providing a host of activities for young people.[91]

These various activities clearly demonstrate that parishioners provided avenues to make children an important part of both the church and the larger community. Moral guidance and education as well as recreation were the means churches used to fight juvenile crime. Although the black churches accepted the notion that recreation was an important way to lessen juvenile delinquency, they did not see children as threatening elements in the community that needed to be kept off the streets. Instead, they viewed recreation as just one aspect of the fight against crime. Many in the churches saw black children as needing direction, moral guidance, and a sense of community.[92]

From the 1920s to the 1950s the black ministers did little to stop the growing ghettoization of Bedford-Stuyvesant. With the exception of a few independent-minded black ministers, like Milton Galamison, the most active were political moderates who did not help establish any long-term movement, forge alliances with grass-roots organizations, or use aggressive tactics to address the problems of housing, health care, education, and employment. More than any other group of leaders, the ministers were in a position to build an independent movement to challenge federal, state, and city governments over the lack of health care facilities, inferior schools, and other evils in the community. They missed their chance to save Bed-Stuy from deteriorating.

There is no doubt that the men who led Brooklyn's black churches should have organized themselves into a much more cohesive group, giving leadership by mobilizing people as a political bloc to assure the election of black candidates, work with grass-roots organizations, and guarantee large demonstrations in the streets. The ministers could have organized thousands of people inside and outside the churches and put pressure on city, state, and federal officials to do something about the dire conditions of Bedford-Stuyvesant and other poor black neighborhoods. Consequently, the record of black ministers as agents who could make a significant impact on Bedford-Stuyvesant during that neighborhood's rapid deterioration is at best disappointing. Perhaps unaware of their real potential strength as a group, the ministers remained a sleeping giant, not taking advantage of their resources to bring about significant change in Brooklyn. African Americans would have to wait until the 1960s before the ministers would act collectively to build an independent forceful protest movement.

Yet it would be inaccurate to conclude that black churches were completely ineffective in the struggle to improve conditions in Bed-Stuy. The countless number of members of Brooklyn's black churches have been an active part of community life by attempting to deliver services and leadership to the black community, especially to the young. Before there was a war on poverty and a commitment by federal, state, and city governments to address the problems of the urban poor, black churches were actively striving to improve the quality of life for blacks.

CHAPTER FIVE

The Ministers' Committee for Job Opportunities for Brooklyn and the Downstate Medical Center Campaign

The civil rights movement of the 1950s and 1960s persisted for more than a decade, dramatically altering the political, economic, and social conditions of America. Civil rights leaders and thousands of ordinary people who participated in civil rights campaigns brought to the attention of the nation the injustice of racism and eventually helped destroy America's apartheid system (more popularly known as Jim Crow). However, this movement expanded beyond the South. Hundreds of communities across the nation launched campaigns attempting to improve the quality of life for African Americans. Each region and community defined its own civil rights issues, developed its own indigenous leadership, and used various methods to address the concerns of black people. This was also true of Brooklyn.

For a brief period black ministers of Brooklyn set aside their moderate approaches and became revolutionaries. They challenged the hegemony of the state and a powerful labor organization by using militant tactics and rhetoric. They sacrificed their comfortable positions as power brokers closely tied to the dominant political order and joined with ordinary people in the streets to eliminate racist union policies that denied people of color employment and to end government inaction on those policies.

In the summer of 1963, one particular demonstration for jobs in Brooklyn became one of the most significant civil rights campaigns in New York City. Between July 15 and August 6, 1963, a ministerial organization called the Ministers' Committee for Job Opportunities for Brooklyn, made up mostly of black ministers from the Bedford-Stuyvesant area, conducted a protest campaign at the construction site of the Downstate Medical Center demanding that one-fourth of all construction jobs at the $25 million construction project be granted to blacks and Puerto Ricans. The construction project was chosen because of its close proximity to the Bedford-Stuyvesant area in hopes of generating jobs for this devastated community. The committee helped organize hundreds of people, led several protests that resulted in the arrest of more than seven hundred protesters, and received extensive news coverage before reaching a settlement with Gov. Nelson Rockefeller. Unlike the Ministers' Committee's attempt in the spring of 1962

July 25, 1963: The police use wire clippers to remove the chain that binds pickets at Downstate Medical Center construction site (Worldwide Associates)

July 23, 1963: Policewomen lift a demonstrator for CORE while another demonstrator reclines on the pavement (Worldwide Associates)

July 22, 1963: Police, some mounted and others on foot,
herd some of the 250 demonstrators toward a
police van (Worldwide Associates)

July 23, 1963: New York City police carry away a demonstrator; Rev. Milton Galamison and Rev. Carl McCall
look on in the background (Worldwide Associates)

to win employment for blacks by boycotting and picketing busi-nesses operating in Bedford-Stuyvesant (see following section), the Downstate Medical Center campaign (hereafter, the Down-state campaign) was much broader. It attempted to build a mass movement that challenged both state government policies and practices of the building and construction trade unions that resulted in excluding blacks from the construction industry. It was a major attempt to break down the barriers of discrimination throughout the entire construction industry and to alter state and city policies. The Downstate campaign differed from the citywide school boycotts of 1964 because of the radical methods used at the construction site and the pivotal leadership role that several black ministers played. The Downstate campaign also differed from the 1964 school boycotts because of its heavy reliance on the black congregations of Brooklyn for financial support and troops for the picket lines. Moreover, because of the many demonstrators involved in the campaign, this was the first major civil rights cam-paign in New York City to capture a national audience. Both newspapers and television covered the events at Downstate. The civil rights movement caused mainline black ministers to stop capitulating to the state. Instead, they adopted a theology of rad-ical activism, stepped out of their usual roles as power brokers, and began to resist the political hegemony of the state. As a col-lective group, the ministers were willing for the first time to use militant measures to pressure government and labor to acquiesce to their demands.

However, despite the fact that this was one of the largest civil rights protests in the urban North during the civil rights decade, the Downstate campaign has been largely ignored by civil rights scholars. Moreover, few works have focused on the black clergy and their churches in northern civil rights campaigns. Although numerous scholars have written on the civil rights movement and black clerical figures during that decade, most of the literature focuses on southern civil rights campaigns.[1] This void has left an incomplete history of the civil rights movement.

By unfolding the historical events of the Downstate campaign, this chapter continues to examine the political activities of sever-al Brooklyn black ministers. It examines how the movement rad-icalized the black clergy, the role that ordinary people played, and why the black ministers eventually moved back into their roles as mediators between the government and African Americans. The chapter shifts the scholarly attention previously given to the South in this area and attempts to broaden our knowledge of a northern civil rights struggle and the role some northern black ministers played during this crucial era in American history. It will trace the activities of the Ministers' Committee, including the strategies and tactics it adopted in order to create a broad mass civil rights movement and its attempt to end racial discrimination in the construction industry in the State of New York.

Origins of the Downstate Medical Center Campaign

By the early 1960s the most militant and vocal organization attempting to improve the quality of life for Bedford-Stuyvesant's poor was the Brooklyn branch of the Congress of Racial Equality (CORE). In 1962 the Brooklyn affiliate teamed up with Rev. Milton A. Galamison and his Parents' Workshop for Equality in New York City Schools and launched a sit-in at the Board of Education's office demanding (and eventually winning) relief in an overcrowded school in Bedford-Stuyvesant. In September of that year Brooklyn CORE launched "Operation Cleansweep." Members of the organization attempted to get city officials to improve the sanitation conditions in Bedford-Stuyvesant and other Brooklyn black ghettos by dumping garbage on the steps of Borough Hall. In 1963 Brooklyn CORE assisted tenants in fighting slum conditions by helping them file complaints with the city's Building Department and urging them to initiate rent strikes.[2]

Brooklyn CORE was considered the most radical chapter in the national organization. It was the first CORE chapter to use direct militant action such as picketing and sit-ins. In 1961 it had held a sit-in at Lefrak Realty Company. And in the summer of 1962 CORE blocked trucks at Ebinger's Bakery, demanding that it hire black workers.[3]

Yet despite its active role in Bedford-Stuyvesant and elsewhere, Brooklyn CORE remained a small organization. As late as April 1963, the Brooklyn civil rights organization had only thirty-five members. The diverse membership consisted of both young black and white adults as well as middle-age militants who had been involved in radical politics since the 1940s. The members' economic status was as diverse as the age makeup of the group.

There were working-class laborers, including a mailman and a bus driver, and white-collar professionals, including a university professor and a medical doctor. The racial makeup of the organization was at least 50 percent white until the Downstate campaign, when the number of blacks dramatically increased.[4]

In the summer of 1963 Brooklyn CORE became a member of the Joint Committee on Equal Opportunity, a coalition of civil rights and labor organizations, whose major goal was to end racial discrimination practices in New York. The Joint Committee, which included the NAACP and the Urban League of Greater New York, initiated a sit-in at Mayor Robert Wagner's office in early July demanding a halt to all construction sponsored by the city until all discriminatory hiring practices were "eliminated."[5]

In early July 1963 Brooklyn CORE mounted a dual campaign against bias in the construction industry and unemployment in the ghetto, demonstrating for jobs for blacks and Puerto Ricans at the Downstate Medical Center project, located on Clarkson and New York avenues. Downstate was also chosen because of the racially discriminatory policies practiced by the numerous building and construction trade unions. Despite claims that race was not a factor, people of African descent were excluded from jobs by a "catch-22" stipulation: work eligibility depended on training in an apprentice program, and admission required the recommendation of two union members. Since scarcely any blacks belonged to the unions, they were effectively shut out of training programs, and thus out of jobs. The system made a mockery of the state's antidiscrimination laws.[6]

Although the power to select apprentices rested with the local unions, New York Building and Construction Trade Council officials made little effort to change the rules. In 1960 African Americans accounted for 22 percent of the city's population but only 2 percent of apprentices in the building and construction trades. Three years later the New York State Advisory Committee of the U.S. Commission on Civil Rights reported that while New York residents of African descent were being denied employment, many white construction workers were "blue-collar commuters," traveling as much as one hundred miles a day to and from their jobs. Of the nineteen craft unions engaged in the construction project, only the carpenters had black workers.[7]

Oliver Leeds, chairperson of Brooklyn CORE, invited Warren Bunn of the NAACP and John Parham of the Urban League to discuss strategies for launching protests against the construction unions. Leeds, Bunn, and Parham first visited the construction site of the hospital and found that, with the exception of a few black carpenters, the work force was "lily-white." Although they attempted to negotiate with the trade unions and convince them to hire more black and Puerto Rican workers, according to Leeds, they were "all but kicked out" of the union's offices. After failing to convince state officials and the Building and Construction Trade Council through negotiation to increase the number of blacks and Puerto Ricans, Brooklyn CORE, along with the NAACP and the Urban League, announced that the organizations would halt construction of the hospital by demonstrating at the construction site of the medical center until the state and city and the construction unions guaranteed that blacks and Puerto Ricans would make up 25 percent of the construction workers and that the building and construction trade unions would open their ranks to people of color.[8]

The Joint Committee on Equal Opportunity agreed to join Brooklyn CORE for this endeavor, but the Brooklyn civil rights group realized from the start that the Downstate campaign would require large numbers of protesters at the construction site. Acknowledging that they were unable to attract these large numbers, members of Brooklyn CORE and the Joint Committee (which as noted included the NAACP and the Urban League of Greater New York) turned to some of the black ministers of the Bedford-Stuyvesant community for support since many of them headed the largest black congregations in the city. Many in CORE believed the ministers would be able to mobilize thousands of people from their churches to participate in the campaign.[9]

Despite their prestige in Bedford-Stuyvesant and their (on the whole) politically mainstream views, fourteen prominent ministers responded to the plea of Brooklyn CORE and the Joint Committee and took part in the civil disobedience campaign on July 15. After hours of picketing at the site, all fourteen ministers, along with Oliver Leeds, had decided to disband and gather again on July 17, when Oliver Leeds suddenly saw a truck heading for the open gate. Leeds turned to the ministers and said, "We can come back Wednesday, but I'm taking this truck today," and sat down in front of the oncoming vehicle. Without a word spoken, all fourteen ministers and many supporters joined Leeds then and there to block any trucks attempting to enter the site. In a scene resembling a southern civil rights protest, the demonstrators sang freedom songs as they were carried into police vans. Later that evening the ministers were greeted by a crowd of two thousand supporters at Cornerstone Baptist Church in Bedford-Stuyvesant. The crowd heard speeches from the clergy and voted to support their efforts to end job discrimination at Downstate.[10]

Although some white ministers joined the effort, the black clergy stepped to the forefront and led the campaign. On the night of July 15, at a meeting at Cornerstone, a group of black ministers formed the Ministers' Committee for Job Opportunities for Brooklyn to help direct the demonstration, selecting Sandy F. Ray as the chairperson. Although it is not clear why Ray was selected, the sixty-five-year-old pastor of Cornerstone Baptist Church might have been chosen because of his close ties with Rockefeller. It was probably believed that the selection of Ray might give the ministers an advantage in negotiating with the governor.[11]

To coordinate the protest, the Ministers' Committee selected Rev. William A. Jones as director of the Downstate campaign. Although Jones was only twenty-nine and just completing his tenth month as pastor of Bethany Baptist Church in Bedford-Stuyvesant, his selection was no accident. The pastor of the 4,500-member church was experienced in civil rights protest. He had been active in a ministerial struggle in Philadelphia to obtain jobs for blacks. He later formed a ministers' group that negotiated with the Bond Bread Company and other businesses for employment opportunities for blacks.[12]

Other members of the committee were Gardner C. Taylor; Walter G. Henson Jacobs, pastor of St. Augustine Episcopal Church in Bedford-Stuyvesant; Carl McCall from the New York City Mission Society; Richard Saunders, pastor of Stuyvesant Heights Christian Church; Benjamin Lowery of Zion Baptist; Milton Galamison of Siloam Presbyterian Church; and A. W. Wilson of Morningstar Baptist Church. With the exception of Carl McCall, all of the executive committee were from Bedford-Stuyvesant and were pastors of churches whose membership exceeded a thousand.[13]

What motivated these clerics to risk their reputations by involving themselves in a militant civil disobedience protest? One important reason is that for decades black ministers and black churches along with numerous community organizations had been addressing a variety of concerns of African Americans—most notably, juvenile delinquency, health care, and education. The struggles of the 1960s should be seen, in part, as a continuation of the ministers' campaign to improve the lives of blacks.

However, the involvement of ministers in crusades of earlier decades does not explain why many ministers were willing for the first time to step out of their roles as power brokers and become involved in a militant civil disobedience campaign, risking their political clout. Another overriding motivation for the ministers' involvement was the inspiration of Martin Luther King, in particular, and the civil rights movement in general. During the middle 1950s and early 1960s, King raised the consciousness of clergy all over the country, moving to the forefront of black protest in the South. King helped smash Jim Crow laws by means of massive, sustained, and non violent demonstrations, boycotts, and sit-ins, and forged a new image of the black minister as militant agent for social change. Bedford-Stuyvesant ministers, sparked by King and the movement, raised money for the Southern Christian Leadership Conference (SCLC) as well as other civil rights organizations, and used their churches as forums by allowing King and others involved in southern civil rights campaigns to address their congregations. Some even attempted to launch a civil rights battle in New York. During the late 1950s and 1960s, Milton Galamison led the struggle for school integration in New York City (notably, by organizing the Parents' Workshop for Equality in New York City Schools, a group that educated parents and worked for a desegregation timetable).

In March and April of 1962 black ministers from Bedford-Stuyvesant formed the Ministers' Movement, which fought for jobs for black residents by boycotting and picketing merchants on Fulton Street. The ministers demanded that local merchants contribute to black agencies in the community and that businesses adopt a "fair employment" program by hiring and promoting black and Hispanic workers. The group crossed denominational lines, consisting of several Baptists, a Presbyterian, and two Pentecostal ministers. Sandy F. Ray, Milton Galamison, Simpson V. Turner (Mount Carmel Baptist), Frank Clemmons (First Church of God in Christ), and F. D. Washington (Washington Temple COCIG) were the most visible members of the group. Calling themselves the "Ministers' Movement," the group used their churches as information centers, kept the community aware of the movement's activities, and organized their members for a one-day boycott. The churches printed more than 100,000 leaflets calling for community support of the boycott and demonstration.[14]

Borrowing tactics from the "Don't Buy Where You Can't Work" campaigns of the 1930s, one hundred ministers and hundreds of demonstrators picketed seven stores on Nostrand Avenue and Fulton Street, the business district of Bed-Stuy, on March 31, 1962. Carrying signs that read "This is a Community and not a Plantation," "Don't Buy Where You Can't Work," and "Upgrade Negro and Puerto Rican Workers," the demonstrators marched from 10 A.M. until 4 P.M. scaring many of the merchants. In fact, one owner of a women's clothing store closed early.[15]

The ministers quickly prepared for another boycott, printing thousands of leaflets and informing their membership of plans for picketing. The threat of a second boycott persuaded merchants to sit down with the ministers and negotiate. The merchants represented by the Fulton Street Merchants Association agreed to hire more blacks, promote them, and contribute financially to community organizations.[16]

Although the Ministers' Movement later targeted Ebinger's Bakery, the group soon disbanded for reasons that are not clear (possibly because the ministers were unable to find the time that a protest movement demanded). However, many of its members would be involved in the Downstate campaign because it offered them yet another opportunity to fight to end Jim Crow in their own backyard.[17]

It should be noted that some Brooklyn pastors were closely associated with Martin Luther King and his efforts. William A. Jones of Bethany Baptist was a member of the SCLC, while Sandy F. Ray of Cornerstone Baptist was a close friend of both Martin King Sr. and Martin King Jr. and had the latter address his congregation. Ray was also committed to the civil rights movement. Besides inviting civil rights leaders to his church to inform Brooklyn residents of their activities, in 1956 Ray was cochair of a city-wide committee for integrated schools to stage a civil rights rally at Madison Square Garden. George Lawrence of Antioch Baptist Church and one of the spokesmen for the Ministers' Committee was regional director of the SCLC at the time of the Downstate campaign.[18]

In Brooklyn, Gardner C. Taylor was probably King's closest political ally. Taylor raised money for SCLC and attempted to win support for King and the civil rights movement within Baptist circles. In 1960 Taylor attempted to move the National Baptist Convention USA, Inc. (NBC), with its five million members (the largest black organization in the country), into the civil rights camp. The pastor of Concord Baptist became part of a group of young ministers who were upset with Joseph Jackson's criticism of the civil rights campaigns and King. Jackson, who was from Chicago and a political conservative, was first elected president of the NBC in 1951. Taylor noted that he and others were upset with Jackson because they "could not get a clear word from our convention on the civil rights matter." He realized that the black Baptists should present a united front in the struggle for civil rights so "enemies of the movement could not use it against us."[19]

Taylor had expressed interest in challenging Jackson for leadership of the NBC in the late 1950s. In a letter to Claude Barnett of the Associated Negro Press in the summer of 1957, Taylor confessed that he would run if nominated. "If, indeed, my denomination were to look to me for leadership, I would approach that responsibility with a sense of humility and honor and commitment to the progress of our denomination." He asserted that the "National Baptist Convention must relate itself on a continuing, day-to-day basis to our Civil Rights struggle, both in fulfillment of our Christian witness and for the sake of our country and Negro Community."[20]

In June 1960 Taylor was selected to run for president of the NBC by three hundred pastors who were critical of Jackson's conservatism and had formed a group within the NBC called the Committee for the Redemption of Our Denominational Harmony. In his acceptance speech, Taylor declared that "the convention must be committed under God to bold and imaginative participation in the Great Crusade for equality." He indirectly criticized Jackson by asserting "There must be no question . . . about

147

our support of the NAACP, the Southern Christian Leadership Conference, the Urban League."[21]

In September 1960 the NBC met in Philadelphia for its annual meeting and to elect its president for the upcoming year. The day before the organization's presidential election, Jackson agreed to Taylor's request that the chief officer would be elected by a roll call of each state delegation. However, on the day of the election, a nominating committee selected by Jackson made a recommendation that the Chicago minister "unanimously be reelected." The Taylor team objected. To practically everyone's surprise, Jackson later claimed that he had been reelected through a voice vote. Martin Luther King, who was present during the morning session when the "voice vote" supposedly occurred, said, "Nobody heard Jackson's voice vote." Despite Jackson's claims, an election by roll call was held and Taylor won by almost a four-to-one margin (1,864 to 536). In spite of this apparent victory by Taylor, Jackson still asserted that he had won and was not giving up power. There were suddenly two National Baptist Conventions.[22]

The Taylor forces were uncompromising. They argued that Jackson had violated the tenure agreement that allowed a person to hold the office of president for a maximum of eight years. Jackson's eighth year was in 1959; therefore, according to the Taylorites, the Chicago minister was ineligible to run in 1960. Determined to take the NBC in a more progressive direction, Taylor declared himself the winner and prepared to run the 1961 convention. King, along with other ministers, supported Taylor.[23]

In order to prepare for that convention, Taylor and his supporters held a secret meeting in April 1961. He sent a letter to King requesting that he attend a meeting in St. Louis of a "select group of men" in order to work out a strategy for the upcoming convention in Kansas City, Missouri. Taylor asked King to come alone and keep the meeting secret.

There is no indication that King attended the session in St. Louis. Twenty-eight years after the meeting Taylor did not recall King attending. However, what is clear is that the SCLC was to play a leading role in Taylor's NBC. Many SCLC officials were appointed to leading positions in the organization. For instance, Ralph Abernathy was named chairman of the social service commission, George Lawrence, a regional director of SCLC, was selected as chairman of publicity, and Dearing E. King, a member of the executive board of SCLC, was named secretary of Taylor's NBC.[24]

In July Taylor sent a letter to members of the NBC with details for registration for the Kansas City convention. Suspecting a confrontation with the Jackson forces, Taylor called on members to pray and to come to Kansas City "determined that we shall show patience and forbearance no matter what attempts may be made to provoke violence." Martin Luther King's itinerary schedule showed that he was scheduled to attend the convention; however, he was missing in action.[25]

Taylor asserted that hours before he entered the hall of the convention on September 6, 1961, he sensed that a physical confrontation was going to occur and he thought he was "going to die." When he and his supporters entered the convention hall, he noticed that the place was filled with Jackson's supporters. Jackson was on the platform and was surrounded by a large number of men. As Taylor and his supporters attempted to walk on the platform, he was grabbed by Jackson's men and a fight broke out. During the melee, a Jackson supporter, Arthur Wright from Detroit, fell from the platform and died of a heart attack.[26]

Jackson never gave up control of the convention, and Taylor eventually conceded. But concession was not enough for the autocratic pastor from Chicago. Jackson took advantage of the event in Kansas City. He blamed King for creating the situation that had led to Wright's death and had the civil rights leader removed from his position in the NBC as vice president of the Sunday School and Baptist Training Union.[27]

Taylor and his supporters responded by leaving the NBC and organizing the Progressive National Baptist Convention. In its platform, the organization dedicated itself to the civil rights struggle and fair elections.[28]

Elements of the Downstate Campaign

Leadership is an important element in a protest campaign. In his work *Political Process and the Development of Black Insurgency, 1930–1970* , Doug McAdam notes that:

All manner of movement analysts have asserted the importance of leaders or organizers in the generation of social insurgency. To do so requires not so much a particular theoretical orientation as common sense. For in the context of political opportunity and widespread discontent there still remains a need for the centralized direction and coordination of a recognized leadership.[29]

Prestige and legitimacy help attract support for a protest. The ministers moved to the leadership of the protest because they were already leaders in the community, had a large audience at their disposal, and were able to use two elements of major importance in creating a mass movement. The first element the Committee for Job Opportunities relied on was ministerial networking. Members of the clerical protest group contacted other pastors throughout the city, urging them to get their congregations involved in the planned demonstrations. Gardner Taylor recalls personally contacting "two or three pastors," urging them to take part in the demonstrations. With enough demonstrators, the ministers hoped to stop construction and force Governor Rockefeller, Mayor Wagner, and Peter Brennan, president of the Building and Construction Trade Council (which consisted of 122 unions), to accept the 25 percent quota.[30]

The second important element was charisma, a basic ingredient in pastoring, used to attract membership and inspire parishioners during religious services. The clergy involved in the Downstate protest relied on their personal charisma to generate support for the campaign. To motivate their congregations to participate in the demonstrations, pastors told parishioners during Sunday morning services (and at other times) that they were part of a moral and patriotic movement: their goal was to make America more democratic by eliminating racism and discrimination. In pulpits and at rallies, ministers appealed for support by linking Downstate to the larger campaign to abolish Jim Crow in America. At a rally in Tompkins Park, six thousand people gathered to hear the ministers explain the significance of the protest. "We are here in response to the call of history," proclaimed Sandy Ray. Linking the Downstate struggle to a larger struggle for human dignity, Sandy Ray contended: "There will be no turning back until people in high places correct the wrongs of the nation." Gardner Taylor, referring to a demonstration planned for July 22, declared that the "Revolution has come to Brooklyn . . . whatever the cost, we will set the nation straight. . . . The protest will be peaceful," he said, "but if the ruling white power structure brings it about, our blood will fill the streets."[31]

Yet leadership was just one aspect of the movement. An examination of any social protest movement should not focus on the leadership alone but also on the concerns and activities of participants on every level. The participants help make up what social scientists call "local center movements." The churches involved in the Downstate campaign became a local center movement, "an interrelated set of protest leaders, organizations, and followers who collectively define the common ends of the group, devise necessary tactics and strategies along with training for their implementation, and engage in protest actions designed to attain the goals of the group." The black churches during the Downstate campaign helped give many ordinary people the opportunity to participate in a civil rights struggle in their own community. The churches became vehicles of empowerment by moving people to respond to the call for street protests and nonviolent civil disobedience. This collective effort to disrupt the operation of the state was an attempt to empower people who were otherwise ignored. The religious activities of parishioners were expanded to include collecting funds to support political protest, attending church rallies, and becoming "jailbirds for freedom," in addition to the traditional rituals, songs and prayers.[32]

There were various reasons why ordinary people became involved in the Downstate campaign. Many were persuaded by their pastors to participate. At Siloam, the pastor appealed to the auxiliaries to give a day on the protest line. Gwendolyn Timmons, a member of Siloam's choir, recalls being on the picket line because the choir had pledged a day to protest at the construction site.[33] Others participated because they were deeply convinced it was their duty. Samuel Fredricks, a member of both CORE and Siloam, knew that black men who served during World War II and the Korean War and were trained as surveyors and bulldozer operators were being denied construction jobs. Fredricks believed that white outsiders were being "imported" for these jobs. Employed as a postal worker, Fredricks would leave work, change quickly, and join the demonstration.[34]

Not all members could or would participate in the demonstrations. Some decided to participate on other levels. For example,

Winifred Fredricks had to take care of small children and was unable to demonstrate but ran bake sales and raised money for the campaign.[35] Thousands participated in nightly rallies held in the churches of Bedford-Stuyvesant, giving support to the campaign. On July 15 some two thousand people gathered at Cornerstone Baptist to declare their support for the campaign. On July 24 fifteen hundred appeared at Mount Sinai Baptist; on July 29 one thousand attended a rally at St. Augustine, and on July 31 two thousand attended Berean Baptist for a rally.[36]

Hundreds helped the protest movement by volunteering to go to jail, while others contributed whatever they could to the campaign. For example, at a rally at St. Augustine, $1,700 was collected in a special offering for the campaign.[37] Moreover, individuals donated whatever they could. In a letter to Rev. Richard L. Saunders, treasurer for the Ministers' Committee, Milton Galamison noted that a Mrs. Lily had contributed ten dollars in August, but the check had been destroyed during the demonstration. "She was, however, kind enough to persist and has renewed her gift." In a letter to Mrs. Dorothy Bostic, Reverend Galamison thanked her for her "generous support of the struggle being waged for equal employment opportunity in the building and construction field. We are greatly encouraged. Your contribution of $100.00 has been forwarded to the movement's treasurer, Reverend Richard Saunders, and will be used to defray the cost of bail and other expenses."[38]

Protest and Settlement

On July 22 more than twelve hundred people took part in the demonstration at Downstate and 211 were arrested, the largest number in New York City since the Harlem Riots of 1943. Protesters sat in front of all entrances to the hospital grounds in an attempt to deny trucks entrance to the work site, thereby causing delays in construction. Police arrested demonstrators, many of whom were carried away singing freedom songs. As one group of demonstrators was taken away by police, another group moved in and took their place. In the police vans, the arrested protesters sang religious songs and prayed. Police later used barricades to deny the protesters access to the entrances. However, many of the defiant demonstrators ran under the police barricades. Moreover, the campaign had gained the support of many whites, who made up an estimated 25 percent of the demonstrators.[39]

Despite the massive turnout on July 22, the ministers were soon to learn that maintaining a protest movement was no easy task. The clergy could not rally as much support in the protests that followed. The following day only two hundred people picketed. By July 26, the number of protesters was estimated at only 150.[40]

One reason for the fading attendance was the scheduling of demonstrations between seven in the morning and the late afternoon, to coincide with construction hours. Because most demonstrators were working people who could not afford to sacrifice more than one or two days' pay, their involvement was restricted. The ministers urged their parishioners to pledge a day to demonstrate. Reverend Saunders strongly suggested that the campaign use children, as in the Birmingham, Alabama, protest, but the idea was rejected. Instead, to compensate for reduced numbers, dedicated activists employed more militant tactics for denying access to trucks—for example, creating a human chain by locking arms and lying down in the path of construction equipment. When arrested, demonstrators went limp; the arresting officers had to carry them to the paddy wagons. Some tied their arms to fences with wire, forcing police to use wire cutters to break them free. By July 29 more than six hundred pickets had been arrested.

For all their efforts, there was little progress in moving state, city, and union officials to accept their demands. Both Governor Rockefeller and Mayor Wagner responded to the demonstration by pledging to enforce existing antidiscrimination procedures, which had so far been ineffectual in breaking down the color line on state and city construction projects. Trade Council president Peter Brennan refused to meet with the ministers and denounced their demands as "blackmail." The day after the July 22 demonstration, he announced that he would attempt to establish a six-man panel to screen job applicants, thereby replacing the old system in which two union members nominated candidates.[41]

Not one official promised a definite number of jobs. Both Rockefeller and Wagner favored increased employment of blacks in construction but neither accepted the 25 percent quota. Recalling a conversation he had with Mayor Wagner shortly after the large demonstration on July 22, Gardner Taylor contends that the mayor begged the question by pointing out his lack of jurisdiction in state programs like Downstate, while the governor publicly condemned the premise as "unlawful and counter to American principles."[42] Brennan's proposed six-man board and Rockefeller's and Wagner's pledges to investigate discrimination in the building and construction trades were dismissed by the protest leaders as inadequate. The ministers and the Joint Committee on Equal Opportunity decided to keep on demonstrating until the state, the city, and the unions accepted the 25 percent quota.

To make matters worse, as the protest continued, violence increased. At one demonstration, a riot nearly occurred when some pickets in a crowd of one hundred taunted the police, calling them "stormtroopers," and teenagers locked hands and stood in front of the trucks. The police then formed a double line and used their night sticks to push protesters away from the entrance and arrested them. Demonstrators reacted to the rough tactics by striking and kicking the police as they were carried away. Two police officers and two women protesters were injured. The following day, a police officer was struck by four young men when he attempted to confiscate their cache of rotten eggs. Twenty police officers came to his defense and carried the four men away. As the demonstrations dragged on, it became clear that the ministers were losing control.[43]

Arrest records suggest that participation by younger demonstrators contributed to the growing militancy. On July 15 only six of 28 pickets were younger than thirty-five. By July 23 this age group accounted for more than half. On July 24 forty-two of fifty people arrested were under the age of thirty-five, and the number of young people kept increasing. Behavior may also have been more aggressive after July 23 because half or more of the younger demonstrators resided outside of Bed-Stuy; they were less inclined to follow the clergy's direction.[44]

Mindful of mounting problems, the ministers began to back off from the quota demand as early as July 28, when Gardner Taylor stated: "Some of us are not particularly wedded to the quota idea." It was a negotiating item, he suggested; the civil rights leaders were open to other ideas. This admission in public could only weaken the protesters' position.[45]

The fear of losing control of the crowd grew among the members of the Ministers' Committee as a result of increasing violence. Yet violence was not their only concern. The strain of the continuing demonstrations created a burden that many were not willing to bear. Some complained that, because of their involvement in the long campaign, their churches were being neglected. At a meeting of the ministers, Oliver Leeds recalls Sandy Ray stating that he was ready to pull out of the protest. According to Leeds, Ray claimed that the campaign was dragging on with no end in sight; it was taking time away from his ministerial duties. Other ministers agreed and added that the decreasing numbers of demonstrators indicated that they could not continue much longer without complete loss of support. This in turn would leave them without any leverage. As a result of these developments, the committee sent letters to the governor requesting that he meet with them to work out a compromise. Although Rockefeller refused their initial request, on August 6 he did grant them a meeting to work out a solution.[46]

Although it is not certain why the governor met with the ministers, the agreement suggests that the ministers were willing to accept his terms and completely abandon the 25 percent quota. During the three-hour meeting, the governor, the Reverends Gardner Taylor, Milton Galamison, William Jones, Walter Offutt (of Bethany Baptist), Benjamin Lowery, Walter G. Henson Jacobs, along with Ramon Rivera of the Urban League, worked out an agreement that provided for laws against bias to be enforced and funds withdrawn from state projects at which discrimination was practiced. The governor would name a representative to oversee the construction industry and report all cases of job discrimination to the State Commission on Human Rights, which in turn would sponsor a public hearing on August 15 to investigate charges of racial discrimination against Sheet Metal Workers International Association Local Union 28. Finally, a recruitment program would be created for finding qualified blacks and Puerto Ricans for apprenticeships and membership in eighteen unions. In return, the ministers agreed to call off the demonstration immediately.[47]

Except for the recruitment provision, the accord was no more than a duplication of proposals previously made by the governor. There was no assurance that the Building and Construction Trade

Council would comply, nor was there any enforceable ruling that specific numbers of black and Puerto Rican workers would get either construction jobs or union cards. At a press conference, Rockefeller made it clear that the 25 percent quota was never considered at the meeting.[48]

Brooklyn CORE reacted unfavorably to the settlement. Although Oliver Leeds had given his approval to the agreement, members of the militant organization voted to reject it and continue picketing. In a letter to the ministers of Bedford-Stuyvesant, Leeds expressed his disappointment with the organization's vote: "It was my judgment that while the accord was less than satisfactory, it was nevertheless, a good beginning. However, neither the membership of Brooklyn CORE nor the Joint Committee of New York City, composed of the civil rights groups, felt this way."[49]

Brooklyn CORE and the Joint Committee publicly condemned the settlement on the following day. A spokesperson said that the settlement was inadequate because the ministers gained no more than "a simple reaffirmation of a promise to enforce state laws against discrimination." Calling the accord between the governor and ministers a public relations device and a substitute for "meaningful" action, the Joint Committee called for continued demonstrations at Downstate. The Joint Committee promised to continue demonstrating until 50 percent of apprentices entering the building and construction trade unions were black or Puerto Rican. A committee of six was established to monitor further discrimination by the building and construction trade unions, and a job-training program in the construction trades was established.[50]

The ministers condemned the call for renewed demonstrations and announced complete withdrawal of their financial and legal assistance. Both Jones and Galamison accused Brooklyn CORE of "bad faith," not only for calling for more demonstrations but also for telling arrested protesters not to follow the advice of the legal counsel hired by the ministers. Consequently, the Ministers' Committee announced its disassociation from the organization.[51]

The ministers' accusation that Brooklyn CORE and the Joint Committee operated in bad faith was unfounded. CORE rightfully complained that, although the two groups were working as a coalition, no CORE members were included in the decision-making process. In fact, the settlement was reached without any member of CORE being present.

Despite the Joint Committee's call for continued demonstrations, the ministers' withdrawal resulted in an almost total loss of support. Only forty-four demonstrators appeared at the construction site on August 8, and the campaign soon died.[52]

The Downstate campaign was the last effort by a wide cross section of Brooklyn's black church community to engage in civil disobedience during the 1960s. With the exception of Milton Galamison, who would lead two citywide school boycotts for integration, and William Jones, who as head of "Operation Breadbasket" led selective patronage campaigns against businesses that discriminated against blacks, demanding and winning more jobs, black ministers ceased to use militant methods throughout the 1960s.[53]

However, they did not neglect the social and economic problems of their community. By the mid-1960s President Lyndon Johnson's "Great Society" program had brought new opportunities that led ministers to address the needs of Bedford-Stuyvesant. In 1964 President Johnson had declared war on poverty and racism by helping to provide funds that would create job-training programs, educational opportunities for youth, improved health care for the aged, civil rights legislation, and urban rehabilitation. The Economic Opportunity Act of 1964, the Food Stamp Act, and the Medicare and Medicaid amendments to the Social Security Act, as well as the Civil Rights Acts of 1964 and 1968, were some of the landmarks of the Johnson administration.[54]

Johnson's "Great Society" helped define a new role for government; it would be at the forefront in the battle against poverty and racism and other evils of inequality. Robert Caro notes:

> [Johnson's] "War on Poverty" was not crowned with triumph like his war on prejudice. Many of the laws he rushed through Congress in such unprecedented numbers—in a frenzy of legislation—as if, it sometimes seemed, he equated speed and quantity with accomplishment, were inadequately thought through, flawed, contradictory, not infrequently exacerbating, at immense cost, the evils they were intended to correct. But his very declaration of that war was a reminder—as was his overall concept of a "Great Society"—of government's responsibility to do more than stand

157

idly by without at least attempting to strike blows against ignorance and disease and want. The presidency of Lyndon Johnson marked the legislative realization of many of the liberal aspirations of the twentieth century: in storming, on behalf of those laws, long-held bastions of congressional hostility to social-welfare programs, he used the power of the presidency for purposes as noble as any in American history.[55]

The Great Society was also the most massive spending campaign to end poverty since the New Deal. As federal funds flowed into New York, a leadership attempting to create and direct programs evolved. Bedford-Stuyvesant ministers, many involved in the Downstate campaign, were among the leaders. In 1964, with the help of federal funds, Mayor Wagner created the Youth in Action (YIA) program, granting the agency $223,225 to examine discontent among the youth and to develop antipoverty programs. Rev. William Jones and Rev. Carl McCall became members of the board of directors. By 1965 YIA had become equivalent to Harlem's Har You Act. Designated as Bed-Stuyvesant's official antipoverty program, YIA received money from the federal government and offered many programs, including job training for unwed mothers, remedial education, and adult on-the-job training. Reverend Offutt of Bethany Baptist became chairperson of the Board of Directors, while Antioch Baptist, Siloam Presbyterian, Concord Baptist, and Nazarene Congregational rushed to house YIA cultural programs. From 1963 to 1966 Siloam housed a Head Start program.

Despite his militant protests after Downstate, by 1967 Galamison had also given up street politics and had become dependent on government assistance. He became founder and chairperson of the Board of Directors of the Opportunities Industrialization Center, a vocational training program that placed thousands of youth and adults in jobs.[56]

The choice of some of Brooklyn's black churches to become conduits for the federal government's War on Poverty was not entirely motivated by the disappointing results of radical street politics. It was also brought about by the change in direction of the civil rights movement. By the mid-1960s many people involved in the movement had become disillusioned with the lack of success in the struggle for an integrated society and began asserting black empowerment. The civil rights movement had failed to address the problems of deteriorating black urban life. Poverty and its related problems could not be answered by attempting to create an open American society. Instead many African Americans began to call for control over the educational, economic, and political institutions in their neighborhoods. Power was the only means of eradicating the ghettos they viewed as the creation of white society in order to control blacks. There was a call for economic self-help and the operation and support of black businesses. The black aesthetic movement also wanted to liberate the minds of black people. In addition, advocates of black empowerment called for cultural liberation. Blacks should identify with Africa by adopting African hair and clothing styles, support African art forms such as music and dance, and study African and "Afro"-American history in order to develop pride in black people. Blacks should no longer look for allies to solve their problems. The white-dominated society was racist and did not have the interest of blacks at heart. Many argued that blacks should instead rely on the collective power of black people.[57]

Brooklyn CORE serves as an illustration of the shift in direction of those involved in the civil rights movement. After the Downstate campaign, new members joined the organization. Included in the new wave of Brooklyn CORE members were people advocating black empowerment and an exclusion of whites from the leadership in the organization. Led by Sonny Carson, the new members contended that "Black Power" was the only way to get rid of ghettos in the urban centers. Blacks had to be in control of the institutions in their community and had a right to self-defense. This nationalist direction taken by the new members also questioned the role of whites in the organization. According to the new members, whites were incapable of leading blacks because they could not understand their plight nor did many truly have the interests of blacks at heart. Instead, blacks must lead their own struggle. White members complained that they were under verbal attack by the new members and excluded from decision-making positions. David Feingold, an active white member of Brooklyn CORE, probably reflected the view of many white members on the new black nationalists.

But along with the youths who wanted to improve their lives came a group of black men who were bitter with the world. They had been so hurt by the white world that they wanted only revenge. Many black persons have felt this way. But in the past they have steered away from CORE's integration philosophy and the nonviolent emphasis. With these out of the way and with the emergence of all black leadership, the bitter persons found CORE a good place in which to work.[58]

Even Oliver Leeds, the chairperson of Brooklyn CORE, came under attack for having a white wife. The push for black power and the expulsion of whites (or at least their reduction to menial roles) led to clear factions within the Brooklyn civil rights group. Besides the new militant members pushing a black nationalist agenda, there were white liberals and an old guard of black workers who advocated integration, and those who attempted to reach an agreement between the two factions.[59]

During this period, black churches came under heavy attack. Many ministers were described as "Uncle Toms" and were accused of preaching the "white man's religion." Gardner Taylor recalls keeping a baseball bat in his office because of the fear that nationalists might attack him because of his moderate views.[60] The growth of the Black Power movement may have led many Brooklyn ministers to look elsewhere to give service to the community. The War on Poverty gave them a good avenue to remain vital economic and political agents in the black community. They were able to move back into their roles as mediators between the black community and the state.

Failure and Success

The Downstate movement gained widespread media coverage but failed to rally effective support for its goal: jobs for blacks and Puerto Ricans in New York's construction industry. The campaign did not generate a substantial number of these jobs. Although hundreds of blacks and Hispanics were interviewed under the agreement, few were hired.

A major reason for failure was the Ministers' Committee's inability to build an effective protest movement. The ministers failed to rally large numbers of blacks and Hispanics, and they were unable to mobilize their own congregations on any lasting basis. Protesting and jail-time meant absence from work and loss of wages, a price few were willing to pay.

More importantly, the Ministers' Committee failed to convince the community at large that the situation in New York mirrored that of the South. Although racial discrimination was a fact of life in the North, New York was a far cry from Alabama or Mississippi. Rockefeller and other government officials convinced the public that they were sympathetic to the cause of fighting racial bigotry and that antidiscrimination laws already existed in the state. The brutality inflicted on civil rights demonstrators in the South, which helped win public sympathy, did not materialize during the Downstate affair. The New York public was not bombarded with images of Bull Conner, fire hoses, police dogs turned on children, or the more overt forms of racism seen in the South. The lack of brutality and the expressed support of government officials for the basic goals of the campaign, if not the means, probably made the public less sympathetic to the Downstate campaign. They may have questioned the need for a civil rights campaign modeled after the Birmingham protest.

Because leaders of the Downstate campaign were eager to create a civil rights movement, they failed to include other community and labor groups. Although the campaign aimed at jobs for Puerto Ricans as well as people of African origin, few Puerto Ricans took part in the demonstrations; nor was there any real attempt to gain support in the Hispanic community, which would have made the movement more broad-based. Likewise, an attempt to gain labor's support would have boosted the campaign; it might have changed the perception that the campaign was an attack by the black community upon labor. On August 6, Leon Davis, president of Local 1199 Drug and Hospital Union, with a predominantly black and Hispanic membership numbering more than 22,000, offered the movement an opportunity to broaden the campaign. He gave his support in letters to both Governor Rockefeller and Mayor Wagner urging a halt to state and city construction projects until discrimination in the industry could be eliminated.[61] Since 1962 Local 1199 had linked the struggle for better working conditions with the struggle for civil rights. The union had cooperated with civil rights groups including King, Adam Clayton Powell, and A. Phillip Randolph to end racial exploitation. Realizing the importance of the redistribution of health care in black communities, the union leadership was willing to join any struggle for racial and economic justice.[62] But by failing to expand the movement and include Local 1199 and community groups, the leaders of the Downstate campaign missed this opportunity to link the job struggle to adequate health services in Bedford-Stuyvesant. The fight for adequate health care would have expanded the cause beyond the issue of employment. Leaders might have focused the Downstate campaign on issues of community empowerment, redefining Downstate in the community not just as a training hospital but as an answer to the health care needs of Bedford-Stuyvesant.

Despite its shortcomings, the Downstate campaign was not unproductive. The campaign helped focus attention on the construction industry, one of the most discriminatory in the country. Although it did not achieve its original goals, the movement forced state, city, and union officials to take action against racial discrimination in that industry. Although some accused the clergy of "selling out," they were perceptive in knowing when to end the protest and negotiate an agreement. If they had continued the campaign, the protest would have fallen apart, and they would have lost leverage in negotiating a settlement.

Moreover, by leading the Downstate campaign, the black clergy helped sensitize citizens to the need to eliminate discrimination in the North as well as in the South. They contended, like CORE, that the struggle for civil rights should not be limited to the South. Consequently, the Downstate struggle afforded many their first opportunity to take direct action against institutional racism.

The Downstate campaign raises the question of the role northern ministers played in the civil rights movement of the 1960s. Although part of an established black elite, the members of the Ministers' Committee for Job Opportunities and the black churches, in leading a civil disobedience protest, challenged state and city governments as well as the construction industry. They were willing to risk their reputations as "responsible leaders" and support from politicians, congregation members, and the community by assuming leadership of a grass-roots movement to end racism. If we are to gain a better understanding of urban black ministers in the civil rights struggle, we must pay more attention

to their role in northern black urban communities during this crucial decade.

Equally significant, the Downstate campaign exemplified the
movement for liberation by black churches across denominational lines. The general public acquired an impression of black religion fostered by King and the SCLC as militant and oppositional,
seeking to address the social and economic plight of people of
African origins. This image would have an impact on people who
were part of the next generation of ministers. By the 1970s and
1980s some black clergy in Brooklyn were willing to regenerate
the role as activist ministers and used various militant tactics in
the struggle for social justice. As King stated, "So the question is
not whether we will be extremists, but what kind of extremists we
will be."[63]

CHAPTER SIX

Driven by the Spirit: African American Women and the Black Churches of Brooklyn

As in all the churches of God's people the women should keep quiet in the church meetings. They are not allowed to speak; as the Jewish law says, they must not be in charge. If they want to find out about something, they should ask their husbands at home. It is a disgraceful thing for a woman to speak in the church meeting.

—1 Corinthians 14:34–35

The Suggestion that women must obtain power before they can effectively resist sexism is rooted in the false assumption that women have no power. Women, even the most oppressed among us, do exercise some power.

—bell hooks, *Feminist Theory: From Margin to Center* (1984)

T hroughout the history of Brooklyn's black churches women have comprised the majority of members; yet as late as the second half of the twentieth century, they were unable to share equally in formal leadership positions of those churches. For the most part they were closed out of the ministry, deacon boards, and with few exceptions, other formal positions of power.

However, individually and collectively African American women have consistently challenged that denial of formal power. They have creatively employed alternative routes to allow them an active voice. This was especially evident in Brooklyn in the 1930s. With the increase in church membership between the 1930s and 1960s, numerous auxiliaries were established to help mold their churches into social welfare and cultural institutions, making them cohesive communities. Through these auxiliaries, women forged a parallel leadership and created alternative routes to power and influence in their churches and communities. Power held by women in these positions was not only used for personal ambition, prestige, and control but was also used to promote public and humanistic concerns.

It is interesting to compare this with the experience of women in the Holiness-Pentecostal churches. Although sexism did exist among some Holiness-Pentecostal groups, many were less rigid than the mainline churches, affording women the opportunity to gain orthodox leadership positions.

Women in the Mainline Churches

Historically, women's roles in the mainline black churches, as in other Christian institutions, have been largely defined by the Pauline view that women are naturally on a lower plane than men, submissive by nature, and incapable of leadership. Thus, it was forbidden for women to preach and lead a congregation. As C. Eric Lincoln and Lawrence Mamiya note:

> The patriarchal values of the larger society and of Christianity itself also added the burden of sexism, including sexual exclusion from the vocation of ministry. As the invisible

underground religion of the slave churches merged into visible, institutional black churches of Baptist and Methodist persuasion, the freedmen and former slaves who founded these churches often accepted in toto the rules, beliefs, hierarchy, structure, and patriarchal conventions of their white counterparts from whose churches they were now separated.[1]

Although the African Methodist Episcopal Zion Church was one of the first major denominations to ordain women (in 1891), most mainline black denominations held on to their conservative views well into the twentieth century. The African Methodist Episcopal (AME) Church did not recognize the ordination of women until 1948, and the Colored Methodist Episcopal not until 1954. The same held true for black churches affiliated with predominantly white denominations. Although the Congregational church accepted the rights of women to preach in the 1890s, the Presbyterian and the Protestant Episcopal churches did not recognize the ordination of women until well into the twentieth century. Similarly, black women have usually found the Baptist churches closed paths to the ministry. Although the black Baptists have no written policy on the ordination of women, they have been restrictive in their practice. Besides being barred from entering the ministry, women have had difficulty gaining positions as deacons and stewards or on the trustee boards, where financial affairs, selection of personnel, and other administrative concerns are commonly discussed and determined. And although women have held positions as deaconesses, stewardesses and "mothers" in the churches, these positions are outside of the administrative and decision-making branches.[2]

The black mainline churches of Brooklyn consistently illustrate this exclusion of women from conventional positions of power.[3] By 1934 the number of Baptist churches had increased to twenty-four. Although the number of AME Zion churches had decreased to two and there was one less Protestant Episcopal, the number of AME churches had increased to five. There was still only one Congregational and one Presbyterian church. Of the twenty-four Baptist churches, all but one still had only male pastors, sixteen reported all-male deacon boards, and the chairs of all the trustee boards were men. A similar pattern was reflected in the other denominations.[4] They were tremendously rare exceptions when

Concord Baptist Church appointed Emma Dillard, a successful mortician, to its trustee board in 1935, and when Naomi AME Zion Church reported having a woman as chairperson of the trustee board in 1936, or when Lucille Brooks Taylor was listed as the sole female trustee board member of the First AME Zion Church in 1942.[5]

In 1947 and 1948 the *Protestant Church Directory* reported twenty-two black Baptist churches, five AME, three AME Zion, two Protestant Episcopal, one Congregational, and one Presbyterian church. Of all the mainline churches providing information on their pastors, ministers, and officials, only four Baptist churches reported women in formal positions of authority. Mount Pisgah Baptist had a woman pastor and Antioch, Concord, and Morning Dew Baptist reported women who were chairs of the trustee board. In 1952 the *Protestant Church Directory* reported that Mrs. Carrie Berry was pastor of Rose Hill Baptist Church in Brooklyn. Although it was not reported in the Protestant directory, it is clear that by the 1940s women served as deacons, elders, and trustees at Siloam Presbyterian Church.[6] These extraordinary rare exceptions demonstrate a persistent pattern of discrimination against women by Brooklyn's mainline black churches. The Pauline view and the social custom that women were not suited to lead was practiced with little deviation. Besides a woman pastor and a few women on trustee boards, women were unable to share in the formal leadership of these institutions.

Salina Perry was among the handful of women able to penetrate the male domain of religious hierarchy. Born in South Carolina in 1882, Perry was raised as a Methodist by her parents Isaiah and Amanda Fair.[7] In 1905, before the Great Black Migration in which hundreds of thousands of African Americans left the South and relocated in northern urban centers, Perry left South Carolina and came to New York, hoping for a better life. She eventually settled in Brooklyn. Unfortunately, life was difficult in New York, especially for African American women. Perry was relegated to the lowest level of employment, performing mostly service work as waitress, cook, chambermaid, and laundress.

Upon her arrival in Brooklyn, Perry became a member of the First AME Zion Church. She soon left and joined Mount Lebanon Baptist Church. Although there is no record as to why Perry changed denominations, it soon became evident that she was thinking about becoming a minister. Because African Methodists required formal education for the ministry and the Baptists did not, the latter offered Perry, who had a limited education, a better opportunity for attaining her goal.

While at Mount Lebanon, Perry stated that she was "driven by the Spirit of the Lord to preach." She decided to attend the Christian Workers Bible School at Concord Baptist Church in order to "train" for the ministry. But when Perry's intentions to preach became known, she met opposition from John Brooks, the pastor of Mount Lebanon from 1910 to 1916, who objected to women becoming ministers. Perry noted, "Many men don't respect a female preacher." She said that Reverend Brooks "started to fight me." Unwilling to accept Brooks's opposition, Perry left Mount Lebanon and became a member of Berean Missionary Baptist Church, where she received a friendly welcome. However, a schism at the church in 1916 caused Perry, along with others, to leave and join Brown Memorial Baptist Church.

In 1929 Perry decided that the time had come for her to go out into the field. Concentrating on her Williamsburg neighborhood, Perry set up a door-to-door ministry, going to people's homes and giving Bible lessons. Eventually, Perry gained a following estimated at twenty-nine to thirty-nine people and decided to rent a storefront at Humboldt Street in Williamsburg. Possessing a dynamic preaching style, Perry attracted others and soon had to move to larger quarters. In 1931 the congregation relocated to 84 Cook Street and officially organized the Mount Pisgah Baptist Church with 150 members.

Perry asserted that soon after the founding of Pisgah, active opposition to her ministry developed. When membership declined in the early 1930s (from three hundred to sixteen), Perry attributed it to male ministers trying to sabotage her leadership by convincing members that a woman pastor was not Christian. Moreover, her ordination in 1935 was held in Manhattan instead of Brooklyn due to the opposition of the all-male Ministers Council of Brooklyn.

Despite the turmoil, by 1935 membership at Mount Pisgah was up to 325, and some Sunday services attracted as many as one thousand people to the church. Due to the church's growth, Mount Pisgah's congregation purchased a large church structure at 756 Quincy Street in Bedford-Stuyvesant, thus becoming the third black church to move into the area.

Church Choir, Bridge Street African Wesleyan Methodist Episcopal Church
(1918) (*Bridge Street AWME Anniversary Book, 1980*)

Bridge Street African Wesleyan Methodist Episcopal Church (purchased in 1854) (*Bridge Street AWME Anniversary Book, 1980*)

Board of Trustees, Bridge Street African Wesleyan
Methodist Episcopal Church (1918) (*Bridge Street
AWME Anniversary Book, 1980*)

Dr. Susan Smith McKinney-Steward, organist for
Bridge Street African Wesleyan Methodist
Episcopal Church (*Bridge Street AWME
Anniversary Book, 1980*)

Church stewardesses, Bridge Street African Wesleyan Methodist Episcopal Church (1918) (*Bridge
Street AWME Anniversary Book, 1980*)

Sandy F. Ray, pastor of the Cornerstone Baptist Church from 1944 to
1979 (*Bridge Street AWME Anniversary
Book, 1980*)

Sunday service, Bridge Street African Wesleyan
Methodist Episcopal Church (June 3, 1951) (*Bridge
Street AWME Anniversary Book, 1980*)

Members of First AME Zion on their way to church (1939) (*First AME Zion Centennial Celebration Book, 1885–1985*)

Concord Baptist Church

Thomas Harten, pastor of Holy Trinity
Baptist Church from 1922 to 1968
(*Holy Trinity Anniversary Book*)

Original choir, organized in 1935, Bridge Street African
Wesleyan Methodist Episcopal Church (*Bridge Street
AWME Anniversary Book, 1980*)

First Baptist Church of Crown Heights

Bishop Frederick D. Washington, founder and pastor of Washington Temple
Church of God in Christ, and his wife Ernestine Washington, gospel singer
(*Bridge Street AWME Anniversary Book, 1980*)

Perhaps because of the example of Salina Perry's difficult success, other women—with the exception of Carrie Berry—did not become pastors or deacons, and only a very few gained positions as trustees. It was apparent that these positions were reserved for men. Unlike their male counterparts, women received no support and encouragement when deciding to become ministers. Instead, they were actively opposed and isolated. For example, as late as 1980, when commemorating its seventy-fifth anniversary, Mount Lebanon Baptist Church in Brooklyn provided a section in its Jubilee book with the revealingly gender-specific title of "Sons in the Ministry." In this section, male ministers who were former members of Mount Lebanon gave thanks for the encouragement and financial support given them by the church. The section also noted those who had attended Mount Lebanon who had gone on to become pastors of other churches. Tellingly, neither Salina Perry nor any other woman was mentioned.[8]

Challenges to Patriarchy

The patriarchal notion that women are to be silent in the churches has always been in conflict with the historical experiences of black women. From slavery to freedom, African American women have always sought their right to preach the word of God. Jarena Lee, Rebecca Cox Jackson, Amanda Berry Smith, and Sojourner Truth were just a few of the women who became preachers in the nineteenth century despite male opposition and attempts to silence them.[9]

Another example of women's consistent active leadership throughout the nineteenth and twentieth centuries is shown in their significant role in the founding of religious institutions. In Brooklyn, African American women helped establish some of that borough's most prominent black churches. For example, in 1847 Concord Baptist was organized in the home of Mrs. Maria Hampton on Fair Street. Along with Rev. Joseph Bacon and two other men, Mrs. Charlotte Bacon, Mrs. Mary Loach, Mrs. Eugenia Nichols, and Mrs. Martha Jackson organized Bethany Baptist in 1883. A group of seven people, including four women, met in the home of Mrs. Nannie Fountain on Herkimer Street in 1916 and decided to organize Brown Memorial Baptist.[10]

The use of power went beyond the notion of privatization or individual aggrandizement. Although women did gain prestige and a certain amount of control, power was also used in both the black mainline and Holiness-Pentecostal churches in a public manner. Ordinary people, especially women, pushed forward a social welfare and political agenda that served the masses. This is not to say that men were not engaged in the broader use of power. Some men were involved in pushing forward a social-welfare agenda in their churches and communities. However, men, unlike women, were also given the option of seeking a greater number of positions in their churches; that would lead to prestige, power, and control of others. Moreover, women made up the majority of the members of the churches; therefore more women were active in the growing number of church organizations that labored to serve the needs of the members of the congregation and neighborhood.

African American women of Brooklyn initiated the creation of clubs and organizations in their churches and communities for social, charitable, educational, and political purposes. These organizations helped them to address issues and problems plaguing their community and to dispute racist images of African Americans. These organizations gave women the opportunity to come together and unite in a common cause exclusive of male influence. Under their own supervision, women addressed their concerns, raised and managed money, and decided their organization's direction. In many cases they provided care and assistance to one another, and to the members of their church and community. Some notable groups were the Women's Christian Temperance Union (WCTU), whose members spoke in churches and communities to promote prohibition; the Equal Suffrage League, whose members participated in the National Association of Women and argued at literary societies and other meetings for the right of African American women to vote; the Women's Loyal League, which provided forums for African American children to "acquaint them with the noted men and women of the race"; and the Auxilian Club, whose major goal was to financially assist worthy young African Americans unable to pay for an education.[11]

One of the most prominent clubs for black women in Brooklyn was the Dorcas Home Missionary Society of Concord Baptist

172

Church. In 1877 Mrs. Elenora Walker Hill organized the Dorcas Home and Missionary Society to provide food, clothing, money, and other assistance to the needy of the church and the community. Although the society was associated with Concord, membership was open to anyone wishing to serve. The society attracted many women and soon began to extend its operation to Africa. By the turn of the century, the Dorcas Home Missionary Society developed into an active agency for women promoting women's rights. For instance, in 1905 the society offered to host the annual convention of the National Federation of Women's Clubs, a group dedicated to the "uplifting and betterment of womanhood." The Dorcas Society organized meetings at Concord and invited members of the Equal Suffrage League, Women's Loyal Union, and other clubs to help plan the activities of the convention.[12] Accordingly, this humanist agenda helped make the black churches into vehicles that addressed needs of working-class as well as middle-class African Americans.

The women of Bridge Street AWME organized the Martinique Linen Shower and the Little Sunshine clubs in order to assist the poor and needy of the church. In 1918 the church described the linen shower as "organized to keep socially in touch with one another, to comfort those in distress, to do all in their power to alleviate the suffering of worthy people and the uplift of fallen humanity." Charging its members a monthly fee of five cents, the club said that it had "fifty financial members and a substantial bank account."[13]

Along with clubs one of the most important sources for developing women's leadership, public-speaking ability, and managerial skills was the Women's Day Celebrations in the black churches. These celebrations became another way women were able to challenge the claim that they were incapable of leadership. Although modeled after the regular Sunday service, they were also a source of pride and consciousness-raising for women, an opportunity to demonstrate their abilities and talents. For example, on one Sunday in March 1905 three services were conducted by women at Concord Baptist Church. Sponsored by the Dorcas Home Missionary Society,

> The regular service began with doxology, invocation, and prayer by Mrs. C. H. Perry. Mrs. Ella A. Boole, a prominent

Women Christian Temperance Union lecturer, spoke on the "Pearl of Great Price." At 3:30 P.M. the services commenced with congregational singing, scripture reading by Miss Christiana Goode and prayer by Mrs. N. B. Dodson. . . . At 7:30 P.M. every seat in the auditorium was occupied and chairs were used in the aisles. Mrs. S. W. Timms read the Scripture lesson and Mrs. M. J. Zeno offered prayer. Miss Pauline E. Hopkins of Boston Mass. was the speaker. Her subject was "Women." She held the interest of her audience for forty-five minutes and closed with an earnest appeal to young women to take a position in the front in the work of temperance, religion and reform."[14]

Another notable practice used by women to gain a voice in the churches was to publicly oppose the leadership of the pastor or other church officials. There is nothing new about disputes between the leadership of the churches and parishioners. In fact, in the late nineteenth century, the *New York Freeman* noted confrontations between pastors and their churches were quite frequent.[15] What is noteworthy is the role women played in these disputes. They were active participants in several confrontations between pastors and the churches; thus their participation contested the image of women as inactive agents.

A case involving Thomas Harten provides a fitting illustration. Despite the popularity of Thomas Harten of Holy Trinity Baptist Church, an incident reported in 1926 pointed out that all was not well at Holy Trinity. Two members of the congregation, Ollie Paige and her husband John, sued the right reverend for slander and assault based on events that occurred in October 1923. The trouble began when Harten delivered a sermon accusing members of Holy Trinity of "immorality"—drinking, gambling, and "shooting crap." Apparently thinking that Harten was referring to her, Ollie Paige, along with her husband, confronted the pastor. During their "discussion," the couple asserted that Harten hit Mrs. Paige with a chair and punched Mr. Paige in the mouth.[16]

Although a large segment of the congregation supported Reverend Harten, the court proceeding revealed that the confrontation between the minister and the Paiges was more than a personal matter. Seated in the court were members of the congregation who accused members of the trustee board of fabricating the

incident and persuading the Paiges to take legal action. According to several members, many church officials were upset over
Harten's strong reign over the church and his growing popularity and wanted to dispose of him. At least half a dozen members
testified on behalf of the Paiges, and a woman parishioner
attempted to strike the flamboyant pastor as he entered the
church one Sunday morning. Eventually the case was thrown out
of court.[17]

In some cases women were in the leadership of attempting to
oust a pastor. The confrontation at Bethel AME Church (also
called Union Bethel) in 1925 is a case in point. A group of "dissenters" of the Bethel AME Church on Dean Street attempted to
stop the new pastor, the Reverend Charles Cole, from entering
the church and conducting Sunday service by chaining the doors.
Although it was claimed that the presiding elder of the Long
Island District of the AME churches, Montrose W. Thornton, was
behind the anti-Cole faction, the dissenters claimed that they
wanted to oust the new pastor because he was too "uppity" and
"stuck up" and "does not want to mix with the common people."
Although the pastor was able to enter the church after his supporters broke the chains, the police had to be called to the scene
in order to stop demonstrators from disrupting the church service.

A few days after the demonstration, fifteen of the thirty-two
church officials sent a letter to Bishop William H. Heard, presiding elder of the First Episcopal District of the AME Church,
demanding that Cole be dismissed and a minister of their choice
be appointed. When Bishop Heard met with the dissenters and
attempted to explain to them why it was difficult to remove a pastor, he was interrupted by a Mrs. Hall, who bluntly stated that
they wanted the pastor removed. Incensed by her action, the bishop ordered her to be quiet. But the group insisted that he read a
letter underscoring their reasons for demanding Cole's removal.
The letter was signed by ten women who were members of the
official board.[18]

When Heard refused their demands, church officials sent a letter to the senior AME bishop demanding the impeachment of
Bishop Heard and accusing him of "fraud and deceit." By late
1925 the dissenters left Union Bethel and established a new
church by the same name.[19]

In another case, a group of members of the Greater Good Will Baptist Church in December 1947 expressed their opposition to the pastor's decision to hold services on a temporary basis in a tent located in an enclosed parking lot while he negotiated the purchase of property to erect a new church. The unhappy members, numbering around thirty-five and led by Vera Joyins, locked themselves in the church and destroyed benches, hymnals, prayer books, and bibles—after the church's piano had been pushed out into the parking lot!

These cases demonstrate that women were not one dimensional but were willing to challenge the authority of the pastor and church officials. These incidents point out that ordinary people in the churches were concerned about issues of power and control and about financial and administrative matters and were willing to go to extraordinary lengths to win their objectives. Like men, women had a view of leadership and were active in attempting to bring this leadership to their churches. Although black women in the mainline black churches did not directly challenge the ideology of patriarchy, they stretched its boundaries so they could include their voices in several aspects of their churches. When challenging the hierarchy of the church, they were assertive, participated in confrontations, and on occasion even moved into leadership positions.

Women and the Increasing Number of Church Organizations

As the twentieth century progressed, African American women were afforded greater leadership opportunities in the mainline and Holiness-Pentecostal churches through newly organized clubs and organizations. With the massive influx of the Great Migration and an increase in the number of blacks in Brooklyn, black churches experienced rapid growth. In response to this growth, churches required new organizations to raise money and serve their growing membership. Women provided their managerial and leadership skills to establish and operate many of these new church groups.[20]

Of the twenty-seven organizations and auxiliaries established in Bridge Street AWME Church after 1930, twenty-three were either formed or headed by women. Sixteen were coed, with 21 percent of their membership male and 79 percent female. Only two of the sixteen groups were headed by men. Of the fifteen organizations and auxiliaries that could be verified as starting after 1930, 19 percent of the membership was male while 81 percent was female.[21]

By 1955 thirty-six of the forty-six organizations and auxiliaries of Concord Baptist Church in Brooklyn were headed by and comprised mostly of women. Eighty-one percent of the coed clubs at Concord were made up of women. In 1966 Cornerstone Baptist Church reported that twenty-five of the thirty-six auxiliaries were headed by women.[22]

These figures raise some important questions about the role of gender and the types of activities that were going on in the mainline black churches of Brooklyn. The growth of the organizations indicate that women continued to be active participants in shaping their churches. These statistics, together with church documents and newspaper accounts, suggest that during this period of rapid growth black women were able to cultivate leadership, rise to important positions, and gain recognition and influence in their churches and communities. They were also able to continue to push forward a social-welfare agenda for the churches, making them not just institutions of supplication but social agencies for the community. Black women were able to alter religious services by creating avenues for parishioners to participate in numerous activities of the churches.

An excellent example of this growing influence of women can be seen in the educational structures of black churches. One of the most concentrated areas of work for black women has been in religious education. In churches throughout Brooklyn, black women either formed or led vacation Bible schools, Bible classes, and Sunday school departments. During the summer of 1944, Concord Baptist's Daily Vacation Bible School provided a full program of recreation, music, and handicrafts for four hundred children in the community, with a staff of eleven teachers, all women, under the direction of Miss Eunice Jackson. In 1954 Mrs. Elizabeth Smallwood, with the help of the church's missionary group, created a successful vacation Bible school that served 142 children. Activities for the children included visits to amusement parks, arts and crafts, and religious training. The Bridge Street AWME Church's Vacation Bible School, also led by women, offered trips to parks, arts and crafts, and lunch to children of the community for twenty-five cents a week.[23]

The concentration of women in the area of religious education has posed a further challenge to the popular racist image of African Americans as irresponsible, childish, and incapable of and disinterested in learning. In churches and communities women were seen as educators with the important task of molding young minds and leading them on the pathway to success. Moreover, as Cheryl T. Gilkes has found in her study of women in the early Sanctified Church, it is incorrect to view women's concentration in educational roles as simply a form of sex discrimination; instead, she argues, it is important to recognize these experiences as the basis for an alternative structure of authority, career pathways, and spheres of influence. Through the publications of the churches and the black press, women received community recognition and praise for their work in religious education. During Women's Day celebrations, for example, black women were praised for being "great educators" and playing an indispensable role in society. At the Brown Memorial Baptist Church's Women's Day celebration in June 1945, women organizers invited as guest speakers women who served as positive role models to African Americans. They included Dr. E. Mitchell Lee, a Brooklyn physician; Ruth Wallace, a ranking dietitian at Halloran General Hospital and the first commissioned dietitian of color in the U.S. Army; and Maude Richardson, a columnist for the *Amsterdam News*. The major theme of the Women's Day celebration at the St. Augustine Protestant Episcopal Church in 1950 was the "community activities of the women of the church."[24]

In discussing black women's important role in church educational institutions, a distinction must be made between vacation Bible schools and Sunday schools. Vacation Bible schools operated only during the summer months for children who were on vacation from school. The churches established vacation Bible schools only if they could afford to operate them; in many cases this was not possible. On the other hand, Sunday schools were year-round operations that served children and adults. Sunday schools met regularly before each church service and were designed to help parishioners read and comprehend the Bible. Their function was essential to practically all black churches. Incomplete evidence suggests that although women dominated the leadership of vacation Bible schools, they did not assume the leadership of Sunday schools until a later period. The Protestant church directories, which published information on area churches including the names of Sunday school superintendents, suggest that the ultimate supervision of Sunday schools was not always left to women. It should be noted that not all churches reported information, so it is difficult to be conclusive.

As late as the 1930s, male superintendents of Sunday schools outnumbered female. Of the fourteen Baptist churches reporting the names of Sunday school superintendents in 1934, nine were men. Moreover, men were in control of the largest Sunday schools: Concord had 895 students; Bethany, 618; Zion, 285; Mount Carmel, 200; St. Paul Community, 200; and Salem, 200. The largest Sunday schools operated by women were Ebenezer, with 150; Evening Star, 150; and Mount Tabor, 120.[25]

Of the four African Methodist Episcopal churches listing names of Sunday school superintendents in 1934, all were men. First AME Zion had 725 students, and Bridge Street AWME had 450 students. Although Siloam reported a female Sunday school superintendent with 215 students, St. Augustine Protestant Episcopal with 375 Sunday school members, and St. Phillip's Protestant Episcopal with 500 members, both reported male superintendents. It is difficult to create a precise picture of the superintendents of Holiness-Pentecostal churches because of the lack of information. However, diminutive data suggest the position of Sunday school superintendent was usually held by men.[26]

Men were appointed as Sunday school superintendents because they were presumably seen as important administrative and management positions in the churches. The superintendent was responsible for managing a staff, students, and a budget. Although not closed out, women were limited to operating Sunday schools in the smaller churches.

By the post–World War II period, the ratio of male to female Sunday school superintendents had changed dramatically. Of the seventeen Baptist churches providing the names of their superintendents in 1947, eleven were women. Of the four African Methodist churches reporting names of superintendents, all were women. Although men still controlled many large Sunday school bodies (including Concord Baptist with 1,274 students, Bethany Baptist with 500, First AME Zion with 583, and St. Phillip's

Protestant Episcopal with 400), women had by this time gained control of others (including Antioch Baptist, with 500 members; Mount Lebanon Baptist, also with 500 members; Zion Baptist with 275; St. Paul Community with 200; Varick Memorial AME Zion with 250; Newman Memorial Methodist with 275; Siloam Presbyterian with 205; and Nazarene Congregational with 200). It should be recognized that Sunday schools and congregations that had women superintendents in the 1930s, like all schools and congregations in this period, experienced significant growth owing to migration, thereby allowing women to manage larger Sunday schools.[27]

The establishment of new churches does not seem to account for the increase in the number of women superintendents. Only one new church, Institutional Baptist formed in 1945, reported a woman superintendent. The increase was probably due to a growing consciousness in the church of the managerial ability of women. As more women gained positions as presidents of church clubs and auxiliaries, male ministers and other men began to acknowledge their leadership ability. The Reverend Clarence Norman, pastor of the First Baptist Church in Crown Heights since 1951, noted that women made good managers. Moreover, unlike those of ministers and deacons, positions as Sunday school superintendents did not directly threaten men's ability to manage the church. This would account for some churches having women Sunday school superintendents early in their existence.[28]

Although women concentrated their efforts in the educational institutions of the church, they were not limited to that area. Many continued to play a major role in fund-raising, which helped pay church debts and mortgages. Through the various clubs and organizations, women developed creative ways to accomplish this goal. They held personal fund-raising drives and pledges—events ranging from fashion shows to talent shows and music recitals. For example, when the Epicurean Club of the Nazarene Congregational Church sponsored a fashion show, it donated all the proceeds to the building fund of the church. Every woman of one particular club at Concord Baptist Church pledged to donate a certain amount of money to help pay for the cost of a new building after the old one was lost in a fire. The annual Women's Day celebrations also became an effective way of raising money for the church.[29]

The money raised was not only used to refurbish the church or pay off the mortgage but also for political purposes. Many churches throughout Brooklyn raised money for voter registration drives and contributed to southern civil rights campaigns. For example, the Social Action Committee of the Antioch Baptist Church not only launched a campaign to make every church member an NAACP member in the late 1950s but also gave generously to that civil rights organization's efforts in the South.[30]

Through church clubs, women have continued working in a collective effort to address the social needs and problems that plague their church and community. In some churches, not only did the missionary societies visit the sick and others unable to attend Sunday services, they also distributed food and clothing to the poor and homeless.[31]

Another community problem women have attempted to address has been juvenile delinquency. By the post–World War II period the black press, black political leaders, and ministers had noted the increase in juvenile crimes. In addition to ministers and community and city agencies, black women were also actively involved in fighting juvenile crimes. They offered children alternatives to street life. Black women kept the church doors open during the week with numerous activities for young people, including junior choir rehearsals, junior usher boards, and junior missionary society meetings. And as noted earlier, black women established and maintained vital summer programs for young people that offered a variety of activities. The chair of Young People's Societies in the black Holiness-Pentecostal churches was usually held by women.[32]

Beyond providing community services to their churches and neighborhoods, an important intent and result of women's organizational work was to help bond church members into a single community. They tried to bring people together on the basis of whatever commonality they could find. One fine example of this has been the formation of state clubs. Most of these clubs, established between 1930 and 1960 at the height of black migration to New York, were composed of people who had come to Brooklyn from one particular southern state.

A close study reveals that these clubs were almost exclusively managed by church women. The Georgia Club of Brown Memorial Baptist Church, organized in 1940, has always had women officers, including its president and vice president. This was also true for the Virginia Club organized in 1940 and the South Carolina Club organized in 1939. Between 1940 and 1966, Brown Memorial Baptist's North Carolina Club had eight presidents, six of whom were women. Of the nine officers serving the club in 1966, all but one were women. Brown Memorial was not unique. Concord Baptist, Cornerstone Baptist, Mount Sinai Baptist, First Baptist, and Bridge Street AWME all reported similar findings.[33]

These clubs were established to embrace and assist newcomers and to create a feeling of attachment to the church. As one member commented of the Virginia Club of Brown Memorial Baptist Church, "We as Virginians pulled together as one big family." Black women wanted to make everyone part of the church, part of the organization as a whole, and an active member not just a passive parishioner.[34]

In addition, the various organizations that were created and managed by women provided them with an opportunity to meet on a regular basis outside of the home. This afforded them a socially acceptable form of meeting and creating support systems. As historian Darlene Clark Hine commented in a similar study of church women in Indiana: "The black women's church clubs also provided essential support for their members as both blacks and women. Black women meeting in each other's homes week after week for ten, twenty, thirty and more years developed much more than leadership skills, positive self images and strategies for organizing communal charity. They nurtured and created a black female community and cultural network identified by its own special style, substance and language."[35]

Black Women and the Rise of Modern Music

As discussed earlier, in the late 1930s gospel choruses became an important ingredient of the churches of New York. This type of music, noted for its rhythmic, hard-driving sound and "otherworldly" message, and derived from the African American music forms of jazz, blues, and spirituals, first became prominent in the Holiness sects that developed at the turn of the century. By the end of World War I, gospel music was heard in the Holiness-Pentecostal churches of the urban centers. These churches had been created by recent black migrants from the South who were attempting to bring a southern style of worship to their new urban communities.[36]

Scholars have noted the reasons for the rise of modern gospel music during the Depression.[37] Yet despite their contribution to our understanding of this African American art form, they have neglected to explore the significance of the relationship between gospel music and black women. Evidence indicates that African American women were greatly responsible for making gospel music an integral part of the larger black Methodist and Baptist churches of New York City. Because of their efforts, African American women were able to organize and maintain gospel choruses in their churches despite opposition from church members who found this art form "primitive." A good example of this determination is the case of Jeannie Epps of Bethany Baptist Church of Brooklyn. In 1937, with the help of several women and a few men, Miss Epps organized the church's first gospel chorus. However, despite her efforts, the church did not provide financial means for the group to hire a pianist. But Epps and the others were undaunted in their efforts to make the gospel chorus a permanent part of Bethany. The members of the group, made up mostly of women, contributed their own money to pay for a pianist, insuring the group's survival.[38]

In the late 1970s Cornerstone Baptist Church acknowledged the contribution women had made in the evolution of its gospel chorus:

> The Gospel Chorus evolved from the membership during the early years of the church on Gates Avenue and Irving Place. Its first President was Mrs. Laura Crafton.
>
> Many persons are responsible for the maturity the Chorus enjoys today. Outstanding among them are Mrs. Maude B. C. Taylor, Mrs. Ethel Cooper Williams, and the present Director, Mrs. Daisy White. Our first concert, given in Atlanta Georgia, was under the leadership of Mrs. Williams. Following her marriage, we were fortunate in having Mrs. Daisy White, a member of our Music Staff, come to us as our Director. It was she who led us from "Gospel to Versatility," which was necessary in many concerts we were to give under her tutelage throughout many areas of the United States.[39]

Largely due to the efforts of black women, by the end of World War II gospel choruses flourished in the black Methodist and Baptist churches in the five boroughs of New York City. This point was illustrated by the first Jubilee and Gospel Song Festival sponsored by the *Amsterdam News*'s Welfare Fund in late December 1945 and January 1946. Of the twenty-one gospel choruses from churches in Manhattan and the Bronx participating in the festival, sixteen were directed by women. In addition, numerous gospel choruses from Brooklyn churches were led by women. The *Amsterdam News* wrote that the most diligent members of the twenty-four Brooklyn church gospel choruses that participated in the festival were women. Fifty-three women were listed as members of the various choirs who had not missed a single rehearsal. Only one man was listed in this category.[40]

The growth of these gospel choruses indicates the impact women had on shaping their churches and culture. Through their efforts they helped connect their churches to the community by bringing to these institutions a popular art form of the African American working class. In addition, gospel choruses created a form of social empowerment for black women. Some women were able to occupy an important church position as director of their church's chorus, while others gained acclaim as solo artists. For example, Ernestine Washington, the wife of Bishop Frederick Washington of Washington Temple Church of God in Christ, became a nationally known gospel singer and recorded several records. Black women helped develop an appreciation for this African American art form with a larger audience by incorporating gospel choruses into the churches and by further promoting it through church and community concerts. As gospel choruses became an integral part of the church, the very nature of gospel music as a participatory music encouraged people to become more active participants in the Sunday service. They were able to sing, clap their hands, and dance to the music. This feeling of exuberance helped create a bonding between members of the church.[41]

Women and the Black Holiness-Pentecostal Churches of Brooklyn

Like mainline churches, many Holiness-Pentecostal churches adopted the view that women should not be allowed to preach.[42]

However, despite the sexism within black Holiness-Pentecostal churches, some women struggled and were able to become leaders of congregations. In their study of Holiness-Pentecostal churches in Bronzeville, Chicago, St. Clair Drake and Horace Cayton confirmed that although men dominated the formal positions of power in the Baptist and Methodist churches, women were able to "rise to the top" in the Holiness-Pentecostal institutions.[43]

Unlike the major black denominations of Brooklyn, in which males had a monopoly on ministerial roles and other positions, some Holiness-Pentecostal churches gave women opportunities to become leaders of congregations and religious organizations. Although men occupied most of the ministerial positions in these churches, by the 1940s there were some women who led congregations and were recognized by their churches and organizations as elders, bishops, pastors, and even ministers. This is not to argue that these institutions were free of sexism. Many women were still limited to more traditional "womanly" duties, such as being secretaries and Sunday school teachers. However the opportunities for women to develop leadership skills were greater in the Holiness-Pentecostal churches, probably because of the belief that the call, which was the primary requirement for ministry (the belief that God contacts believers through visions, dreams, and sometimes miracles and assigns them the task to preach), was not limited by gender. Women, like men, could claim that God had spoken to them and had bidden them to preach His word. Women could also assert that they were given gifts by God, such as the ability to heal the sick. This claim helped give them legitimacy. Because of their claims of receiving the call, and in some cases because they were less restricted by institutional and doctrinal pressures, several women gained leadership authority within the Holiness-Pentecostal movement of Brooklyn. Some women were even able to increase their following and move to larger quarters.

Women who led Brooklyn congregations in the 1930s and 1940s had backgrounds similar to that of Salina Perry. They were usually born in the South, married, and some had a limited formal education. But unlike men who had the opportunity to become pastors of established churches, women who received the call usually had to organize new congregations. Although the evidence is incomplete on the success rate for these women, it is clear that their determination helped some flourish as leaders of successful congregations.

Priscilla Proctor, elder of the Elect Church on Fulton Street and Grace Haven-Waller, reverend of Tabernacle Healing Temple on Clifton Place, both in Brooklyn, serve as examples. Elder Proctor began preaching in the 1920s after she "received" the call. She probably preached in the homes of followers and gave guest sermons in some churches. She apparently developed a small following but had no church. Proctor and her followers, or "small caravan," went "door to door to collect funds and do good for those in need." Proctor and her caravan later organized a "praying band" and visited churches and the sick. She practiced healing and claimed to have cured "many souls." Probably due to both the growing membership and increasing financial assets, Proctor was able to establish the Elect Church on Fulton Street in 1936.[44]

Born in Virginia at the turn of the century, Grace Haven-Waller attended high school. Although there is no indication that she graduated from high school, she later took a nurse's training course in Georgia. She joined the armed services and was stationed at Fort Jackson, South Carolina. While in the army, Haven-Waller experienced a terrible accident that left her crippled. However, she asserted she was "healed" by God and claimed that this was the call that persuaded her to go into the ministry. Haven-Waller decided to attend Bible classes at the Bible Institute in North Carolina. She was ordained a minister in 1957 and soon after married Edwin Waller. Haven-Waller intended to open a grocery store in 1957 but was persuaded by an associate who was also "called" to preach, "Mother" Irene Lewis, to let her use the store as a church. Haven-Waller assisted Mother Irene in building the congregation and, after a few months of the church's operation, Haven-Waller took over as the pastor. By 1967 the Tabernacle Healing Temple under Haven-Waller's leadership moved to larger quarters in Brooklyn and opened a prekindergarten center with a trained staff for neighborhood children.[45]

During the 1940s and 1950s, many women founded Holiness-Pentecostal churches, including Pastor Ethel Crump (Jesus Christ's Triumphant Church of the Apostolic Faith), Reverend Carrier (the Sanctified Church in Christ), Bishop Eva Lambert (St.

Mark's Holy Church), and Bishop Mary Martin (the Life and Time of Jesus Pentecostal Church of the Apostolic Faith)[46]

Along with being pastors of congregations, women were found in other formal positions of power in black Holiness-Pentecostal churches. The House of Prayer for All People, located on Fulton Street, had women in the positions of Sunday school superintendent and chairperson of the trustee board. Besides having a woman pastor, Jesus Christ's Triumphant Church of the Apostolic Faith had women holding positions as associate minister, church clerk, and treasurer. In 1939 the Church of God, located at 1637 Bergen Street in Bedford-Stuyvesant, had women in prominent positions, including assistant pastor, music director, director of religious education, church clerk, and treasurer. The Church of God on Sumpter Street in Bed-Stuy had two associate ministers, a director of music, and a Sunday school superintendent who were women. Women held positions as educational director and musical director in the Church of God in Christ on the Hill.[47] Thus, many women in the Holiness-Pentecostal churches challenged the Pauline concept and social custom practiced by many denominations and gained positions of authority.

Although it is possible that men abandoned or refused to join churches with women in leadership positions, we do know that some men accepted and even served in leadership with women. At least two men served as elders of St. Mark's Holy Church under the pastorship of Eva Lambert during the 1940s. During its twelfth anniversary celebration, St. Mark's Holy Church had several men on the arrangement committee, including "Elder" Isaac S. James, overseer; "Elder" William T. Young, ruling elder; and "Brother" Milton Grayson, assistant to the secretary. Jesus Christ's Triumphant Church of the Apostolic Faith, under the leadership of Ethel Crump, had at least two men serving as assistant ministers. Some women were appointed to high positions, demonstrating the congregations's willingness to accept women in leadership positions. Sister Grace Haven-Waller was ordained by Bishop Samuel Sapp of the Church of God and later "ordained" by Bishop Charles Poole of the Bethlehem Healing Temple, thus allowing her to establish her own church. Without a doubt, credit must be given to these women for convincing others of their authority and right to lead.[48]

Black women in the Holiness-Pentecostal churches spoke with authority, leading congregations, interpreting the Bible, and dealing with financial matters and other organizational concerns. Like women in the mainline black churches, they were role models, confronting the dominant society's stereotypical images of black women.

People in subordinate social, political, and economic conditions attempt to alleviate their oppression whether it be in the workplace, church, or community. A defining part of the history of America is the story of the struggle by African Americans to overcome this country's insistence that they remain in a subordinate position. For African Americans, the black churches have been used as vehicles to struggle against racial inequality. African American women in the black churches have broadened that struggle to include the fight for gender equality. The history of the black church in Brooklyn importantly demonstrates that feminism has never been a strictly white middle-class project. Black women have a long but generally ignored history of working for gender equality.

African American women have struggled both individually and collectively for a voice. They have had a long history of leadership and organizing in their churches and communities. They have consistently opposed attempts to keep them silent and powerless. By creating alternative paths for social empowerment, black women were also able to oppose both the racist image of African Americans as nonthinking beings and the sexist image of women as passive. Moreover, through their leadership, they adopted a collective method to address what they perceived to be the problems plaguing their churches and communities.

Although the fight for equality continues, black women in their effort to gain power in their churches and communities have already made a major contribution toward that goal and have raised the consciousness of many Americans. They have made many of us realize that if equality remains an important goal among African Americans, then the attempt to eradicate sexism within the churches and African American communities must be a key component of that struggle.

CONCLUSION

Continuing the Legacy

From their founding in the nineteenth century to the civil rights era, Brooklyn's black churches have attempted to address the plight of black people by struggling for a variety of goals. Those goals have ranged from social and moral uplift to economic and cultural independence and political empowerment. In doing so, Brooklyn's various religious institutions and leaders, while often falling short of their full goals, have proven themselves successful in remaining integral parts of their communities.

As the 1970s approached, Brooklyn faced numerous difficulties. Old problems such as crime, drugs, inadequate health care for the poor, and a failing public school system still plagued the black communities. In addition, new problems such as the critical loss of industrial jobs, the erosion of government-support programs, the exodus of the black middle class (which, together with white flight, contributed to an eroding tax base), the growth of the urban poor, the crack epidemic, gang wars, and the AIDS epidemic all added to the deterioration of Brooklyn's black communities.[1] These problems continue to create greater challenges and demands for black churches. How have the ministers and their churches addressed these challenges?

Brooklyn still remains the center for some of the most politically active ministers and churches in the nation. It is beyond the scope of this study to examine the full range of contemporary activities of the entire body of ministers in Brooklyn. This chapter will instead seek to concentrate on an exploration and evaluation of the careers of six of these ministers, their roots in Brooklyn's religious life, and their attempts to connect and adapt this religious heritage to the many socioeconomic problems currently afflicting their communities. These ministers discussed here are Herbert Daughtry of House of the Lord Pentecostal, Fred Lucas of Bridge Street AWME, Johnny Youngblood of St. Paul Community Baptist Church, Clarence Norman of First Baptist Church of Crown Heights, and Wilbert Jones of Beulah Church of Our Lord Jesus Christ, but I place particular emphasis on the career of Al Sharpton.

Herbert Daughtry

Herbert Daughtry, pastor of the House of the Lord Pentecostal Church, located at 415 Atlantic Avenue in Brooklyn, has become one of the more noted militant pastors of Brooklyn in his attempt to address the social, political, and economic concerns of African Americans.

Daughtry was born in Savannah, Georgia, in 1931, the son and grandson of ministers. In the early 1940s the young Daughtry and his family moved to Brownsville in Brooklyn where his father first established the House of the Lord Pentecostal Church on Fulton Street.[2]

Despite growing up in a religious household, negative environmental pressures proved to be a strong pull in the new urban setting. Influenced by the excitement of the streets, Daughtry dropped out of school and joined a youth gang. The gang offered the positive influence of companionship and a strong identity. However, the choice of gang activity also involved a path of crime and violence, ultimately resulting in confinement to a youth detention center. Unfortunately, these centers were not rehabilitative but breeding grounds for hardened criminals. After leaving the detention center, Daughtry became more deeply involved in drugs and crime. By the age of seventeen he was a heroin addict. To support his addiction, he robbed and forged checks. When he was twenty-two Daughtry was convicted of armed robbery and check forgery and sent to Trenton State Prison.[3]

While in prison, Daughtry decided to turn himself around by pursuing religious and academic studies. He worked hard in prison, earning a high school diploma and a B.A. He also became an ordained minister. After his release in 1958, Daughtry succeeded his father as pastor of House of the Lord Pentecostal Church. Through his diligence, he increased the congregation from less than a dozen to hundreds of members.[4]

Inspired by the growing civil rights movement and his own personal experience, Daughtry decided to become an activist pastor and work to improve the conditions of black Brooklyn. He became involved in numerous community struggles in the 1960s, including the fight for community control of neighborhood schools.

In 1968 a harsh confrontation erupted between the United Federation of Teachers and the black and Hispanic community of Ocean Hill in Brownsville. Responding to a growing demand from the black and Hispanic communities of New York to control their own public schools, the Board of Education established a number of experimental community governing boards, including one in Ocean Hill Brownsville. Officials of the governing board were elected by the community, giving parents a stronger and more direct voice in their children's education.

Soon after its election, the Ocean Hill Brownsville governing board, led by Rhody McCoy, asserted its right to hire and fire school personnel by dismissing thirteen teachers and some administrators whom the board claimed were incompetent. Reacting to the decision of the governing board, the United Federation of Teachers called a strike, demanding the reinstatement of the thirteen teachers.[5]

Daughtry joined the battle with other ministers in support of the governing board. He asserted that the community had a right to control the education of its children. Daughtry used his church for community meetings and for organizing demonstrations. The *Amsterdam News* noted his involvement in the "memorable struggle" by labeling him a member of the "troops" fighting alongside other community activists and leaders of the community school board in Ocean Hill Brownsville.[6]

Daughtry soon became involved in a number of other important movements. He became an active member of "Operation Breadbasket," attempting to win jobs for blacks in Brooklyn. He served as its vice president and helped direct the A&P boycott campaign. In 1977 the Pentecostal minister, along with a group called the Coalition of Concerned Citizens, organized a boycott demanding increased black employment and led demonstrations against three Fulton Street department stores: Abraham and Straus, Martin's, and Mays. Daughtry and the coalition also attempted to force the stores' managements to support their call for a federal investigation of the killing of Randolph Evans, a fourteen-year-old African American Brooklyn resident fatally shot by New York City police officer Robert Torsney. Torsney never denied shooting Evans but claimed that he himself had a rare epileptic seizure. He was acquitted.[7]

As in the church-based boycotts of previous eras, the boycott was justified on the grounds that blacks spent their money in these businesses; therefore the stores had a moral obligation to the black community. In this case it was further demanded that these businesses use their influence to guarantee jobs not only in their stores but also in the new Fulton Street Mall then being built.[8]

In spite of Daughtry's efforts, his goals and tactics were ineffective. His target was too big. A&S, Mays, and Martin's were all large businesses where thousands of people shopped every day. The task of persuading thousands of people to stay out of the stores was overwhelming for a lone organization unsupported by other ministers and civil rights organizations. For better results, Daughtry might have more effectively employed the selective boycott approach used by the Reverend Leon Sullivan in Philadelphia in the late 1950s and early 1960s.

Sullivan's approach called for organizers to select one store that they felt was discriminating against blacks. Ministers or representatives would contact store owners or management and ask how many blacks they employed, how many were in supervisory positions, and other questions about their contribution to community organizations. If the business did not respond, or reported that it hired or promoted few or no blacks, ministers would make the public aware of the store's policy and call for a boycott and demonstration. One important factor in Sullivan's "Selective Buying" campaign was the establishment of a ministerial network. This network allowed organizers of the boycott to reach a broader public. Ministers who were organizers of the boycott first contacted fellow clergy, urging them to inform their congregations about the discriminatory policy and about possible boycotts and demonstrations. The next step called for informing the selected target of the demands of the organizers and the consequence if it failed to meet those demands. If the owner of the targeted business refused to negotiate, a boycott of the business and demonstrations would take place.[9] Unfortunately, in this later instance, Daughtry made no attempt at either effecting a single-target strategy or of networking for a broader coalition.

After the Randolph Evans murder and the failed boycott, Daughtry decided to establish a more broad-based group to help organize the black community and to lead campaigns for various civil rights causes. The organization, known as the Black United Front (BUF), launched a series of campaigns, demonstrations, and meetings on the issues of ending police brutality, increasing jobs for African Americans from Bedford-Stuyvesant merchants, and supporting the aims of the Palestine Liberation Organization (PLO). For example, in September 1978 BUF demonstrated at City Hall, demanding an end to police brutality, better health care in Bed-Stuy, and for city officials to rehabilitate abandoned housing and make it available to the poor.[10]

BUF tried to keep the community informed by distributing flyers and holding weekly meetings at the House of the Lord Church. For example, one flyer distributed throughout black areas in Brooklyn called for blacks to "wake up." It listed a series of beatings and murders of blacks by police, Hasidic Jews, and gangs of young whites. "How much more blood are we prepared to shed?" It called on blacks to attend Tuesday night meetings of BUF and gave a phone number for "information on how to prepare and protect your community."[11]

By December 1978 Daughtry, along with other community leaders, claimed he had won a major victory through negotiation with some of the downtown Brooklyn department stores, including A&S, Martin's, J. W. Mays, and Korvettes. At a press conference, BUF said it had "attained" a promise from the merchants to give $15,000 annually to a scholarship fund for Brooklyn's black high school seniors in order help them pay for college. Daughtry claimed that $80,000 was earmarked for the creation of a "Randolph Evans Community Crisis Fund aimed at providing assistance to organizations and individuals in the Brooklyn areas who may be desperately in need of help." In an interview with the *Amsterdam News*, the Pentecostal pastor also claimed that he had gotten merchants to agree to purchase from minority suppliers and to encourage contractors in the Fulton Mall to comply with an affirmative action program. Despite these claims, Daughtry gave no details on how the money for these efforts was going to be provided. Moreover, no one representing the merchants attended the press conference.[12]

Daughtry's announcement was premature. Although he was able to win two hundred summer jobs for disadvantaged youths in the summer of 1979, the other items of the agreement never materialized. Moreover, by the summer of 1980, BUF threatened to launch not only a new boycott against these same businesses it claimed to have "won" agreements with but, further, the activist minister vented his anger at Con Edison, Brooklyn Union Gas, the

Dime Savings Bank, and other downtown Brooklyn companies, as well as at nine community service organizations and the Brooklyn Chamber of Commerce, because of their part in the creation of the Carter Opportunities for Brooklyn Youth (COBY). This organization was created in order to give 142 jobs to disadvantaged teens. Daughtry complained that COBY was created by the business coalition just to avoid negotiations with BUF. He accused the mayor of New York, Edward I. Koch, of undermining the agreement between the merchants and BUF by attempting to strike a deal between the city and the companies for summer jobs for youths. Daughtry claimed the merchants felt that making a deal with the city would relieve them of their obligation to BUF and the black community.[13] The episode demonstrated that more than promises were needed to obtain political empowerment and jobs for African Americans.

BUF did not limit its focus to local events. While it was attempting to win jobs for blacks, criticizing Mayor Koch for not paying enough attention to the concerns of African Americans, and attacking police brutality in New York, Daughtry and his organization also concentrated on global issues. BUF became an outspoken advocate for ending apartheid in South Africa. Daughtry, BUF, and the House of the Lord Church were quite active in the push for divestment and were major critics of Ronald Reagan's publicly silent policy of "Constructive Engagement."[14]

BUF also became an outspoken advocate for the Palestine Liberation Organization. The pro-PLO position became extremely controversial because of the arguments used by Daughtry to define that position. Those arguments smacked of anti-Semitism and were damaging to Daughtry's and BUF's reputations.

In August 1979 Daughtry led a demonstration in front of the Israeli Consulate in Manhattan to protest what he called the "Zionist racist pressure which resulted in the dismissal of Ambassador Andrew Young" from his position as U.S. ambassador to the United Nations. Young had resigned the position after it was publicized that he had violated U.S. policy by holding secret meetings with representatives of the PLO. Carrying signs that read "Zionism-Racism," Daughtry and the demonstrators chanted "Long Live the PLO."[15]

In an article in the *Amsterdam News*, Daughtry justified the demonstration and his support of the PLO by pointing out that

BUF was a longtime supporter of the organization. He argued that "since Arab States and Mayors have unanimously affirmed the Palestine Liberation Organization as the legitimate representative of the Palestinian people, the Black United Front sees no other choice but to accept their decision." He also argued that African Americans should be involved in world events because "it is our world and we will be blessed or cursed by decisions made by human beings regarding it."[16]

In an effort to demonstrate that his actions were not anti-Semitic, Daughtry argued that he was only attacking "Zionist leaders" or Jews who "embrace a particular Ideology." In an article in the *Amsterdam News* on November 3, 1979, he incorrectly asserted that although President Truman had wanted to receive 400,000 Jews in the United States, "Zionist leaders" rejected the plan. According to Daughtry, they were willing to sacrifice millions of Jews for a Jewish State.[17]

Daughtry's objective was not just support for the PLO. He wanted to lambaste the NAACP and the Urban League for their criticism of his position on the Middle East, and Jews for their lack of support of African American empowerment. In a stinging attack, Daughtry accused national black leadership of being pro Zionist because it wrongly believed that Jews loved and supported blacks. Daughtry attempted to justify his position by citing the UN resolution equating Zionism with racism and the Zionist support for the South African government. However, midway through the article Daughtry abandoned his discussion of Zionism and wrote only about Jews in general, asserting that Jews only supported blacks when it benefited them. He argued that Jews did not support a black candidate for mayor or affirmative action. "If Jews really wanted to show their support of Black interests, here were some golden opportunities to do so. But, Jews chose to support only their own interests."

In the same article Daughtry noted that while a number of powerful political positions were held by Jews, including mayor, four of the five borough presidents, and controller, they refused to support black candidates. Daughtry concluded by asserting that Jews were not true friends of African Americans.

Indisputably, the Jews have enormous clout, politically and economically, etc. in New York. Yet, Blacks are powerless and the situation grows worse daily. When true friends arrive in positions of power, they bring their friends with them. Friends help create situations in which their friends become independent. If Jewish support were genuinely altruistic, then Jews would rejoice in Black assertiveness, realizing it is the inevitable result of the independence which they helped to create.[18]

The article was inflammatory and divisive—just the type of rhetoric that fuels the flames of anti-Semitism. This is not to say that people who support the PLO or a Palestinian homeland are anti-Semitic. It is one thing to declare one's support for people struggling for a homeland but quite another to single out a particular group and accuse that group of working against the interests of African Americans. Although Daughtry attempted to make a distinction between Zionists and the "average Jew," his often blurry distinctions and sloppy history were clouded by anti-Semitism. This approach did great harm to the historic relationship between African Americans and Jewish Americans. Instead of promoting unity, Daughtry's comments could only increase tensions between Jews and blacks.

To Daughtry's credit, he has given serious thought to how black leadership should serve ordinary people. In 1979 he presented a model of how various groups could work together to bring about positive results. According to Daughtry, organizations such as BUF could initiate confrontation with a target, such as a business or a government agency, that is practicing racial discrimination. Another group, such as the NAACP, could attempt to negotiate with the target. Once an agreement is reached between the negotiating group and the target, another group, such as ministers, should act as an "ongoing monitoring agency to make certain that the agreed-upon objectives are accomplished." Black elected officials should act to "safeguard" gains by working to increase the political involvement of the masses and gain "political control over the political process." According to the Pentecostal pastor, there should also be an attempt by community groups to work to create greater ties between native-born and Caribbean blacks. Daughtry's model was imaginative and smart. It recognized that there exist various civil rights and community organizations with different political views and approaches. Nevertheless, they all can work together for black people.

Complaining that BUF lacked a "Christian leadership," Daughtry left the Black United Front in the early 1980s. The complaint was an odd one, especially since he had been a founder and leader of the organization and had been in the forefront of its campaigns. A more realistic explanation may be that he was attempting to distance himself from BUF's unsuccessful campaigns and its identification with unpopular national and international positions. Also, Daughtry did not have complete control over the organization. Other community leaders were actively involved in the front.[19]

Although Daughtry left BUF, he did not end his political activism. Influenced by the doctrine of Black Theology, he decided to create the African People's Christian Organization (APCO) in 1983. Asserting that Africanness and Christianity are reconcilable and that "Biblical Christianity" originated in Africa, APCO became a black Christian nationalist organization. Its major objective was to build educational, social, and economic institutions in the black community that were solely controlled by blacks. Borrowing heavily from theologian and author James Cone's view of the function and significance of the Bible to people of African origins, APCO stresses: "Theologically, the God of the Bible identified with the oppressed masses and with their liberation. Both the Old Testament and the New Testament relate statements and stories confirming God's presence with any deliverance of poor subjugated humanity." APCO further asserts that it is attempting to build a black nation. "By pooling and expanding our skill, talents, and resources, we will be able to govern, educate, communicate with, protect, house, feed, clothe and employ ourselves."[20]

The fact that Daughtry resides in the predominantly white community of Teaneck, New Jersey, may raise questions of his sincerity about nation building and community self-help. However, the Pentecostal minister is too smart to believe that African Americans in Crown Heights and elsewhere can build an independent black nation. Daughtry sees black nationalism as a cultural tool to instill pride and encourage personal initiative, stimulate support for black businesses, and help create a stable black community. In order to reach its goals, APCO attempts to reach the masses by getting them involved in the various activities of the group, including its Timbuktu Learning Center, voter education and registration drives, prison ministry outreach, various lecture series, and regular membership meetings. In addition to these, APCO operates its own radio show, broadcasting on the all-black radio station WWRL on Saturday mornings.[21]

Despite its noble goals, APCO has failed to develop as a mass movement, perhaps because it is too closely associated with Reverend Daughtry. It is seen by many as being just an extension of his House of the Lord Church. Moreover, its call for nation building is seen as unrealistic and probably discourages people from joining the organization. Despite these weaknesses the organization has been a tremendous service to the community by becoming involved in voter registration and in offering lectures that focus on strengthening the black family, as well as in honoring both men and women who give their time to serve the black community.[22]

A more realistic and effective program coming out of the House of the Lord Church is "Man to Man, Incorporated," which attempts to address the problem of young African American boys growing up in single-parent households headed by women. Modeled after the "Big Brother" program, "Man to Man" strives to introduce positive male role models into the lives of black males six to sixteen years of age. Male volunteers, twenty-five years or older, endeavor to develop a strong relationship with young black males through recreational activities such as softball games, outings, and various sporting events; cultural events include trips to museums, concerts, and the library, and educational activities involve tutoring and homework assistance. "Man to Man" challenges the social problems facing black males by attempting to instill in them sound judgment for daily decisions, cooperation, respect for others, awareness of the benefits of hard work, and the importance of family. This innovative program needs to be established and supported by more community organizations.[23]

Daughtry has shown some growth as a leader. He is still committed to "lone gun" confrontational activities but also has incorporated workable programs for the community. His "Man to Man" program and some aspects of APCO strongly suggest that he has tried to build an institutional church that offers workable solutions to specific predicaments of African Americans.

Fred Lucas

A Brooklyn pastor who has decided to work for the betterment of African Americans within the confines of the institutional church is the Reverend Fred Lucas of Bridge Street AWME Church. Unlike Daughtry, Lucas grew up in a middle-class home in Washington, D.C., where his parents provided him with a stable environment. His father, a photographer. and his mother, a typist, both devout Catholics, decided that their son should become a priest. They sent him to parochial school in order to help prepare their son for the priesthood.[24]

However, at the height of the civil rights movement in 1964, the young Lucas, then in the seventh grade, began questioning the doctrine of the Catholic church. He believed that the Catholic church and its doctrine were not addressing the pressing social and cultural issues of the period. He concluded that the Catholic church was "irrelevant" to those concerns. It was presumably at this period in life that he decided not to pursue the Catholic priesthood.[25]

Successful in secondary school, Lucas went on to Harvard University where his life was greatly changed. At Harvard he was exposed to a number of political activities and ideas. He was drawn into a number of campaigns, such as divestment of Harvard stock in companies doing business with the racist regime of South Africa, the fight to increase the number of black students on campus, and the demand that the university increase the number of courses in black studies. This period had a tremendous impact on Lucas. He later told a *Newsday* reporter that it was there that "I was imbued with the philosophy of Marcus Garvey, Kwame Nkrumah, Frederick Douglass, W. E. B. Du Bois." Lucas contended that "I came away realizing that God did not send me there to join the black bourgeoisie, to leave the masses of black people to fend for themselves." He gained a deeper spiritual awareness, combined with a deeper political commitment to improving the lives of black people.[26]

He decided to abandon the Catholic church but not religion. Instead, he turned to the African Methodist Episcopal because it was an "independent black church operated, controlled, administered and owned by blacks." The AME church promoted a doctrine of "self-help, black pride, and dignity."[27]

After graduating from Harvard in 1972, Lucas enrolled at Harvard Divinity School where he graduated with honors. He became a pastor first at an AME church in Philadelphia and later at an AME church in Buffalo. In 1982 Lucas, together with his wife Barbara, who had earned degrees at Tufts University and Rochester Colgate Divinity School, moved to Brooklyn where he became the pastor of Bridge Street AWME.[28]

Lucas has helped transform Bridge Street AWME into one of the city's leading churches with a significant outreach program. Unlike some churches that only open for church services and choir rehearsals, Bridge Street AWME opens its doors from nine in the morning until ten in the evening most days of the week. It has sixty clubs and auxiliaries which meet on a regular basis and give members of the church the opportunity to become active. Its outreach programs include distributing food and conducting services at shelters for the homeless, missionary work at both men and women prisons, walk-in counseling at the church, Al-Anon meetings, and counseling for people overcoming drug and alcohol dependency, resumé writing programs, and employment services. In addition to this extensive outreach program, Bridge Street AWME, in conjunction with the New York City Public School Auxiliary Services, offers classes for adults wishing to gain a high school equivalency diploma.[29]

Sociologists C. Eric Lincoln and George Mamiya describe Bridge Street AWME as part of a movement in the AME church known as "neo-Pentecostalism" (that is, a movement by some historically mainline black churches to adopt a charismatic approach). "Neo-Pentecostalism in black churches tends to draw upon the reservoir of the black folk religious tradition which stressed enthusiastic worship and Spirit filled experiences." According to Lincoln and Mamiya, the "neo-Pentecostal movement in the A.M.E. Church concerns its curious combination of a deep Pentecostal spiritual piety and the A.M.E. tradition of involvement in progressive politics and political activism." They note that a major reason for the rise of this movement is that the majority of the pastors involved in the movement are politically progressive. Many were veterans of the civil rights movement. "Some of these activists felt burned out by the continuous struggle and sought a deeper, spiritual side" without giving up their politics.[30] Lucas fits into this category. As noted, he was involved in a number of political struggles, was influenced by black nationalist doctrine, and left the Catholic church looking for a deeper spiritual fulfillment.

The response to the neo-Pentecostal approach at Bridge Street AWME has been overwhelming. By the late 1980s Bridge Street AWME claimed four thousand members, making it one of the largest and most active churches in New York City.[31]

Johnny Youngblood

Like Reverend Lucas, the Reverend Johnny Youngblood, pastor of St. Paul Community Baptist Church, has also adopted the approach of building an extensive church outreach program. Located in East New York, one of the most devastated neighborhoods in Brooklyn, St. Paul has become one of the most stabilizing forces in that community.

Youngblood, who came to the church in 1974, has a B.A. from Dillard University and an M.A. from Colgate Rochester Divinity School. The histrionic Youngblood is a dynamic preacher able to excite the congregation with his loud, deep voice and charismatic manner. Youngblood uses simple language, including profanity, in his sermons in order to bring complicated thoughts "down to earth" so all can understand. He contends that it is okay to have vices, as long as you "give yourself to the Lord." Because of his charisma and his church's outreach programs, Youngblood has managed to increase its membership from less than one hundred in 1974 to over three thousand by the late 1980s.[32]

Under Youngblood's leadership, the church has built both an elementary school and secondary school. St. Paul also offers a scholarship fund to college-bound youth. St. Paul has also joined with other churches in the area and the Industrial Area Foundation to help build the Nehemiah Project, low-income housing in Brownsville and East New York.[33] With the most cutbacks in federally funded low-income housing since 1980, this has been a particularly important if smaller scale contribution to an escalating unmet need.

In an attempt to bring black men into the church, Youngblood and St. Paul have reached out to black men across social and economic lines by offering them gender-segregated services. These services for black men offer them a chance to come together and express their problems, concerns, emotions while at the same time receiving moral support. The service includes scripture readings, songs by the men's choir, poetry reading, dramatic performances, and testimonies in which men may stand and voice their personal problems. Throughout the service, white men are usually blamed for the plight of the black man because they refuse to share power, while black women are usually accused of not being understanding.[34]

There are no concrete solutions offered at these services, so blaming white men and black women for the conditions of black men without offering explicit solutions to their plight is too simplistic an approach. Nevertheless, despite this criticism, the service has attracted a large number of men including professionals, entrepreneurs, the working-class poor, and drug and alcohol abusers. It is at least a place where black men can gather to vent their anger, encourage and offer hope to each other, and gain self-esteem.

Youngblood and St. Paul have made dramatic strides in serving the community, and the church has become an essential institution in the depressed East New York area. Youngblood has managed to become an important player and leader in New York City, and he has done this without compromising the needs of the poor. In fact, he has used his increasing prestige to help provide needed services. Accordingly, he has gained the respect of city officials and the powerless.

Clarence Norman

The Reverend Clarence Norman, pastor of the First Baptist Church of Crown Heights, is one of the most politically active ministers in Brooklyn. Although he has been pastor of First Baptist since the early 1950s, it was not until the 1970s that Norman and his church became major forces in Crown Heights. Since the 1970s, Norman and First Baptist have been in the vanguard of a number of enterprises, attempting to better the lives of black people in the community. He asserts that a major priority of his church is to address the various needs of blacks in his community, including race relations, housing, and juvenile delinquency.

In March 1953 Norman, along with nineteen other people, founded a Baptist mission. Although he was not an ordained minister at the time, Norman was selected as its spiritual leader. The group rented a storefront on Throop Avenue in Williamsburg and renamed itself the First Baptist Church of Williamsburg. It organized a deacon board, trustee board, Sunday school, usher board, Baptist Training Union, and choir, and selected officers to head each group. In April 1953 First Baptist held its first service and attracted seventeen new members.[35]

Norman, who possesses an outstanding speaking voice, was able to attract other members, and the church experienced tremendous growth. Another important factor helping to increase the membership of First Baptist was the growing black population of Williamsburg. Unable to accommodate the growing congregation, First Baptist moved to larger quarters in 1954. The church made several other moves before it purchased its present home at 450 Eastern Parkway in 1967 (formerly Park Manor Caterers, Inc.). The church built a magnificent edifice, able to seat hundreds. In 1987 the church reported having 1,600 members (with nineteen auxiliaries and five choirs). Norman noted that on any given Sunday some 750 to 800 people attend Sunday morning service.[36]

Norman said that he has been greatly influenced by the advocates of Black Theology and that the doctrine of Black Theology has led him to his view that the black church must be involved in improving social conditions. Arguing that Black Theology helps return the black church to its original goals of gaining liberation and freedom for black people, Norman claims that there are today two black churches. The first has been deradicalized and has bought into the dominant culture. He said that he was part of this group for many years. The second emphasizes "liberation and freedom," and Norman now sees himself as part of the second group.[37]

To make his church an active political and social force in the black community, Norman has worked to address some of the most serious issues facing blacks in Crown Heights. In the 1970s the church operated a social service agency on Rogers Avenue whose purpose was to help people gain housing, assist those who had disputes with their landlords, and organize tenant councils.

Norman has also worked to ease tensions between people of African descent and the Jewish community. Since the early 1980s tensions between blacks and Jews have been dangerously escalating in that neighborhood. The pastor of First Baptist has been an active member of the Crown Heights Coalition, a group of black and white ministers and rabbis who came together in order to "promote dialogue" and help develop ways of alleviating the tension between the two groups. The coalition has adopted a "trickle down" approach to race relations. Norman said that if ordinary people see their religious leaders discussing problems, they might adopt the same approach and hold discussions. Norman maintains that the clergy must try to bring about peace. "If blacks and Jews can't live together in Crown Heights, I can't see how they are going to live together in any place." One problem with this approach is that there does not seem to be any way to measure its success. Despite Norman's optimism, an added problem for the black clergy is that so many of the people who are involved in violent incidents are young people who do not attend church services. An important step that this group must take if it is going to be successful is to make the group more inclusive. Not only clergy but neighborhood leaders and ordinary residents could be included to broaden discussion. In addition, a broader agenda for jobs, improved educational and recreational facilities, and better police protection could be included as goals for the Crown Heights Coalition.

Along with race relations, Norman has addressed the problem of housing in Crown Heights and has met with some success. First Baptist has built and operates a building for senior citizens that provides housing for 152 people. In 1985 First Baptist Church won a state-funded grant of $3 million to build a housing project for the homeless. The church renovated a building on Pacific Street and is making it a transitional residence for ninety-six homeless men and women who previously lived in shelters and were either drug or alcohol addicts. The major goal is to get people back on their feet. A support team of social workers has been assigned to the project in order to assist the residents and to identify those who might be able to leave the project and join the mainstream. Norman asserted that those who are marginal can be brought back into the mainstream with a little work.

This is a bold endeavor, however, as Norman admits it is only "scratching the surface because the needs are so great." A greater effort must be made by government and community agencies to help the growing homeless population. In the meantime, he said that the church must not make up excuses for inaction. "If the black church does not start addressing the problem, who will?"

The First Baptist Church also operates a "Meals on Wheels" program funded by the Community Development Agency. This program provides a meal a day for the elderly and people who are physically restricted to their homes. In addition to "Meals on Wheels," the Missionary Circle, an auxiliary of the church, provides 125 lunches every Wednesday to men who live in the homeless shelter on Bedford and Atlantic avenues. The group also provides baskets of food and clothing to the needy.[38]

Another activity of the church is promoting higher education. The Hospitality Club of First Baptist provides small scholarships to high school graduates who go on to college. It also assists students in seeking additional sources for college scholarships.[39]

Since the 1970s, First Baptist has been involved in political campaigns. Norman admits that his church is partisan. In 1976 he himself ran for a state senate seat. Although he lost his race, his son Clarence Norman Jr., running for a state assembly seat, won with the support of the church. The church has also supported and campaigned for Jesse Jackson, who addressed the congregation in his bid for the presidency in both 1984 and 1988. Norman frequently preaches politics from the pulpit, informing and urging his members to get involved.[40]

Like other churches, First Baptist has organized boy scout and girl scout units in order to combat juvenile delinquency. And it helped organize the Comprehensive Youth Program, a Crown Heights organization that provides summer jobs for neighborhood teenagers. Norman concedes that he has had trouble getting young people of his church involved in these activities,[41] and he recognizes that these efforts still fall short of addressing the vast range of problems confronting teens, from drug and alcohol use to violence, crime, and dropping out of school.

The church is extremely active. Programs for housing the homeless and providing meals for the disadvantaged are resourceful, but First Baptist, like other black churches, still needs to construct programs that more effectively reach the vast number of Crown Heights teens who remain outside the church.

Wilbert Jones

Wilbert Jones, pastor of Beulah Church of Our Lord Jesus Christ (COOLJC) represents an emerging black clerical leadership within the Pentecostal church. As Holiness-Pentecostal bodies grow and become dominant institutions in the black communities, they confront the same conditions that older mainline churches have faced over the decades. Providing broader services to the congregation has become of paramount importance for black Pentecostal churches, thus some have modified their position on opposing "worldly" activities. Some churches have deliberately sought ministers who are more educated and socially active. This ministerial class has been educated in institutions of higher learning including seminaries. In common with earlier generations of Pentecostal ministers, they hold firmly to a fundamentalist faith that stresses an otherworldly doctrine and paints the world as evil, while accepting such practices as healing and speaking in tongues, and encouraging a strict code of behavior. But unlike earlier generations, they are more willing to take an active role in addressing the broader social conditions of African Americans.

Jones, born in the Bronx in 1944, has long had affiliation with churches. He attended religious instruction at St. Anthony's Roman Catholic Church in the Bronx, joined the Cadet Corps at Caldwell AME Zion Church, and was an usher and junior deacon at a local Baptist church. However, it was not until the age of sixteen, Jones said, that he was "baptized with the Holy Spirit" and joined a Pentecostal church. Jones said that his call to preach and subsequent training as a minister occurred at Refuge Temple in Harlem, and his more formal training was at the American Bible College. With a B.A. and an M.A. in theology, he was also a chaplain in training at Harlem Hospital in New York City and a pastor/counselor for the Harlem Interfaith Counseling services.[42]

Jones, who came to Beulah COOLJC in 1972, said that while he is committed to the teaching of the scriptures, speaking in tongues and healing are also important components of Beulah services. His church upholds a dress code that forbids women from wearing pants and insists that they cover their heads during service. Members of the church are prohibited from card playing, moviegoing, gambling, "sensual dancing," drinking alcoholic beverages, and smoking. According to Jones, sticking to these principles and declaring oneself at war with the world has not hurt the church. In fact, Jones claimed that since he became pastor of Beulah, its membership increased from five members to a size currently requiring he hold three services on Sunday in order to accommodate all members. The first service, which takes place at eleven in the morning, usually draws about 750 people. The

Sunday afternoon service attracts 400, and the evening service usually has 600 worshipers. In addition, the Sunday morning service is broadcast by the black radio station WWRL.[43]

In keeping with the new generation of Pentecostal members, Jones has not isolated the church from the larger Christian community in Bedford-Stuyvesant, despite the strict adherence to Holiness-Pentecostal faith. He has preached at Washington Temple, First AME Zion, and a number of Methodist churches, and Beulah COOLJC's choir has sung in an Episcopalian church. Together with Rev. Fred Lucas, he has become involved in community activities. The church has a food program, using government-subsidized food. Beulah also offers a free literacy program for adults, a job-training program, and a computer literacy program. In addition, the church offers counseling to community residents.[44]

The church has also been involved in voter registration campaigns. Although it is the policy of the Pentecostal group to discourage ministers from running for elected office, others were allowed to run. Jones makes it clear that while he is not as demonstrative as Reverend Daughtry, he agrees that the struggle for upward mobility and justice for the oppressed is high on the church's agenda. Members of the church have gone to Albany to lobby for legislation.[45]

Despite his church's professed commitment to equality and social change, Jones upholds the banning of women from the pulpit. He said that this is not an attempt to be sexist but rather an attempt to follow the teachings of the Bible. He further defends this view by explaining that women of the church hold other important positions as trustees, social workers, bookkeepers, secretaries, mothers of the church, missionaries, and officers of auxiliaries. Despite Jones's defense that it is just a matter of following scripture, not all Pentecostals agree with his reading and its effect of restricting women to traditional roles and away from positions of power. Without a doubt, this justification of discrimination has hindered the progressive steps taken by the Pentecostal pastor.[46]

Al Sharpton

One cannot conclude even a brief look at Brooklyn's active ministerial leadership without discussing the most controversial minister in the borough, the Reverend Al Sharpton. This articulate, publicity-savvy, and still young minister has become one of the most charismatic, and at the same time divisive, forces in New York City politics—and for that reason his career requires lengthy attention. Sharpton has drawn people with his radical street politics. His black nationalist insistence that blacks rely on their own community and resources has won him the admiration of many working-class blacks. He has given people a sense of empowerment through forums that have allowed them to actively express their anger. But to the detriment of his cause and to his own reputation, as well as to the broader community he seeks to represent, he has frequently allied himself with questionable characters and has taken part in activities that have cast doubts on his credibility and leadership.

Alfred Sharpton Jr. was born in the Brownsville section of Brooklyn in 1954, the youngest child of Alfred and Ada Sharpton. Sharpton has an older half brother and half sister and an older sister. His father was a contractor who owned several houses in both Brooklyn and Queens and provided a comfortable life for his family. In 1959 the Sharptons moved into a large private house in the middle-class neighborhood of Hollis, Queens.[47]

Before moving to Queens, the Sharptons began attending Washington Temple Church of God in Christ (COGIC) regularly. At an early age, Sharpton was impressed with the charismatic preaching style of its founder and leader. Bishop Frederick D. Washington. Sharpton decided to become a minister and at the age of four gave his first sermon at the church entitled, "Let Not Your Heart Be Troubled." By the time Sharpton had reached the age of ten, he was ordained as a COGIC minister by Bishop Washington. He became an itinerant preacher, giving guest sermons in various churches in New York. By the time he was thirteen, he started traveling with the famed gospel singer Mahalia Jackson. Sharpton would open her shows with a sermon. Because of his youth he became known and billed as the "wonder boy preacher."[48]

Despite his success in the ministry at such an early age, Sharpton was confronted with personal difficulties as a child. Because of marital problems, his father decided to leave. He left the family the home in Queens but nothing else. This forced the family out of their middle-class existence and into poverty. Sharpton has said that the breakup between his parents nearly led to his mother's having a nervous breakdown. The young minister asserted that his family lived for six months in the Hollis home without utilities. Sharpton's mother was forced to take a job as a domestic worker. She sold the house and moved the two remaining children, Al and his older sister, to an apartment in East Flatbush, Brooklyn. The young Sharpton helped keep the family afloat with his earnings from preaching. This was a heavy burden for a child. More positively, his preaching at such an early age and the responsibility of taking care of a family probably helped him develop his independence and outspokenness. But his father's desertion has left Sharpton bitter and resentful. As recently as 1991, when Sharpton was stabbed at a demonstration in Bensonhurst, Brooklyn, and was recuperating in a hospital, aides of the Pentecostal minister had to convince him to accept a phone call from his father.[49]

Sharpton's political activism was probably sparked by Rev. Adam Clayton Powell Jr. of Abyssinian Baptist Church in Harlem. Sharpton, who was twelve when he met Powell for the first time, recalled that he was amazed at how Powell handled the press during an interview he attended. "It was the most amazing show I had ever seen in my life," Sharpton said. Shortly after the first encounter between the two ministers, they became friends. Powell took the young Sharpton to his first Broadway show and to the island of Bimini for a vacation. He even counseled the "wonder boy preacher." Sharpton would tell the *New York Times* years later that he had decided he wanted to be like the militant pastor from Harlem and become an activist preacher.[50]

Growing up in the 1960s, Sharpton was aware of many black clerical figures who were in the forefront of the civil rights movement. Their example probably helped shape his views on the relationship between the ministry and social issues. According to Sharpton, the minister must address and try to seek solutions for the social conditions of the economically disadvantaged and powerless. The role of the minister cannot be limited to the spiritual realm. Sharpton decided to become less active in Washington Temple because he thought that Bishop F. D. Washington and the church were not in the vanguard of the struggle for economic and social justice. Although he still claims to be a member of the church, he has dedicated more of his time to civil rights than to preaching.[51]

By the time Sharpton was twelve, he developed a close connection with more activist ministers such as Rev. William Jones of

Bethany Baptist Church. In the late 1960s Jones had become the head of the New York branch of "Operation Breadbasket." The national organization, which struggled for economic justice for blacks, was headed by the Reverend Jesse Jackson. Jones introduced Sharpton to Jackson.

In 1969 when Sharpton was fifteen, Rev. Jesse Jackson appointed him youth director of the New York City chapter of "Operation Breadbasket." The young activist minister participated in a number of campaigns including a boycott against the Atlantic and Pacific Tea Company (A&P), which operated a national chain of supermarkets. The boycott was launched by Jones and the New York chapter of "Operation Breadbasket." It involved numerous ministers and won the support of several religious groups and a significant segment of the population. However, despite the fact that A&P reported a drop in its stock because of the boycott, the New York chapter of "Operation Breadbasket" failed to win the support of the national organization for a nationwide boycott against the corporation. In the end, no agreement was reached between the opposing sides.[52]

Sharpton's involvement in the boycott radicalized him, and he acquired a taste for street protests. In 1971, while still in high school, Sharpton told a *New York Post* reporter that he had been arrested four times in protest demonstrations.[53]

While attending Samuel Tilden High School in the late 1960s and early 1970s, Sharpton's political activism grew. He became president of the Afro-American Club and the Martin Luther King Plaque Committee, Chair of the Vietnam Moratorium, and associate editor of the school newspaper. In 1971, while serving as a student intern to New York City's Human Resources administrator, Sharpton decided to leave "Operation Breadbasket" and form his own organization, the National Youth Movement (NYM). The organization stated that its goals were to help register young people to vote, increase youth employment, fight sickle-cell anemia, and wage a war against drugs.[54]

Throughout the 1970s and 1980s Sharpton experimented with a variety of techniques—negotiation and threats, demonstrations and sit-in—in order to accomplish his goals and also to attract media attention. Sharpton, along with the NYM, held demonstrations at City Hall and other places demanding summer jobs for teens. In 1970 he held a sit-in at City Hall, calling on city officials to provide jobs for African American youths. He later held a sit-in at the Board of Education's office to demand the hiring of blacks for top positions. He was eventually ejected by security officers. On another occasion he and members of the NYM marched on Wall Street and painted X marks on office buildings where they claimed drug sales were taking place.[55]

Sharpton also tried his hand at politics. In 1978, at the age of twenty-three, the young minister decided to run for state senator in Ocean Hill Brownsville. He claimed that he had been approached by several local leaders, including Sam Wright, former district leader of the 54th Assembly District to run for office against the incumbent, Major Owens. Owens was the former head of the Brooklyn branch of the Congress of Racial Equality (CORE) and a well-known grass-roots fighter who has since become a member of the U.S. Congress.[56]

Sharpton's ambitions for political office were put on hold when Brooklyn Supreme Court Judge Gerald Beldock knocked him off the ballot, citing the young minister's registration in two different districts. Judge Beldock said that Sharpton was "hopping and bopping" from different addresses in order to run for office. Beldock asserted that it was "one of the strangest" cases he had ever witnessed.[57]

In the early 1980s the flamboyant minister stopped subway traffic and gained significant press attention. On these occasions he twice blocked tracks in Manhattan to publicize his demand for more black representation on the Metropolitan Transit Authority (MTA). He also publicly threatened to lead a demonstration of five thousand in order to stop the MTA from raising its fare. No shift in MTA policy resulted.

In 1985 the *Amsterdam News* reported that a research team for the NYM had disclosed that few contracts were given by record companies to black promoters representing black artists. Sharpton referred to this as "economic Apartheid." By going public, Sharpton embarrassed CBS, Electra, RCA, and MCA into negotiations.[58]

Sharpton and NYM also held weekly forums in Brooklyn in order to win the loyalty of young people. One such forum held in 1986 featured choir singing, civic leaders speaking on the issues facing black Brooklyn, and a police captain warning of the dangers of crack-cocaine.[59] However, despite Sharpton's assertion that he was working in behalf of oppressed people, his activities often seemed to be more geared to generating personal publicity. In contrast to his headlines, his accomplishments have been sparse.

In November 1986 Sharpton tried yet another tactic to gain public attention. He and a group from NYM, who called themselves "crackbusters," marched again on Wall Street in order, they claimed, to expose crack houses. This time he told reporters that he had the names of dealers and the addresses of crack houses and he was personally going to give the information to federal authorities.[60]

At the same time that Sharpton was leading protests, he was developing ties with well-known celebrities and some unsavory characters as well. In 1973, through a local disk jockey, Sharpton met singer James Brown, who, according to the Pentecostal minister, became a major contributor to the National Youth Movement. Brown also agreed to financially assist Sharpton by investing in the carting industry when, in 1980, Sharpton tried to form a joint business with the Consolidated Carting Company. Sharpton claimed that his goal in establishing this venture was to generate jobs for blacks. However, when he attempted to gain a contract with Consolidated Edison, the company refused to negotiate, asserting that it was not Sharpton but Matthew ("Matty the Horse") Ianiello, "a reputed captain in the Genovese crime family," who had real control over the Consolidated Carting Company. In 1988 *New York Newsday* reported that Sharpton had acted as a "front" for Ianiello "in an attempt to win a lucrative garbage collection contract with the Consolidated Edison Co."[61]

Sharpton first met boxing promoter Don King in 1974, but it was ten years later that he began developing a close relationship with King. Don King is a man with a notorious past. Between 1951 and 1966 King was arrested thirty-one times for various charges, including gambling and assault. In the early 1960s he became a numbers boss in Cleveland, grossing $15,000 a day. The FBI has reported that King had "kicked back" a portion of his earnings to organized crime figures in Cleveland in exchange for protection of his numbers operation. In 1960 King kicked a man to death because he owed him six hundred dollars. Although convicted of second degree murder, the judge reduced the charge to manslaughter. King served four years in prison and was released in 1971, receiving a full pardon from the governor of Ohio in 1983 (under somewhat suspicious circumstances, according to reporter Jack Newfield).[62]

King began a new career as a boxing promoter in the early 1970s but was once again connected to organized crime figures. Joseph Spinelli, a former head of an FBI boxing investigation, noted that Don King had had business meetings with reputed mobsters. King has also been accused of making lucrative closed-circuit television deals for boxing matches with organized crime figures. And he has been sued by several boxers managed by his stepson Carl King, for cheating them out of their proper share in profitable boxing matches.[63]

In 1984 Sharpton and King teamed up to work on the singer Michael Jackson's "Victory" tour. King was the national promoter, and Sharpton became head of the tour's community relations office. King also donated money to the NYM. Sharpton has acknowledged his relationship with King and is frequently King's guest at celebrated boxing events.[64]

Despite Sharpton's activism, he did not gain truly widespread prominence until 1986 with the Howard Beach case. In the winter of 1986, three young black men were beaten by a gang of white youths in the Howard Beach section of Queens, New York. One of the black men, twenty-two year-old Michael Griffith, was beaten and chased by the gang onto a highway, where he was struck by a car and killed. Although a group of white youths were arrested shortly after the incident, Sharpton, who became the spokesperson for Michael Griffith's family, and the family's attorneys, C. Vernon Mason and Alton Maddox, encouraged witnesses not to cooperate with the Queens district attorney. Instead, they demanded that Gov. Mario Cuomo appoint a special prosecutor to handle the investigation. The lawyers claimed that the Queens district attorney's office and the police had mishandled the investigation from the beginning by not arresting the driver of the car that killed Griffith. The driver had left the scene of the incident and washed the car before surrendering to authorities. The driver was never charged with any crime.[65]

In order to bring pressure on the governor, Sharpton held highly publicized demonstrations in Howard Beach, including one in which he went to the pizza shop the three black men had visited before they were attacked. In front of news cameras,

Sharpton ordered a slice of pizza and said he and any other African American had a right to buy and eat pizza anywhere they wanted. When Mayor Koch met with other black leaders at City Hall to talk about ways to ease the racial tension in the city, Sharpton held a press conference and called the mayor's meeting a "coon show." Eventually, Governor Cuomo appointed attorney Charles Hynes as special prosecutor. Hynes won a conviction.[66]

Sharpton, Maddox, and Mason were revered by many as heroes. Their effective strategy won praise from the black press and radio and from New Yorkers who had previously seen a number of highly publicized racial incidents in which blacks had been beaten or killed resolved without a single conviction. Sharpton in particular gained media attention because of his outspokenness.

In spite of his notoriety and prominence, questions about his integrity were again raised. In January 1988 *New York Newsday* revealed that Sharpton had worked for the Federal Bureau of Investigation by supplying information on organized criminals, Don King, and black politicians. The minister admitted that he had supplied information to federal authorities on organized crime figures and crack dealers, but he emphatically denied spying on black leaders. According to federal authorities, Sharpton had a two-hour interview with an undercover agent, Victor Quintana, posing as a rich South American. The undercover agent reportedly asked Sharpton to "introduce me to somebody in drugs." According to Sharpton, he told the undercover agent that he does not deal with drugs nor does he deal with people who sell drugs. However, federal authorities stated that Sharpton agreed to assist.[67]

Sharpton claimed that two or three weeks after the meeting with Quintana, FBI agents approached him and said they had a tape of him attempting to make a drug deal. He said that after he told the agents he was innocent, he agreed to work with them. He then claimed the agents asked him to provide information on Don King and Michael Franzese, a reputed Columbo family crime person. Apparently, Sharpton had come into contact with mob figures during his earlier involvement in the entertainment world. He agreed to provide information on the mob because "the problem I have with the entertainment world is that I represent a lot of blacks at the bottom, and these mobsters have used us." Sharpton claimed that because he threatened to boycott the Michael Jackson concert in 1984, that Sal Posillo, an alleged crime figure connected with the tour, threatened to kill him. According to Sharpton, this also explained his decision to work with the FBI.[68]

Sharpton also participated in a sting operation against Danny Pagnano, a reputed member of the Genovese crime family, who was scalping tickets for concerts by black artists. Sharpton claimed that he knew Pagnano because he owned a record company and "one of my guys worked for him."[69]

The most disturbing part of the interview with *Newsday* came when Sharpton asserted that, unsolicited, he went to the regional U.S. attorney's office in the Eastern District and gave them information "proving" that Major Owens and Al Vann, the Brooklyn assemblyman representing Bed-Stuy, were involved in election fraud. Sharpton said, "I called for a meeting and said I had information on some election fraud—I had information on Al Vann and Major Owens being involved in a vote ring." Although it is not clear why he decided to provide federal authorities information on Owens and Vann, Sharpton did admit that they were political enemies, which might prompt us to question both his motive and evidence. He also may have wished to get even with Owens, whose previous challenges had forced Sharpton off the ballot for state senator in 1978.[70]

Despite his denial about making a drug deal, FBI officials claimed that they had a videotape of Sharpton inquiring about buying cocaine. They also said that the reason he was not indicted was because he agreed to cooperate. Wearing a hidden microphone, he attended meetings between Don King and crime figures. Along with organized crime people, King, and Owens and Vann, the FBI also said Sharpton gave information on black activist Sonny Carson and a local African American minister.[71]

The episode was bizarre. Why was Sharpton dealing with organized criminals such as Matthew ("Matty the Horse") Ianiello, Danny Pagnano, and Michael Franzese? Why did he cooperate with federal officials on a probe of two of the most highly regarded African American politicians in New York? Why did he agree to work with an agency that had a notorious history of opposing civil rights leaders and activities? These actions clearly suggested that he was a man who could not be trusted.

But the impact of Sharpton's undercover work with federal authorities was relatively mild when compared to his actions in the notorious Tawana Brawley case. On November 28, 1987, fifteen-year-old Tawana Brawley was found near an apartment building in Wappingers Falls. She was wrapped in a plastic bag with "KKK," "bitch," and "nigger" scrawled on her chest in charcoal, and with feces smeared over her body. The jeans she was wearing had been burnt in the crotch, thus suggesting that she might have been deliberately burned. She was taken to the emergency room of St. Francis Hospital in Poughkeepsie, New York. While in the hospital, she indicated to a police officer that she had been kidnapped and taken to the woods and raped by white men. She said that one of the rapists was a "white cop." According to Brawley, the men had made her perform oral sex.

Numerous law enforcement officials were assigned to investigate the alleged sexual assault and apparently racially motivated incident. Among the officials were African Americans, women, and people with experience in sexual assault cases. In addition, Dutchess County District Attorney William Grady, who was handling the case, contacted the FBI to inform the agency that civil rights violations may have occurred. The Bureau responded and assigned to the case a female special agent who handled civil rights cases.[72]

Dutchess County law enforcement authorities attempted to interview Brawley on several occasions. Although she spoke to a deputy sheriff and detectives (on November 28), and to two assistant district attorneys, an FBI agent, and two people specializing in child abuse cases (on November 30), by early December Brawley and her family refused to cooperate further with the investigation.[73] Why were the Brawleys refusing to cooperate?

One reason being offered was that the Brawley family had asserted from the beginning that white police officers were responsible for the incident. Brawley's stepfather, Ralph King, was heard to have yelled in the hallway of St. Francis Hospital, "Don't talk to those white fucking cops, they're not going to help us. We're going to hire a lawyer and get all those white cops in court and make them tell us what they done." Also, when Tawana's aunt, Juanita Brawley, called for an investigation of the December 1 death of part-time officer Harry Crist, Jr., it left the impression that he might have been involved in the case.[74]

But by early December the principal reason explaining their refusal to cooperate was the advice the family received from their legal counsel. On the second of December, the Brawley family announced that it had hired attorney Alton Maddox to represent Tawana because, they claimed, authorities were not properly handling the investigation. Maddox immediately advised the Brawleys not to speak to local law enforcement officials. He claimed that, from his experience in the Howard Beach case and other racially motivated incidents, local law enforcement personnel could not be trusted. He cut off all access to Tawana and demanded that Governor Cuomo appoint a special prosecutor to handle the case.[75]

For five consecutive days, from December 7 to 11, Dutchess County District Attorney Grady's office attempted to reach Maddox, leaving several messages. Maddox did not return any of his calls. When two New York State police officers went to Maddox's office to inform him that the Dutchess County district attorney was trying to reach him, he replied that he was aware of it and would get in contact with Grady. He never called or visited the Dutchess County district attorney.[76]

On December 8, Grady and an assistant went to the Brawleys' home and spoke to Glenda Brawley. They asked to speak to Tawana, but Mrs. Brawley stalled, saying that she needed the consent of the family's attorney. In addition, on the evening of that day, a state police lieutenant, the state police senior investigator, and an assistant district attorney also visited the home of the Brawleys, hoping to question Tawana about the incident. Her mother gave them the same answer that she had given to Grady.[77]

After these failed attempts by law enforcement authorities to make contact with both Maddox and Brawley on December 14, 15, and 17, the district attorney wrote a letter to Mrs. Brawley and Maddox to notify them that a grand jury was "being impaneled and that he would like to prepare Tawana Brawley on January 5 for her Grand Jury appearance." They did not respond. When they failed to appear before the district attorney, he issued subpoenas for Tawana, her mother, and her aunt for their appearance before the grand jury on January 13. Again, they did not show up for the session.[78]

Al Sharpton decided to get involved in the Brawley case in early December 1987. In the first place, his involvement in what

219

seemed to be a brutal racially and sexually motivated crime could help enhance his reputation in the black communities of New York. It would give him an opportunity to portray himself as a defender of the victimized. The Brawley case had the potential of bringing him the type of media coverage he desired. After Howard Beach, it was clear that he was seen as part of the team with Maddox and Mason. The Brawley case allowed him once again to be seen as part of this heroic trio.

Another important reason for Sharpton's involvement in the Brawley case was his decision during the Howard Beach case to work for a permanent special prosecutor to handle racially motivated incidents. Past cases in New York City and throughout the State of New York had demonstrated to many that it was extremely difficult to work with local law officials and win a conviction in racially motivated cases; therefore, a permanent special prosecutor was needed to handle such cases.

Sharpton, along with Maddox and Mason, pressed Governor Cuomo to appoint a special prosecutor. The flamboyant Pentecostal minister's rhetoric was increasingly inflammatory. At a rally held in Newburgh, he said that blacks were being attacked and murdered daily in New York State, and he referred to Governor Cuomo as a symbol of "urban racism." The governor refused Sharpton's request, arguing that local officials were capable of handling the case. He contended that the system should be given a chance. The governor did not want to undermine the authority of Dutchess County District Attorney William Grady. However, on December 18, Grady announced that his investigation had hit an impasse because Brawley refused to talk. Brawley's representatives said that she would not cooperate with any investigation handled by the Dutchess County office. They began to make claims that certain police officers were involved in the abduction and rape, including Harry Crist Jr. (the part-time police officer who had committed suicide on the first of December).[79]

On January 20, 1988, District Attorney Grady announced that, due to a conflict of interest, he could not continue his investigation. He never explained the nature of the conflict, allowing Brawley's representatives to allege that Grady was simply hiding details about police involvement. (It was later learned that a member of Grady's staff, deputy district attorney Steven

220

Pagones, was a suspect in the alleged rape. Pagones was a friend of Harry Crist Jr., and the two had been together on November 28. Pagones asserted that he and Crist had gone shopping in Danbury, Connecticut, that day.)[80]

In order to ensure an investigation without any appearance of impropriety, Grady decided not to continue his investigation. He consulted with state and federal justice officials. On January 21, he asked a Dutchess County court to appoint a special district attorney. The court appointed David B. Sall, a lawyer with a private criminal law practice in Poughkeepsie, and local attorney William T. Burke as his assistant. Sall immediately made contact with Glenda Brawley, attempting to set up a meeting to talk to her daughter. Although Mrs. Brawley had first agreed to the meeting, she later called him to cancel on advice from her attorney.[81]

On January 22, after a meeting with Grady and learning why he had bowed out of the case, Sall announced that he and his assistant were also bowing out of the case, claiming a conflict of interest. Sall asserted, "I believed it would be incumbent upon me if I continued as special district attorney to investigate, to any extent, the very office that was prosecuting defendants that I was representing."[82]

On January 26 Governor Cuomo appointed state Attorney General Robert Abrams as a special prosecutor for the case. Despite the apparent victory of Brawley's representatives, they announced that Tawana would not cooperate because Abrams was not devoting his full time to the case. Abrams had appointed state assistant district attorney John M. Ryan to handle the day-to-day investigation. Alton Maddox claimed that Ryan had no experience prosecuting civil rights cases and was therefore not qualified to handle the Brawley case. Abrams acknowledged this but pointed out that Ryan, who headed the attorney general's prosecution bureau, was an experienced trial lawyer, while he was not. He had also assigned an eight-member team of lawyers, three of whom were African Americans, to assist in the investigation. Abrams pleaded with Brawley to cooperate with the investigation and provide information about her claims.

In early February, Abrams visited Poughkeepsie in an attempt to meet with Brawley. However, Sharpton, Maddox, and Mason refused his request. They insisted that Abrams, not Ryan, would have to handle the entire investigation.[83]

Brawley's advisers appealed to Representative John Conyers Jr., chairman of the House Judiciary Subcommittee on Criminal Justice. They asked him to request that the Justice Department appoint a special prosecutor to investigate recent cases of racially motivated crimes, including the Brawley case. After a telephone conversation with Abrams, Conyers publicly expressed confidence in the state attorney general. As it turned out, because of the allegation that police officers were involved in the Brawley incident, Abrams had already requested assistance from the Justice Department.[84] Responding to Abrams's request, on February 4 the Justice Department publicly announced that in December it had launched an investigation of the Brawley case to determine if civil rights laws were violated. This proved a mixed victory for Brawley and her advisers. They apparently had won a demand that they had publicly requested. But it made their charge of a cover-up by state officials harder to sell to the public. They had no evidence to claim that the investigation was not going to be fair. Besides having the Justice Department involved, Abrams also assured Maddox that he would have an "extreme" role in the investigation. Yet despite reassurances from the attorney general, Maddox refused to respond. In fact, Maddox decided to increase the demands in order to get Brawley to cooperate with state officials. On February 9, Maddox told reporters and a crowd of supporters at the Star of Bethlehem Baptist Church in Ossining, New York, that Brawley would not cooperate until arrests were made. It was clear that the attorneys for Brawley were stalling. They were raising demands that any legal expert knew would be rejected by the attorney general. They also rejected assistance from the state NAACP and other lawyers.[85]

Finally, after months of impasse, Abrams directed assistant attorney general John M. Ryan to begin the investigation. In defiant language, Brawley's advisers denounced both Abrams and Ryan and insisted that the Wappingers Falls teenager would not cooperate in the investigation unless Abrams was removed as special prosecutor. In the most divisive language, Sharpton compared Abrams, a man whose objectivity he had earlier praised, to Hitler. He said that asking Brawley to cooperate with the grand jury is "like *asking* someone who watched someone killed in the gas chamber to sit down with Mr. Hitler." To compound the hysteria, Mason, furious over a television station that showed pictures taken of Tawana's partially clad body when she was at St. Francis, lashed out at Abrams and accused him of "masturbating" over the pictures of Brawley.[86] Despite the growing criticism of their strategy, Sharpton and the lawyers continued to refuse to allow Brawley to cooperate. In fact, they attempted to stall the investigation through a series of legal moves, making up new demands that included having the governor appoint yet a new special prosecutor, and seeking limits on inquiries into the case.

While they were busy legally delaying the investigation, Sharpton attempted to remove Abrams by threatening "a day of civil disobedience" and calling on the governor to meet with him. But Cuomo refused to remove Abrams. Instead he made a public appeal to Brawley and her advisers for complete cooperation. When it became apparent that Brawley would not cooperate, Abrams impaneled a grand jury on February 28 to determine if any crimes had been committed against the Wappingers Falls teenager.[87]

Despite the fact that, initially, a large percentage of people throughout the state were outraged at the alleged rape, Brawley's advisers made it clear they were not interested in building a coalition with white sympathizers. In a speech at Bethany Baptist Church in Brooklyn in late April, Maddox said that he saw this as an exclusively black struggle. He asserted that "liberal whites and Hispanics" looked out for themselves, and it was time that black people do the same. He said that in 1989, "We will coalesce with ourselves. We don't need white folks to win."[88]

In spite of this claim, neither Sharpton nor Mason or Maddox were particularly interested in building a coalition, even with other black groups. Instead, they invested their time in escalating racial tensions and the anger of black people with increasingly wild allegations. On March 6 Sharpton alleged that an informant had told him that a white racist cult connected with the Irish Republican Army was responsible for Brawley's abduction. However, he was later unable to provide any information when pressed for more details or the name of his informant. Even blacks were not spared from attacks. Responding to criticisms from the state NAACP on how the lawyers were handling the case, Maddox called the oldest civil rights organization "the National Association for Coon People."[89]

By the early summer it was clear that Brawley and her advisers had declining support. In June a CBS/*New York Times* poll showed that a majority did not find Brawley, Sharpton, Mason, or Maddox credible. Sixty-two percent of white New Yorkers and 37 percent of black New Yorkers believed the Brawley team was lying. Another 35 percent of black New Yorkers said that they were unsure. Only a disturbing 28 percent of black New Yorkers believed Brawley's allegations.[90]

The Brawleys' advisers further failed in legal terms when Glenda Brawley was requested to appear in court by a Poughkeepsie judge to explain why she refused to appear before the grand jury. Instead of appearing before the court, they advised Mrs. Brawley to wait outside the courthouse with supporters while inside Mason and Maddox gave the judge a lesson in African American history. They explained that blacks had suffered for four hundred years, and it was impossible for Mrs. Brawley to receives a fair hearing. The judge responded to her lawyers' refusal to offer a defense by ordering her arrest for defying the subpoena. Sharpton responded by moving Glenda Brawley to a church in Queens and then to Bethany Baptist Church in Brooklyn for "sanctuary."

The lawyers' intransigence suggested to many that they were trying to hide the fact that they had little or no case. It further suggested that they were willing to go to any length to continue what was now seen by many as a hoax.[91]

Two events took place in June that in the short run aided Brawley's accusation. Perry McKinnon, a former aid to Sharpton who claimed that he was an "insider," told reporters that he knew that the Brawley team was lying. He told CBS reporter Mike Taibbi that he knew for certain that Mason, Sharpton, and Maddox were aware that Brawley had made up the abduction and rape, but that they were attempting to fool the public in order to enhance their popularity. Sharpton, Mason, and Maddox responded with witnesses that claimed McKinnon was emotionally disturbed, had lied about his army record, and was guilty of bigamy. McKinnon later stated before the grand jury that he knew nothing of Brawley's whereabouts between November 24 and 28.

In the other instance, Samuel McClease, a self-proclaimed surveillance expert, came forward claiming to the media that he had secretly taped the three advisers and heard them say that they were aware that Brawley was lying but that they could become prominent with this case. However, it was revealed that

McClease had nothing on tape. The McKinnon and McClease episodes convinced Brawley's remaining supporters that the media and Abrams were desperately attempting to discredit Brawley.[92]

However, despite these two incidents, evidence presented to the grand jury demonstrated that Brawley was lying. On October 6, 1988, after an eight-month investigation, the grand jury released its report on the allegations made by Tawana Brawley. The grand jury relied on 180 witnesses, 6,000 pages of testimony, 250 exhibits brought into evidence, and testimony from experts in forensic serology, chemistry, pathology, and psychiatry. Moreover, experts in fiber and hair analysis, and handwriting analysis testified and medical evidence was used. The grand jury concluded that Brawley had fabricated the abduction and rape. Between November 24 and 28, as grand jury testimony reconstructed the event, Brawley hid in an apartment that she and her family had been evicted from months earlier—the Pavilion Apartments at 19A Carnaby Drive in Wappingers Falls.

The grand jury noted that Brawley's stepfather had punished her for staying at a party, and a witness testified that Brawley had said she did not want to go home that night because she was in trouble. Witnesses living in the Pavilion reported hearing noises in the apartment, including loud music.[93]

On November 28, at 1 P.M., witnesses saw Brawley outside of her former apartment. They said they saw her take a large plastic bag, step into it, and pull it up around her neck. She then hopped a few feet before lying in a fetal position. A witness also testified that she saw Glenda Brawley, Tawana's mother, sitting in a car during this time. Mrs. Brawley told police she had gone to the apartment to see if her daughter was there and to collect unforwarded mail. However, a mail carrier testified that no one had picked up the mail for days (p. 6).[94]

Also on November 28 at 1:30 P.M. another witness who lived in the apartment and had observed Brawley getting into the bag called the police. At 1:44 P.M. Dutchess County Deputy Sheriff Eric Thurston arrived at the Pavilion. He and the witnesses approached Brawley. They said that she appeared unconscious, but they saw her open and close her eyes twice. After seeing her covered with feces, dirty, and in torn jeans, Thurston called for an ambulance (p. 7).

The ambulance arrived around 2 P.M. with two emergency medical technicians (EMTs). One EMT who ripped open the plastic bag found no injuries. During the EMT's examination, Brawley "grabbed, with both hands, the hand of one of the EMTs," a clear sign that she was conscious. Moreover, the EMT found no signs of exposure, low body temperature, dehydration, or undernourishment—in spite of the fact that temperatures during the days she claimed to be in the woods were below freezing (pp. 8, 34–37). The ambulance crew took her to St. Francis Hospital in Poughkeepsie. In contradiction to her claims, medical witnesses from St. Francis who examined Brawley reported that she was never unconscious. A specialist in emergency medicine who examined the patient reported that Brawley had resisted opening her eyes, indicating that she was conscious. Moreover, the physician administered a "consciousness test by raising Ms. Brawley's arm directly above her face and letting it fall. If the patient is unconscious, the arm will strike his or her face; a conscious patient will be aware of the threat to his or her face and will alter the course of the arm's fall," according to the physician. In Mrs. Brawley's case, her arm "did not strike her face." She also responded to vocal commands, including one that told her to sit up. The grand jury report also noted Brawley's physical condition:

> Her teeth were clean, and her mouth did not have a bad odor. In her testimony, the emergency room physician noted that a typical person who came into the emergency room having been out in the environment would not have brushed her teeth or have good hygiene of the mouth. This would result in a dab odor, even if the person was out only overnight. Ms. Brawley's good dental hygiene was inconsistent with not having brushed her teeth in three or four days. (pp. 35–36)

The grand jury report pointed out that there was no evidence that plant substance or hair other than her own was found on her. This refuted Brawley's and her advisers' claim that she was raped in the woods. Moreover, a psychiatrist "ruled out post traumatic stress disorder because Ms. Brawley showed no symptoms of reliving the experience (pp. 45–50).

Other evidence pointed to additional inconsistencies in Brawley's story. On December 7 a psychiatrist saw Brawley in a wheelchair at her home. A friend of the Wappingers Falls teenager testi-fied that, on December 8, the alleged victim could not walk. How-ever, the following day a police officer visiting the house noticed Brawley "get up, walk out of her living room and go upstairs." Moreover, there was no medical evidence showing "organic or neurological evidence for her medical complaints" (p. 52).

Also, there was not any indication that part-time police officer Harry Crist Jr., assistant district attorney Steven Pagones, or any other law enforcement officials had been involved in the alleged rape. The advisers had publicly accused Pagones of taking part in the kidnapping and rape of Brawley, although they never pro-duced any evidence for such claims. In addition, after the suicide of Harry Crist, Glenda Brawley asked for an investigation into his death. Maddox later asserted the Crist death was not a suicide but a murder. According to Maddox, Crist was going to reveal the names of those who took part in the incident. However, the "cul-prits" killed him before he could talk (pp. 64–65).

Despite these claims, witnesses testified that between Novem-ber 24 and November 28, Crist and Pagones were seen by dozens of people. Moreover, the death of Crist in December was not a murder and was not connected with the Brawley case. He had left a suicide note, and it did not mention Brawley. Crist had been despondent over the breakup with his girlfriend and at failing to meet the qualifications to become a New York State trooper (p. 77).[95]

Furthermore, experts pointed out that the dog feces Tawana was covered with were the same feces found in the area where Tawana was found, and that identical feces were also found in the former Brawley/King apartment at Pavilion. In addition, an FBI special agent who was an expert in forensic chemistry testified that he had cut off the tips of a pair of gloves that were also found under the plastic bag that Brawley was found in. The special agent found charred cotton fibers "inside the middle and pinky fingers of the right glove and bundles of such fibers in the thumb." He also found charred cotton fibers in the ring finger and in the thumb of the left glove. These same materials were found in the Pavilion apartment. The grand jury report concluded that Brawley's claim was fraudulent (pp. 60–63, 84–88).

This summary has not been and is not meant to be an in-depth examination of the Brawley case. The full content and ramifications of this event cannot be adequately plumbed in a few short pages. Instead it is an attempt to present another example in a disturbing pattern. The Brawley case and other incidents involving Al Sharpton clearly point out that, despite his notoriety, he has offered little in terms of positive leadership. Instead his agenda seems to focus on remaining in the limelight.

Although Maddox was the architect of the Brawley defense "strategy," Sharpton's role was clear. He not only supported the defense, he went to great lengths to encourage reckless behavior. His role in the case was central in promoting and perpetuating the hoax with theatrics, threats, and wild accusations. The conclusions of the grand jury report indicate that the Tawana Brawley incident was a clear case of manipulation on the parts of Al Sharpton, Alton Maddox, and C. Vernon Mason of the feelings of African Americans on the subject of race and sex. One of the most sensitive issues among African Americans is the rape of black women by white men. African Americans are familiar with the history of the sexual exploitation of African American women in bondage and in freedom by white men. Black women were subject to rape, and both black women and black men were powerless to react. By portraying Brawley as part of a continuing legacy of racial and sexual exploitation, they touched a collective nerve in black America. The fact that she was fifteen only added to the fury. It is little wonder that her early support in the black community was so vast.

Their divisionary tactics, the smokescreen of lies, the use of inflammatory racial rhetoric, the concocted images of white public leaders masturbating over pictures of an African American child, all helped hold the black community hostage to a complex web of feelings. They put people of African origins in the position of choosing between questionable evidence and racial pride. After the Howard Beach incident, Sharpton, Mason, and Maddox had emerged as heroes for racial justice. After the Tawana Brawley case, they emerged either as liars or else as remarkably incompetent advocates. They claimed that their goal was to build a new civil rights movement by using Brawley to galvanize people. It was clear from their actions that the "three advisers" to Brawley had little understanding of the movement. The objectives of the leaders and participants in the civil rights movement was not to cause racial division but to unite people.

The greatest victims in the Brawley case were and are the victims of real racially and sexually motivated criminal acts. By "crying wolf" these three men undermined the legitimate claims of those who have been sexually assaulted and physically attacked because of their race. Abrams was fully aware of the damage that Brawley and her advisers caused. He asserted that " the issue of racial violence is one of extraordinary difficulty and sensitivity. Our nation's history has been tarnished by racism, and racism and racial violence are facts of life we must confront and address."[96]

Recently, some people have claimed that Al Sharpton has done an about face. His racial rhetoric has toned down, and he has apparently become more moderate. This change has been noted by the media covering his recent 1992 bid for a U.S. Senate seat. Sharpton finished third in a four-person race in New York's state Democratic primary. He had been endorsed by the largest black weekly in the country, the New York–based *Amsterdam News*. *New York Newsday* contended that "Sharpton the campaigner has gained credibility." His talk has grown more statesmanlike, and his acceptance in the black community seems to be broadening beyond the ready-to-march street protesters he has attracted for years. Sharpton credits this more moderate image to growing up.[97] He also claims to be broadening his approach. This new image was not born in the election of 1992 but began emerging years earlier.

When he was jailed for protesting the release on appeal of some convicted Howard Beach defendants, Sharpton wrote a well-crafted letter to Mayor David Dinkins from a maximum security cell at Rikers Island. In an attempt to echo Martin Luther King's "Letter from a Birmingham Jail," Sharpton in his letter from prison offered a vision of new unity. He also claimed responsibility for the Dinkins victory in 1989. "I was in the forefront of a movement that finally, successfully defeated your predecessor. Secondly, I played a major role in events that many experts admit led to your primary and general election victory."[98]

Sharpton asserted his credibility as a leader by pointing out that a CBS/*New York Times* poll released in June 1990 reported that 30 percent of black New Yorkers supported his leadership. "Though they claim more are against me, the fact that one third support anyone is substantial." In an attempt to show his concern for universal brotherhood, he called on Dinkins to do away with institutional racism and work for "equal protection under the Law." He contended that "both whites and blacks voted for you in the hopes that you would deal with the racial polarization question." He ended the letter with an urgent plea. "I urged you in the case of Bensonhurst and I urge you now, to immediately sit down with a cross section of Black leadership and deal with the issue of racial justice."[99]

This universalist theme of racial unity was also emphasized by Sharpton in an article entitled, "The Need for a New Alliance," which appeared in the *National Alliance,* the magazine of the New Alliance Party, in April 1990. Sharpton claimed that Martin Luther King was able to bring a diverse group of people and groups together—such as the Student Non-violent Coordinating Committee (SNCC), CORE, peace activists, and environmentalists—in order to save the world. He asserted that such a coalition is needed today in order to save the world:

> We need to unite, as Dr. King attempted to, the Black, and the Native American and the Latino and the progressive white and the outcast and the rejected and the homeless and people from all walks of life who have endured pain and neglect only because the lifestyle they choose or the color of the skin they were born with. Yes, it is time for a new alliance that will bring elected officials into office who represent their constituency, not those who go downtown and come back to represent downtown to their constituents.[100]

In spite of his stress on unity, Sharpton continues to use divisive language and to associate with people who work to divide people, not heal racial scars. In a speech delivered at a conference on "Blacks and Jews" in Brooklyn in 1990, he accused the "power elite" of attacking him, Louis Farrakhan, and Fred Newman. "There is a frank difference between the Martin Luther Kings and the Abraham Hesses, who were in the trenches fighting together, and who now sit on Madison Avenue writing up hit lists on people like Farrakhan and me and Newman." Denying that he has ever made anti-Semitic remarks, Sharpton argued that "key Zionists" were moved into "key positions" in the city government. He asserted that black leaders such as Dinkins are always forced by Zionists to denounce grass-roots black leaders:

In the Black community, being that we are at the bottom of the economic and political and social ladder, if we need mass organizers, people that can inspire our people to remain conscious and disciplined, to move toward real liberation, that is not just a pleasure, that is a need we have. So how can we be asked to enter into a relationship with another group of people—for the sake of this discussion, enter into a relationship with Jews—if we have to sacrifice the only mass leaders that we have and need? How can we enter a relationship and be told we have to leave Farrakhan, who can draw more Black masses than anybody in the United States tonight? Or you've got to leave Jackson out, or you've got to leave Sharpton out or Fulani out."[101]

In that same speech, he accused Mayor David Dinkins of favoring Jews over blacks. For Sharpton, the real problem facing black America was "capitalist Zionists" and black politicians like Dave Dinkins and Virginia's Governor Doug Wilder who sell out black people. "So Dave Dinkins may be the first black mayor in the city, but he's also the first Black mayor in this country who ran on a platform complete with commercials denouncing Louis Farrakhan which means that while he fills one need, he robs another need from the black community."[102]

Calling black elected officials "sellouts" and accusing Jews of gaining power and using it to manipulate African Americans is an ongoing theme. Although he attempts to claim a "new" image, the old one is still with us. Despite the rhetoric of unity he too often remains a divisive force.

An important force behind the emergence of the "new" Al Sharpton has been the New Alliance Party (NAP). NAP was founded by Fred Newman, a therapist with a Ph.D in philosophy and a former ally of right-wing extremist Lyndon LaRouche, a self-styled Marxist. Newman runs a therapy group that argues that only a proletarian revolution can be successful in ending individual neuroses. Writer Bruce Shapiro contends that

Newman and his original associates (all of them white and most of them women) were political hard-liners who argued that only a revolution of the working class could resolve the individual psychic crisis; at the same time, like practitioners of EST and other distinctly unMarxist products of the nascent human potential movement, they believed that the road to their revolutionary new age lay in an extreme version of confronting the oppressor within, stripping the ego of its bourgeois, individualistic detritus. . . .

In place of bourgeois patterns of thinking came "new revolutionary patterns of consciousness." Sexual relationships, employment and other aspects of human existence were questioned. Disturbingly, Newman as part of a potentially abusive therapeutic process, required his "patients" to recruit, donate money and do political work. Out of this social therapy collective based in New York, Newman formed the International Workers Party in the mid-1970s, which formed an alliance with Lyndon LaRouche for a brief period in 1974, and by 1979, it had changed its name to the New Alliance Party.[103]

As part of its vanguard networking with oppressed minorities, NAP has embraced the Nation of Islam leader and anti-Semite, Louis Farrakhan. In fact, Newman and NAP have also espoused anti-Semitism. According to Shapiro, Newman blamed Jewish attacks on Farrakhan for anti-Semitism in the black community. Moreover, Newman and NAP argue that capitalist Zionists and the United States have created Israel, not as a Jewish State but as a military base, therefore arguing that Jewish desire to escape oppression has nothing to do with the formation of Israel.[104]

Sharpton acknowledges that NAP has attempted to reshape him in order to make him more appealing to the public. And he has credited the chairperson of the party, Dr. Lenora Fulani, for helping him to tone down his inflammatory language.[105]

But the relationship between NAP and Sharpton goes far beyond providing demonstrators, increasing the Pentecostal minister's income, and rhetorical cosmetics. NAP is involved in molding Sharpton's political ideology. Although he contends that he has ideological disagreements with NAP, it is clear from his own speeches and writings that he has adopted aspects of NAP's philosophy and jargon. He credits Newman for his view that Israel is a "military base for the United States."

In response to an article that appeared in the newspaper of the Communist Party attacking Sharpton for his role in demonstrations against the police killing of an African American teenager in

Teaneck, New Jersey, Sharpton accused the American Communist Party of defending the "establishment bourgeois leadership against the grass-roots challengers." He defended himself from the accusation of not meeting with the established black leadership in Teaneck by claiming that he had been invited to the city by students and "lumpen proletariat groups." Using simplistic Marxist jargon, Sharpton declared, "One wonders whether Mr. Johnson [Ron Johnson, writer for the *People's Daily World*] is just a regular Democrat—he seems to feel the legitimate constituency is the petit bourgeoisie and not the masses one would assume that he at least rhetorically would represent." Sharpton even refers to Johnson as a "corporate communist."[106] Despite the jargon Sharpton has never claimed to be a Marxist or socialist. Over the years he has presented himself strictly as a black nationalist.

Still, NAP has formed a strong alliance with Sharpton. The organization provides him with a standing "army" for his demonstrations. Newman has estimated that NAP members account for 50 percent of the troops at Sharpton-sponsored demonstrations. Newman has also made Sharpton a partner in his nationwide teenage talent competition business. In 1988 the business brought Sharpton $12,000 in revenue. And *The New York Times* reported in February 1988 that NAP's lecture- and media-booking company arranged twenty speaking engagements for Sharpton which earned him an additional $20,000.[107]

Is Sharpton's new image legitimate? Unquestionably, he cannot throw off his past as an FBI informant spying on black elected officials, or as a man involved with organized underworld figures, or as a member of the inner circle that attempted to perpetuate the Brawley hoax and play on the fears and angers of African Americans without better explanation. Despite the media's surprisingly positive coverage of his 1992 campaign for the U.S. Senate, Sharpton should not simply be excused for his past and present activities. Why was he involved with alleged organized crime figures? And so these questions persist. Why did he continue the Tawana Brawley fiasco? What is the justification for his close relationship with the cultish NAP? Until these questions are better answered, his rhetoric and efforts will continue to be viewed with suspicion. After a long meeting with Sharpton, the philosopher Cornell West asserted that the minister's leadership is an open question. "'He has the courage and the talent. Does he have the perseverance, the humility? Or will he fall back into opportunistic practices?"'[108]

The ministers examined in this chapter have continued the legacy of the black ministerial class and black churches of Brooklyn by providing leadership, services, and solutions to the black community. Some ministers and churches are more successful, less self-serving, and less divisive than others in this enormous task. But all continue to make black churches pivotal in the lives of African Americans by addressing the shifting set of problems that have afflicted black communities. Black ministers and churches have never neglected or turned away from the social, economic, or political challenges facing the black community. On the contrary, they have consistently been in the forefront of grappling with these problems. At the very least, the black Christian community of Brooklyn has offered the intangible but real existential value of hope and struggle.

During the 1980s and early 1990s, cities have experienced growing problems and shrinking tax bases because of the federal government's cutbacks in social services and the continuing flight of the middle class to the suburbs. Cities have been forced to cut their budgets by reducing social services, thus making an already difficult life even harder for the working poor. The need for black churches to help in this time of crisis is greater than ever. Many in Brooklyn's black churches continue to experiment and continue to work for the cause of social and economic justice. We see this in the listing of sagging mainline as well as burgeoning new Pentecostal churches. This latter development is perhaps the most exciting. As Pentecostalism has become the dominating, or at least fastest-growing, denomination in Brooklyn, their mistakes have shifted their perspective from their own immediate congregants to seeing the entire neighborhood, borough, and city as their parish. They have joined with mainline ministers in seeking to guide and represent the interests of not just their own congregations but also the wider community. Some have been more flamboyant, self-serving, and divisive than others in the process, but it is still early in the careers of many of this new generation of ministers. It remains to be seen whether these self-serving or community concerns will dominate. Whatever the case, for all its faults and failings the black church remains the most critical institution in the black community.

APPENDIX

Table 1 *Black Churches of Brooklyn (1920)*

Churches (Dates organized)	Pastor	Church Members	Sunday School Members	Money Raised	Property
Baptist					
Berean (1851)	A. C. Mathews	549	275	$ 6,218	75,000
Bethany (1893)	K. L. Warren	700	285	10,085	75,000
Bethel (1907)	Timothy White	200	150	2,510	18,000
Concord (1847)	Vacant	900	557	15,000	110,000
First Baptist (1899)	J. H. Dennis	98	45	1,128	12000
Friendship (1910)	R. E. Edwards	N.A.	N.A.	N.A.	N.A.
Holy Trinity (1898)	C. D. Patterson	500	300	6,500	32,000
Mount Calvary (n.d.)	S. W. Timns	N.A.	N.A.	N.A.	N.A.
Mount Lebanon (1900)	J. W. Hamlin	700	325	7,500	12,000
African Methodist Episcopal (AME)					
Bethel (1848)	C. E. Wilson	166	98	5,060	25,000
Bridge Street (1818)	W. S. Carpenter	1,200	800	15,000	70,000
AME Zion					
First AME Zion (1890)	A. L. Lightfard	N.A.	N.A.	N.A.	N.A.
Fleet Street (1885)	P. A. Wallace	986	428	16,159	58,500
Congregational					
Nazarene (1873)	H. H. Proctor	135	175	1,440	25,000
Protestant Epiccopal					
St. Augustine (1875)	Supply	390	100	4,489	16,500
St. Phillip's (1899)	Supply	220	225	2,479	N.A.
Presbyterian					
Siloam (1848)	Supply	215	135	8,000	160,000

SOURCES: *Brooklyn Daily Eagle Almanac* (1920).

Table 2   Black Churches of Brooklyn (1929–31)

Churches (Dates organized)	Pastor	Church Members	Sunday School Members	Money Raised	Property
Baptist					
Antioch (1918)	Moses Paylor	3,000	300	N.A.	N.A.
Berean	S. T. Eldridge	921	605	$11,000	129,000
Bethany	K. L. Warren	1,600	700	19,231	175,000
Bethel	Timothy White	700	150	N.A.	N.A.
Concord	James Adams	2,700	700	33,500	260,000
First Baptist	James C. Brown	98	90	6,800	25,000
Friendship	R. E. Edwards	30	75	1,287	5,000
Holy Trinity	Thomas Harten	2,100	600	N.A.	100,000
Mount Calvary					
Mount Lebanon	J. W. Hamlin	669	350	10,000	50,500
African Methodist Episcopal (AME)					
Bethel	C. P. Cole	350	200	33,000	60,000
Bridge Street	E. Ernest Tyler	1,450	600	20,300	100,000
AME Zion					
First AME Zion	A. L. Lightfard	N.A.	N.A.	N.A.	N.A.
Fleet Street	William C. Brown	2,500	1,126	N.A.	N.A.
Methodist					
Newman Memorial	L. S. Perry	131	260	N.A.	N.A.
Congregational					
Nazarene	H. H. Proctor	800	156	26,000	150,000
Protestant Episcopal					
St. Augustine	F. Miller	650	342	19,887	99,000
St. Phillip's	N. P. Boyd	326	263	5,178	N.A.
Presbyterian					
Siloam	George S. Stark	589	290	12,000	43,000

SOURCES: *Brooklyn Eagle Daily Almanac* (1929); *Brooklyn Federation of Churches Year Book* (1930–31).

Table 3   Black Churches of Brooklyn (1950–1952)

Churches (Dates organized)	Pastor	Church Members	Sunday School Members	Money Raised	Property
Baptist					
Antioch	M. Paylor	10,000	500	N.A.	125,000
Berean	H. L. Dames	1,301	201	N.A.	N.A.
Bethany	T. Goodall	3,606	500	N.A.	156,900
Bethel	L. T. Chapman	N.A.	N.A.	N.A.	N.A.
Ebenezer (1913)	A. W. Wilson	650	100	N.A.	20,000
Evening Star	M. Logan	400	200	N.A.	18,000
First Baptist	Lynwood Taylor	N.A.	100	N.A.	N.A.
Friendship	V. B. Whitfred	450	75	N.A.	50,000
Holy Trinity	Thomas Harten	N.A.	N.A.	N.A.	N.A.
Institutional (1912)	W. B. Scott	480	75	N..\.	50,000
Morning Dew (1936)	H. B. Womak	500	150	N.A.	12,000
Mount Carmel (1936)	J. Carrington	300	150	N.A.	12,000
Mount Lebanon	C. L. Franklin	4,500	500	N.A.	350,000
Mount Pisgah (1930)	S. A. Perry	N.A.	N.A.	N.A.	N.A.
Mount Sinai (1919)	Paul E. Jones	N.A.	N.A.	N.A.	N.A.
Mount Zion (1923)	A. Murphy	N.A.	N.A.	N.A.	N.A.
New Hope (1935)	J. P. Sawyer	N.A.	N.A.	N.A.	N.A.
Pilgrim (1941)	F. D. Harris	N.A.	N.A.	N.A.	N.A.
Rose Hill (1943)	Mrs. Carrberry	N.A.	N.A.	N.A.	N.A.
St. Paul Community (1929)	A. S. Smith	N.A.	N.A.	N.A.	N.A.
Zion Baptist	Benjamin Lowery	2,562	398	N.A.	426,000
African Methodist Episcopal (AME)					
Bethel	Samuel Grumbs	330	190	N.A.	80,000
Bridge Street	R. C. Henderson	3,000	500	N.A.	275,000
People's Institutional	Charles Stewart	1,786	742	N.A.	85,000
Williams Mission	N.A.	N.A.	N.A.	N.A.	N.A.
Wright Memorial	Harry F. Berry	86	56	N.A.	10,000
AME Zion					
First AME Zion	William Patterson	9,006	550	N.A.	500,000
Naomi	N.A.	N.A.	N.A.	N.A.	N.A.
Varick Memorial	S. H. Williams	450	225		75,000
Methodist					
Newman Memorial	D. W. Jones	659	N.A.	N.A.	N.A.
Congregational					
Nazarene	Vacant	N.A.	N.A.	N.A.	N.A.
Protestant Episcopal					
St. Augustine	Charles England	1,189	381	N.A.	90,000
St. Phillip's	John Coleman	1,250	400	N.A.	100,000
Presbyterian					
Siloam	Milton A. Galamison	1,020	250	N.A.	110,000

SOURCES: Protestant Council of the City of New York, *Protestant Directory for Metropolitan New York* (1950, 1952).

NOTES

Introduction

1. The noted exception is Samuel Freedman, *Upon This Rock* (New York: Harper and Row, 1993).

2. The view that black Holiness-Pentecostalism culture was a form of militancy challenges the view that religious fundamentalism is a hindrance to militancy. See Gary Marx, *Protest and Prejudice* (New York: Harper and Row, 1969).

3. Although I use the terms *pastor* and *minister* interchangeably, there is an important distinction between the two. A pastor is an ordained minister who leads a church, while a minister is ordained and can conduct religious services but may not administer a church.

4. W. E. B. Du Bois, *The Souls of Black Folks* (New York: Dodd, Mead, 1961), p. 144.

1. The Formation and Development of Brooklyn's Black Churches from the Nineteenth to the Early Twentieth Centuries

1. *New York Freeman*, November 7, 1885.

2. Gayraud S. Wilmore, *Black Religion and Black Radicalism* (Maryknoll, N.Y.: Orbis, 1986), p. 142.

3. A few exceptions are Carter G. Woodson, *The History of the Negro Church* (Washington, D.C.: Associated Publishers, 1945); James H. Cone,

Black Theology and Black Power (New York: Seabury, 1969); W. E. B. Du Bois, *The Philadelphia Negro* (1899; rpt., New York: Schocken, 1967); and Wilmore, *Black Religion and Black Radicalism*.

4. Albert Raboteau, *Slave Religion* (New York: Oxford University Press: 1978), pp. 97–110; Mechal Sobel, *Trabelin' On: The Slave Journey to an Afro-Baptist Faith* (Princeton: Princeton University Press, 1979), 59–71.

5. Raboteau, *Slave Religion*, pp. 128–34; Sobel, *Trabelin' On*, p. 85; Gary Nash, *The Urban Crucible* (Cambridge: Harvard University Press, 1979), pp. 204–12.

6. Lawrence W. Levine, *Black Culture and Black Consciousness* (Oxford and New York: Oxford University Press, 1977), p. 157.

7. Levine, *Black Culture and Black Consciousness*, pp. 30–31.

8. Ibid., pp. 22, 33.

9. Raboteau, *Slave Religion*, pp. 231–39.

10. William Wells Brown, "Black Religion in the Post-Reconstruction South," in Milton C. Sernett, ed., *Afro-American Religious History: A Documentary Witness* (Durham, N.C.: Duke University Press, 1985), pp. 240–41.

11. Harold X. Connolly, *A Ghetto Grows in Brooklyn* (New York: New York University Press, 1977), pp. 2–4.

12. Connolly, *A Ghetto Grows in Brooklyn*, pp. 4–5.

13. Ibid., pp. 6–8, 16–17.

14. Ibid., pp. 8–9; David Ment and Mary Donovan, *The People of Brooklyn: A History of Two Neighborhoods* (New York: Brooklyn Arts and Cultural Association, 1980), p. 21; U.S. Census Bureau, Ninth Census (1870), Population Schedule; Tenth Census (1880), Population Schedule.

15. *The African Wesleyan Methodist-Episcopal Church Anniversary Book* (New York: Church Publication, 1980), pp. 13–18 (hereafter, *Bridge Street AWME Anniversary Book*); Leonard P. Curry, *The Free Black in Urban America* (Chicago: University of Chicago Press, 1981), p. 183.

16. *Bridge Street AWME Anniversary Book* (1980), pp. 16–21.

17. Bethel AME Church is sometimes called Bethel Tabernacle, Union Bethel AME, or just Bethel AME. *Black Churches of Brooklyn*, exhibition brochure (New York: Long Island Historical Society, 1984). The Long Island Historical Society changed its name in 1985 to the Brooklyn Historical Society.

18. Records of Church Incorporation at Kings County Clerk's Office: *Black Churches of Brooklyn* and *First African Methodist Episcopal Zion Church Centennial Celebration, 1885–1985* (New York: Church Publication, 1985), p. 14.

19. Curry, *The Free Black in Urban America*, p. 177.

20. *Amsterdam News*, June 4, 1855.

21. *Berean Missionary Baptist Church Anniversary Book* (New York: Church Publication, 1976), pages unnumbered.

22. Stanley M. Douglas, "The History of the Siloam Presbyterian Church," in the *Centennial Yearbook of the Siloam Presbyterian Church (1849–1949)*; *Black Churches of Brooklyn*; *Amsterdam News*, July 8, 1925.

23. *Amsterdam News*, October 9, 1948, and October 21, 1950; *Black Churches of Brooklyn*.

24. For the early history of Concord Baptist Church see *Amsterdam News*, June 4, 1955; *Bethany Baptist Church Centennial Celebration: Commemorating Our History—Celebrating Our Hope, 1883–1983* (New York: Church Publication, 1983); *Black Churches of Brooklyn*; Douglas, "The History of Siloam"; *Book of Memories: The Holy Trinity Baptist Church, Inc., 1899–1972* (Hackensack, N.J.: Custombook, 1972); *New York Age*, February 13, 1892.

25. *Brooklyn Daily Eagle Almanac* (1889), pp. 96–103.

26. *New York Age*, October 25, 1906.

27. Douglas, "The History of Siloam"; *Bridge Street AWME Anniversary Book* (1980), p. 40.

28. *Amsterdam News*, June 4, 1955; Douglas, "The History of Siloam"; *Bridge Street AWME Anniversary Book* (1980), 53–54.

29. Connolly, *A Ghetto Grows in Brooklyn*, p. 14; *Weekly Anglo-African*, February 2, 1861.

30. *Annual Report of the Board of Managers of the Brooklyn Sabbath School Union* (1858–59).

31. *Brooklyn Daily Eagle Almanac* (1891).

32. U.S. Census Bureau, Ninth Census (1870), Population Schedule.

33. Ibid.; *New York Times*, July 14, 1895; Allan Kulikoff, *Tobacco and Slaves* (Chapel Hill: University of North Carolina Press, 1986), p. 9.

34. *Brooklyn Daily Eagle Almanac* (1892), pp. 104–10; (1896); (1900), pp. 348–56.

35. Connolly, *A Ghetto Grows in Brooklyn*, pp. 23–24, 27.

36. *Amsterdam News*, January 17, 1943.

37. William Seraile, "Susan McKinney Steward: New York State's First African-American Woman Physician," in *Afro-Americans in New York Life and History* 9, no. 2 (July 1985): 27–40; *New York Times*, July 14, 1895, and June 5, 1887.

38. Maritcha Remond Lyons, "Memories of Yesterday: All of Which I Saw and Part of Which I Was: An Autobiography," pp. 5–38, Harry A. Williamson Papers, Schomburg Center for Research in Black Culture, New York (Harlem).

39. Woodson, *History of the Negro Church*, pp. 219–21; Connolly, *A Ghetto Grows in Brooklyn*, p. 25.

40. *New York Age*, February 27, 1908.

41. *New York Age*, June 10, 1909.

42. Charles E. Wynes, "T. McCants Stewart: Peripatetic Black South Carolinian," *South Carolina Historical Magazine* 80 (1979): 311–17.

43. Seraile, "Susan McKinney Steward," pp. 27–40; *New York Times*, June 5, 1887, and July 14, 1889.

44. *New York Age*, 2/27/1892.

45. *Brooklyn Daily Eagle*, September 16, 1892; *New York Times*, July 14, 1895.

46. *New York Age*, July 20, 1905.

47. *New York Globe*, February 1, 1885.

48. Maritcha Lyons to May Loeb, August 17, 1918 (Harry A. Williamson Papers).

49. *New York Globe*, February 1 and February 17, 1883; *New York Freeman*, October 10 and October 31, 1885.

50. *Annual Report of the African Civilization Society* (May 31, 1865).

51. Ibid.

52. *Brooklyn Howard Colored Orphan Asylum Annual Report* (1912–13); Carleton Mabee, "Charity in Travail: Two Orphan Asylums for Blacks," *New York History* 55, no. 1 (January 1974): 55–77.

53. *Brooklyn Howard Colored Orphan Asylum Annual Report* (1912–13).

54. *Brooklyn Directories* (1893–1918).

55. Woodson, *History of the Negro Church*, p. 196.

56. *The Twenty-Third Quadrennial General Conference of the African Methodist Episcopal Churches* (1908), p. 64.

57. *Berean Missionary Baptist Church Anniversary Book* (1976); *Brooklyn Daily Eagle Almanac* (1891); *Weeksville Then and Now* (New York: Society for the Preservation of Weeksville and Bedford-Stuyvesant History, 1983), p. 30.

58. *New York Freeman*, January 24, 1885; *Bridge Street AWME Anniversary Book* (1980), pp. 38–40.

59. *New York Globe*, March 31, 1883; *New York Freeman*, April 11, 1885.

60. *New York Globe*, February 3, 1885; *New York Age*, October 31, November 21, and December 5, 1891; *Brooklyn Daily Eagle*, September 17, 1892.

61. Lawrence Levine, *Highbrow Lowbrow* (Cambridge: Harvard University Press, 1988), p. 158.

62. *New York Age*, April 1, 1909. For Holy Trinity Baptist see *New York Age*, August 3, 1909. For St. Augustine see *New York Age*, February 20, 1892; *Bridge Street AWME Centennial Book: 1818–1918* (New York: Church Publication, 1919); *New York Freeman*, November 22, 1884. For Nazarene Congregational Church see *New York Age*, April 1, 1909; for Concord see *New York Age*, January 23, 1892.

63. For choir experts see *New York Age*, April 20 and June 1, 1905, April 2 and May 21, 1908. *Bridge Street AWME Centennial Book: 1818–1918*; Douglas "The History of Siloam"; *New York Globe*, August 23, 1924; *New York Freeman*, January 24 and October 17, 1885.

64. *New York Globe*, August 23, 1884; *New York Freeman*, November 22, 1884.

65. Woodson, *History of the Negro Church*, pp. 181–97.

66. C. Eric Lincoln and Lawrence H. Mamiya, *The Black Church in the African American Experience* (Durham, N.C.: Duke University Press, 1990), p. 53; *Twenty-third Quadrennial General Conference* (1908), pp. 50–51.

67. Woodson, *History of the Negro Church*, pp. 180–82.

68. Ibid., pp. 219–21; *New York Age*, February 20, 1898, June 15, 1905, July 12 and July 19, 1906, and June 10, 1909; *Flatbush of Today* (1908; published on the occasion of the tricentennial celebration of the coming of the Dutch to Flatbush), p. 57.

69. *New York Globe*, September 22, 1883.

70. *New York Globe*, August 4, 1883, and February 2, 1884; *New York Age*, October 31, 1891.

71. *New York Freeman*, December 5, 1885, and February 27, 1886; *New York Globe*, September 27, 1884.

72. *Constitution and By-Laws of the Brooklyn Literary Union* (1886); *New York Age*, September 26, October 17 and 31, 1891, February 27 and March 26, 1908; *New York Freeman*, September 26, 1885, and February 27, 1886; and Douglas, "The History of Siloam."

73. Rufus L. Perry, *The Cushite; or, The Children of Ham, as Seen by the Ancient Historians and Poets* (published by the Literary Union in 1887, a copy of this paper is at the Schomburg Center for Research in Black Culture); *New York Age*, October 31, 1891; *Brooklyn Daily Eagle*, September 17, 1892.

74. *Constitution and By-Laws of the Brooklyn Literary Union* (1886).

75. Ibid.; *Brooklyn Daily Eagle*, December 18, 1892.

76. *New York Age*, February 27, 1908.

77. Daniel Walker Howe, "American Victorianism as a Culture," *American Quarterly* 27 (December 1975): 521–31.

78. Levine, *Highbrow Lowbrow*, p. 199.

79. George M. Fredrickson, *The Black Image in the White Mind* (Middletown, Conn.: Wesleyan University Press, 1971), pp. 1275–82.

80. Wyn Craig Wade, *The Fiery Cross: The Ku Klux Klan in America* (New York: Simon and Schuster, 1987), 119–39.

81. John Hope Franklin, *From Slavery to Freedom* (New York: Knopf, 1988), pp. 238, 312–13.

82. Franklin, *From Slavery to Freedom*, pp. 238, 312–313.

83. *Thirty-Fifth Annual Session of the National Baptist Convention USA Incorporated* (1915), pp. 234–35.

2. The Rise of Black Holiness-Pentecostal Culture in Brooklyn

1. *Amsterdam News*, January 18, 1947.

2. *Amsterdam News*, July 19, 1958.

3. George Hobart, "The Negro Churches of Brooklyn, N.Y.: Study Made in 1930–31" (New York: Brooklyn Federation of Churches and the Greater New York Federation of Churches, 1931), pp. 5–10; First Church of God in Christ (COGIC) reported 700 members in 1952; Overcoming COGIC reported 350 members (New York: Protestant Church Directory of Brooklyn, 1952), p. 95.

4. Sydney E. Ahlstrom, *A Religious History of the American People* (New Haven: Yale University Press, 1972), p. 326.

5. Arthur E. Paris, *Black Pentecostalism* (Amherst: University of Massachusetts, 1982), pp. 17–18; Hans A. Baer and Merrill Singer, *African-American Religion in the Twentieth Century* (Knoxville: University of Tennessee Press, 1992), p.148.

6. Baer and Singer, *African-American Religion in the Twentieth Century*, p. 150

7. E. Myron Noble, "Genesis of W. J. Seymour in Perspective," *MAR Gospel Ministries Newsletter* 10, no. 1 (Spring–Summer 1990): 3.

8. Ibid.; James R. Goff, *Fields White Unto Harvest: Charles F. Parham and the Missionary Origins of Pentecostalism* (Fayetteville: University of Arkansas Press, 1988), pp. 62–111.

9. Leonard Lovett, "Black Holiness-Pentecostalism" (Ph.D. diss., Emory University, 1979), pp. 57–60. Neely Terry, who had invited Seymour to preach in Los Angeles, had been exposed to Holiness teaching while visiting Houston and wanted Seymour to become an associate pastor to the church. Noble, "Genesis of W. J. Seymour," pp. 4–6; Sherry Sherrod DuPree, *Biographical Dictionary of African American Holiness-Pentecostals, 1880–1990* (Washington, D.C.: Middle Atlantic Regional Press, 1989), pp. 207–208.

10. Elenora L. Lee, *C. H. Mason: A Man Greatly Used by God* (Memphis, Tenn.: Women's Department of COGIC), pp. 1–6; Lovett, "Black Holiness-Pentecostalism," pp. 4–5.

11. Charles Price Jones, "Autobiographical Sketch of Charles Price Jones, Founder of the Church of Christ (Holiness) USA," *Journal of Black Sacred Music* 2, no. 2 (Fall 1988): 52–58.

12. Morris E. Golder, *History of the Pentecostal Assemblies of the World* (Indianapolis, Ind.: Published by Golder and Grace Apostolic Church, 1973), pp. 65–70, 139.

13. *Census of Religious Bodies, 1936, Church of Christ (Holiness) USA* (Washington, D.C.: Department of Commerce, 1940), p. 5. Divisive issues were not always racial. Mason and Jones split over the issue of speaking in tongues. Another issue dividing groups was the concept of the Trinity. According to many Holiness-Pentecostal groups (including COGIC, the United Holy Church of America, Inc., and Fire Baptized Holiness Church of God of the Americas), God appears in

three forms: the Father, the Son, and the Holy Spirit. The Trinitarian doctrine, a major tenet in most Christian denominations, claims that there are three distinct personalities in the Godhead, each with a specific role.

However, by 1913 the Trinitarian view was under attack by some Holiness-Pentecostal leaders. Ministers who attended a 1913 Pentecostal camp gathering at Arroyo Seco in southern California questioned the validity of the Trinity. The Reverend Frank J. Ewart, a Pentecostal minister from the West Coast, asserted that the only personality in the Godhead was Jesus Christ and that the Father and Holy Spirit were only titles for God to reveal his personality. This belief, known as the "Jesus Only" or the oneness doctrine, was soon adopted by some Holiness-Pentecostal groups, including the Pentecostal Assemblies of the World and the Church of Our Lord Jesus Christ of the Apostolic Faith. Lovett, "Black Holiness-Pentecostalism," pp. 90–94.

14. Elmer T. Clark, *The Small Sects in America* (New York: Abingdon, 1937), pp. 117–24; DuPree, *Biographical Dictionary.*

15. *Pentecostal Assemblies of the World* (Washington, D.C.: U.S. Department of Commerce, 1936), p. 36; *Fire Baptized Holiness Church of God of the Americas; Statistics, Denominational History Doctrine, and Organization* (Washington, D.C.: GPO, 1940), p. 4; Lovett, "Black Holiness-Pentecostalism," pp. 70–71.

16. Lovett, "Black Holiness-Pentecostalism," pp. 76–79.

17. Ibid., p. 84.

18. Ibid., pp. 81–84.

19. Wilbur L. Jones, "Tongue-Speaking (Glossolalia): A Biblio-Historical Account" (New York: Beulah Church of God in Christ Jesus, n.d.).

20. Jon Michael Spencer, *Protest and Praise* (Minneapolis: Fortress Press, 1990), p. 153.

21. Spencer, *Protest and Praise,* p. 155.

22. Lawrence W. Levine, *Black Culture and Black Consciousness* (Oxford and New York: Oxford University Press, 1977), pp. 179–80.

23. Morris E. Golder, *The Life and Works of Bishop Garfield Thomas Haywood* (Indianapolis, Ind.: Published by Golder and Grace Apostolic Church, 1977), p. 23.

24. Charles Price Jones, "The History of My Songs," *Journal of Black Sacred Music* 2, no. 2 (Fall 1988): 62.

25. Mary Tyler, *The Bridegroom Songs,* (Indianapolis: Christ Temple Bookstore, n.d.), pp. 17, 35, 39, 91; Charles Price Jones, "The History of My Songs," p. 61.

26. Tyler, *The Bridegroom Songs,* p. 93.

27. Arthur W. Fauset, *Black Gods of the Metropolis* (New York: Octagon, 1970), pp. 17–18.

28. Robert C. Spellman and Mabel L. Thomas, *The Life, Legend and Legacy of Bishop R. C. Lawson* (Scotch Plains, N.J.: Published by the authors, 1983), p. 42; Bishop Smallwood Williams, *This Is My Story*, pp. 50–51.

29. G. Norman Eddy reported visiting numerous House of Prayer of Our Lord churches in Harlem and described a typical testimonial service at one such institution: "Perhaps the most distinctive thing about their services is the frenzied congregational participation. After a brief period of spontaneous singing, the young and old line up to take their turn at the microphone to offer testimony. It may be a long or short effort, but occasionally it becomes so emotional that a few lose control of themselves completely. They start to clap their hands while the speaker moves around in ever-increasing tempo until eventually he jumps high off the floor. He throws back his head as if from a violent spasm. His actions are contagious and those waiting in line to offer testimony begin to imitate him," G. Norman Eddy, "Storefront Religion," *Religion in Life* 28 (1958–59): 77.

30. Allan H. Spear, *Black Chicago: The Making of a Negro Ghetto, 1890–1920* (Chicago: University of Chicago Press, 1967), p. 175.

31. Hobart, "The Negro Churches of Brooklyn," pp. 5–11.

32. *Protestant Church Directory of Metropolitan New York* (1948), pp. 136–37, *Protestant Church Directory* (1952), pp. 137–39; *Amsterdam News*, June 29, 1957.

33. Ithiel Clemmons and Alonza Johnson, "The History of the First Church of God in Christ" (New York: Published by the First Church of God in Christ, n.d.); *Amsterdam News*, May 30, 1964.

34. Clemmons and Johnson, "The History of the First Church of God in Christ."

35. Author interview with Ulysses L. and Louise Corbett, Brooklyn, April 20, 1990.

36. Author interview with Taffie Brannon, Brooklyn, July 25, 1990.

37. *Protestant Church Directory* (1950), pp. 142–50.

38. Blanche Redd, "History of Washington Temple Church of God in Christ, Inc. in Brooklyn New York" (New York: Church Publication, 1989); *Amsterdam News*, February 1, 1957.

39. *Protestant Church Directory* (1950), pp. 142–50; Charles Emmanuel Grace, popularly known as "Sweet Daddy Grace," was formerly a member of COGIC but left over financial differences with Charles Harrison Mason. Grace founded the United House of Prayer in the 1920s. The group stressed sanctification, baptism of the Holy Spirit, and healing. Fauset, *Black Gods of the Metropolis*, pp. 22–30; DuPree, *Biographical Dictionary*, pp. 104–105.

40. Author interview with Maritcha Harvey, Brooklyn, May 3, 1990 (Harvey is the daughter of Peter J. F. Bridges).

41. *Protestant Church Directory* (1963) and *Protestant Church Directory* (1966).

42. Author interview with Samuel Gibson, Brooklyn, May 8, 1990. Gibson had met Skinner at Mother Horn's church in the 1940s. He later joined Skinner's church in Newark and was one of the founding members of Deliverance Tabernacle in Brooklyn; DuPree, *Biographical Dictionary*, p. 251.

43. Arturo Skinner, *Nine Gifts of the Spirit* (Newark: Deliverance Evangelistic Center, 1975).

44. Author interview with Samuel Gibson; *Deliverance Voice* 9, no. 1 (January–February 1975); author interview with Henri Ann (Penny) Hooks, Brooklyn, August 22, 1990; Esther Hooks, *The Penny Hooks Story: God Specializes* (New York: Hooks Publishing, 1986), pp. 14–25; *Amsterdam News*, February 8, 1964.

45. Cynthia E. Hedgepeth, *Lord Why Me? The Making of an Apostle* (New York: Tabernacle of Prayer Publishing, 1989), pp. 32–52.

46. Hedgepeth, *Lord Why Me?* pp. 32–52.

47. Huey C. Rogers, *The Dynamics of Christian Faith* (New York: Total Truth Publications, 1982), pp. 7–17.

48. Author interview with Taffie Brannon; author interview with Maritcha Harvey.

49. Author interview with Morry Bryant McGuire, Brooklyn, July 25, 1990.

50. Author interview with Nettie Kennedy, Manhattan, May 24, 1986.

51. Author interview with Nettie Kennedy.

52. Author interview with Ulysses L. and Louise Corbett.

53. Lovett, "Black Holiness-Pentecostalism," p. 104.

54. Author interview with Maritcha Harvey.

55. Author interview with Evelyn Smith, Brooklyn, April 30, 1991.

56. T. J. Jackson Lears, "The Concept of Cultural Hegemony: Problems and Possibilities," *American Historical Review* 90, no. 3 (June 1985): 571.

57. Author interview with Taffie Brannon.

58. Author interview with Taffie Brannon.

59. Author interview with Maritcha Harvey.

60. Lafayette Avenue Church of God, *50th Anniversary, 1928–1978* (New York: Church Publication, 1978), p. 46.

61. Lafayette Avenue Church of God, *50th Anniversary*, p. 34.

62. Ibid., pp. 35–36.

63. Esther Hooks, *The Penny Hooks Story*, pp. 1–25; author interview with Penny Hooks.

64. Hooks, *The Penny Hooks Story*, pp. 1–25; author interview with Penny Hooks.

65. Author interview with Maritcha Harvey.

66. Ian Robertson, *Sociology* (New York: Worth, 1987), pp. 64–65.

67. Baer and Singer, *African-American Religion in the Twentieth Century*, p. 172; author interview with Maritcha Harvey.

68. Author interview with Samuel Gibson.

69. Author interview with Ruby Richards, Brooklyn, June 16, 1991.

70. Author interview with Ruby Richards.

71. *Church Directory of Greater New York* (1938); *Protestant Church Directory* (1944–1955); author interview with Maritcha Harvey.

72. Melvin Williams, *Community in a Black Pentecostal Church: An Anthropological Study* (Pittsburgh: University of Pittsburgh Press, 1974), p. 157.

73. Joseph R. Washington, Jr. *Black Religion* (Lanham, Mo.: University Press of America, 1984), p. 115.

74. Williams, *Community in a Black Pentecostal Church*, p. 162.

3. Brooklyn's Black Churches and the Growth of Mass Culture

1. *Amsterdam News*, September 20, 1941.

2. Lawrence Levine, "The Folklore of Industrial Society: Popular Culture and Its Audiences," *American Historical Review* 97, no. 5 (December 1992): 1369–99; Lizabeth Cohen, *Making a New Deal* (Cambridge: Cambridge University Press, 1990), p. 148.

3. Kathy Peiss, *Cheap Amusement* (Philadelphia: Temple University Press, 1986), pp. 11–16; John F. Kasson, *Amusing the Million* (New York: Hill and Wang, 1978), pp. 4–8; Roy Rozenweig, *Eight Hours for What We Will* (Cambridge: Cambridge University Press, 1983), pp. 208–21.

4. Sam J. Slate and Joe Cook, *It Sounds Impossible* (New York: Macmillan, 1963), pp. 41, 43–45, 49, 51, 57–58, 105–106, 149–51, 163–67.

5. *Brooklyn Daily Eagle*, January 26, 1907, and September 27, 1942.

6. Rozenweig, *Eight Hours for What We Will*, pp. 204–20; *New York Age*, January 26, 1907, and September 27, 1942; *Brooklyn Daily Eagle*, May 16, 1910.

7. *Brooklyn Daily Eagle*, January 26, 1907.

8. Ibid.

9. *Brooklyn Daily Eagle*, May 16, 1910.

10. *Brooklyn Daily Eagle*, May 18, 1910.

11. Ibid.

12. Ibid. Not all prominent citizens opposed the new establishments. Realtors who were putting up new buildings on Pitkin Avenue were not opposed because they could collect high rents for the double stores needed for movie houses. *Brooklyn Daily Eagle*, January 26, 1907.

13. *Brooklyn Daily Eagle*, April 21, 1918.

14. For example, the Brooklyn Apollo advertised a Little Rascals com-

edy short, along with "The Adventures of Galahad" and five cartoons. Saturday matinees were nearly an all-day affair, beginning at noon and lasting until five or six o'clock in the evening. By the late 1930s, Brooklyn residents were spending a great deal of their leisure time in movie palaces, engrossed in comedy, horror, western, romance, and cartoons. *Amsterdam News*, August 6, 1938, June 14, 1941, July 25, October 10, and December 19, 1942, February 27 and November 27, 1943, March 18, 1944, November 16, 1945, and January 25, 1947; *New York Age*, September 25, 1937, and September 10, 1938.

15. *New York Age*, September 10, 1938, October 28, 1939, and December 19, 1942. See also G. Williams Jones, *Black Cinema Treasures Lost and Found*, pp. 31, 203, and 215.

16. *New York Age*, October 28, 1939, and November 14, 1942; *Amsterdam News*, December 19, 1942.

17. *Amsterdam News*, February 16, 1946; *Amsterdam News*, Ike McFowler's "Brooklyn's Tavern Jottings," January 5, 1946.

18. *Amsterdam News*, July 26, 1947; *Amsterdam News*, McFowler's "Brooklyn's Tavern Jottings," June 1, 1946.

19. *Amsterdam News*, Clyde Williams's "Nite Life," March 18, 1944; *Amsterdam News*, February 24, 1945, and February 16, 1946.

20. *Amsterdam News*, April 28, 1959.

21. *Amsterdam News*, McFowler's "Brooklyn Tavern Jottings," February 16, June 22, and July 19, 1946, July 26, 1947, and April 8, 1950.

22. *Amsterdam News*, McFowler's "Brooklyn Tavern Jottings," February 16, June 22, and July 19, 1946, July 26, 1947, and April 8, 1950; *New York Age*, February 5, 1955.

23. *Amsterdam News*, McFowler's "Brooklyn Tavern Jottings," March 2 and June 8, 1946; *Amsterdam News*, September 13, 1952, and May 29, 1959.

24. *Amsterdam News*, McFowler's "Brooklyn Tavern Jottings," July 27, 1946. McFowler, in an interesting potential conflict of interest, also managed and presented entertainment groups. In June 1946, Ike McFowler Enterprises presented "Five Hilarious Sessions of Entertainment Each Week," including star musicians of radio, stage, and screen every Monday night. On Tuesday evenings there were big-name acts and an amateur contest. Sunday matinees featured a "great show," dance music, music by "John English and his Society Orchestra, Clint Smith and his Clintonians, and Rector (Wizard of the Strings) Baily and his sensational combo" (*Amsterdam News*, June 15, 1946).

Bedford-Stuyvesant became such a popular entertainment spot that black weeklies carried regular columns highlighting Brooklyn's nightlife. In the 1940s the *Amsterdam News* featured not only McFowler's column but also Clyde Williams's "Nite Life," and Tommy

Watkins's "Escapading in Brooklyn." The *New York Age* ran both Larry Douglas's "Swinging in Brooklyn" and Buddy Franklin's "Brooklyn After Dark."

25. *Amsterdam News*, November 16, 1946, and January 18 and 25, 1947.

26. U.S. Census Bureau, *Negroes in the United States, 1920–32* (Washington, D.C:, GPO, 1935), p. 525.

27. Lerone Bennett Jr., *The Shaping of Black America*, (Chicago: Johnson Publishing, 1975), pp. 221–22; *New York Age*, March 16, 1905, February 27, 1908, September 8, 1945; *Amsterdam News*, May 16, 1931, November 17, 1945, July 5, 1952, December 8 and 22, 1956. For hair and skin products see *New York Age*, April 15, 1944; *Amsterdam News*, October 14 and November 4, 1944, March 22, 1947, July 12, 1952, May 23, 1959. For Anthony George see *Amsterdam News*, July 14, 1945, and January 3, 1948.

28. L. Eldridge Cleaver, "Black Is Coming Back" in John H. Bracy Jr., ed., *Black Nationalism in America* (Indianapolis: Bobbs-Merrill, 1970), pp. 429–42.

29. S. Michelson, "The National War Veterans Association," WPA Research Papers, Schomburg Collection, Schomburg Center for Research in Black Culture, New York (Harlem); Harold X. Connolly, *A Ghetto Grows in Brooklyn* (New York: New York University Press, 1977), p. 9.

30. *New York Age*, June 24 and July 29, 1933.

31. *New York Age*, August 28, 1937.

32. *New York Age*, August 3, 1940.

33. *New York Age*, September 25, 1937.

34. Cohen, *Making a New Deal*, p. 153.

35. It should be noted that even before the turn of the century some black ministers and churches were involved in the temperance movement, condemning establishments that sold alcohol of morally corrupting African Americans. William T. Dixon of Concord Baptist was an advocate of prohibition. He addressed the Prohibition Party of Brooklyn, noting the negative impact alcohol had on the black community. Concord Baptist had a Women's Christian Temperance Union (WCTU) that met on a regular basis, and a series of "Gospel Temperance" meetings were held at Siloam Presbyterian on Sunday evenings, while the WCTU of Berean Missionary Baptist Church met on Monday evenings. Bars, taverns, and other places that sold alcohol were blamed by these groups for corrupting the morals of African Americans. *New York Freeman*, October 17, 1885; *New York Age*, March 23, 1905, and February 27 and September 2, 1908.

36. *New York Age*, March 8 and 15, 1930; *Amsterdam News*, March 5 and 12, 1930; William H. Welty, "Black Shepherds: A Study of the Leading Negro Clergy in New York City, 1900–1940 (Ph.D. diss., New York University, 1969), p. 187.

37. *New York Age*, May 16, 1925.

38. Hans A. Baer and Merrill Singer, *African-American Religion in the Twentieth Century* (Knoxville: University of Tennessee Press, 1992), p. 177.

39. Darlene Clark Hine, *When the Truth Is Told* (Indianapolis: National Council of Negro Women, 1981), pp. 19–27; *Bridge Street AWME Centennial Book: 1818–1918* (1919), pp. 33, 37, 41.

40. *Amsterdam News*, June 4, 1955; *Bridge Street AWME Centennial Book: 1818–1918* (1919); *Bridge Street AWME Historical Brochure* (1951); *Church of Mount Sinai Sixtieth Year Retrospective* (New York: Church Publication, 1979); *Brown Memorial Baptist Fiftieth Anniversary Journal* (New York: Church Publication, 1966).

41. *Brooklyn Daily Eagle Almanac* (from 1920 to 929); George Hobart, "The Negro Churches of Brooklyn" (New York: Brooklyn Federation of Churches and the Greater New York Federation of Churches, 1931).

42. *Brooklyn Daily Eagle Almanac* (1929); Hobart, "Negro Churches of Brooklyn"; *Cornerstone Baptist Church Sixtieth Anniversary Book* (New York: Church Publication, 1977); *Protestant Church Directory of Metropolitan New York* (1952); *New York Age*, April 3, 1943.

43. Hobart, "Negro Churches of Brooklyn"; *Church Directory of Greater New York* (1936); *Protestant Church Directory* (1945, 1950, 1952).

44. Connolly, *A Ghetto Grows in Brooklyn*, pp. 65–66; *Protestant Church Directory* (1945, 1950, 1952).

45. *Communities Population Characteristics and Neighborhood Social Resource*, vol. 2 (New York: Bureau of Community Statistical Services, Community Council of Greater New York, 1959).

46. *Cornerstone Sixtieth Anniversary Book* (1977); *Brown Memorial Fiftieth Anniversary Book* (1957); author interview with George Beard Sr. (member of Brown Memorial), Brooklyn, May 5, 1988; author interview with Rev. Clarence Norman Sr., pastor of First Baptist Church of Crown Heights, Brooklyn, February 8, 1988.

47. *Amsterdam News*, June 4, 1955; *Bridge Street AWME Sunday Bulletin* (May 18, 1952); *Bridge Street AWME Annual Women's Day Program* (May 5, 1957); *First AME Zion Church Bulletin*, "Tenth Anniversary of the Occupancy at Tompkins Avenue" (October 5, 1952).

48. *Amsterdam News*, February 3 and March 22, 1944, January 13, February 3, and June 2, 1945, January 26, 1946, December 2, 1950, and April 14, 1956; *Bridge Street AWME Anniversary Book* (1980); *Concord Weekly Bulletin* (October 13, 1957); *First AME Zion Bulletin* (October 5, 1952); Siloam Presbyterian Church brochure (no date); *Protestant Church Directory* (1950); *Brown Memorial Fiftieth Anniversary Book* (1957); First Church of God in Christ, "A Congregation Designed for the Eighties" (New York, n.d.).

49. For Intercultural Club, the First AME Zion Church, see *Amsterdam News*, January 26, 1946; for the Talent Guild of Siloam see *Amsterdam News*, December 2, 1950; for Mount Sinai see *Church of Mount Sinai Sixtieth Year Retrospective* (1979); for Concord's annual Spring Concert see *Amsterdam News*, May 6, 1950.

50. Baxter R. Leach, "Important Negro Churches in Brooklyn," *Amsterdam News*, October 10, 1942, December 2, 1946, and April 14, 1956.

51. Anthony Heilbut, *The Gospel Sound* (New York: Limelight, 1985), pp. xii–xvii; Kenneth Morris, "If I Can Just Make It In," in Langston Hughes and Arna Bontemps, eds., *The Book of Negro Folklore* (New York: Dodd, Mead, 1983), p. 322; Mellonee Burnim, "Music in the African-American Religious Tradition" (Paper presented at the conference on "African American Religion: Research Problems and Resources for the 1990s," May 26, 1990, Schomburg Center for Research in Black Culture, New York/Harlem).

52. Lawrence W. Levine, *Black Culture and Black Consciousness* (Oxford and New York: Oxford University Press, 1977), pp. 180–88.

53. Paul Oliver, Max Harrison, and William Bolcom, *The New Grove: Gospel, Blues and Jazz* (New York: W. W. Norton, 1986), p. 203.

54. Oliver, Harrison, and Bolcom, *The New Grove Gospel*, pp. 210–14; Levine, *Black Culture and Black Consciousness*, pp. 174–79.

55. Author interview with Myra M. Gregory, Brooklyn, July 1, 1987. Ms. Gregory has been a member of Berean Missionary Baptist Church since 1912.

56. Author interview with Myra M. Gregory; *Bridge Street AWME Anniversary Book (1980), p. 118; Brown Memorial Baptist Fiftieth Anniversary Journal* (1966); *Cornerstone Sixtieth Anniversary Book* (1977); *Amsterdam News*, November 17, 1945.

57. Levine, *Black Culture and Black Consciousness*, p. 174. Wyatt T. Walker remarks, "The creation of Gospel music is a social statement that, in the face of America's rejection and economic privation, Black folks made a conscious decision to be themselves. It was an early stage of identity awakening and identity nourishing." Walker, *"Somebody's Calling My Name": Black Sacred Music and Social Change* (Valley Forge, Pa.: Judson Press, 1979), p. 144.

58. *Amsterdam News*, August 16, 1941, and August 26, 1944; *New York Daily News*, January 30, 1965.

59. *Brown Memorial Baptist Fiftieth Anniversary Journal* (1966); *Cornerstone Sixtieth Anniversary Book* (1977); *Amsterdam News*, August 16, 1941, June 4, 1955, March 2, 1958, and May 4, 1963.

60. *Amsterdam News*, November 10 and 17, 1945.

61. *Amsterdam News*, May 10 and August 16, 1933, May 17, 1944, January 12 and November 17, 1945, March 22, 1947, and February 2, 1951.

62. *Brown Memorial Baptist Fiftieth Anniversary Journal* (1966); *Amsterdam News*, April 17, 1929, February 20 and July 20, 1957.

63. Watkins's "Escapading in Brooklyn," *Amsterdam News*, June 8, 1938.

64. Many churches built kitchens and served inexpensive meals after the morning service, and church clubs sponsored dinners. The St. Phillip's Protestant Episcopal's June Birthday Club gave dinners in the lecture room of the church. On July 14, 1958, Friendship Baptist Church held a southern-style barbecue. The *Bridge Street AWME Sunday Bulletin* announced weekly dinners given by various clubs; *Amsterdam News*, June 10, 1944, June 3 and June 30, 1957, and June 14, 1958.

65. *Amsterdam News*, April 21, 1934, May 4, 1940, and August 25, 1956; *First AME Zion Centennial Celebration Book, 1885–1985* (New York: Church Publication, 1985), p. 29; *Brown Memorial Baptist Fiftieth Anniversary Journal* (1966); *Bridge Street AWME 187th Anniversary Book* (New York: Church Publication, 1953).

66. *Bridge Street AWME 187th Anniversary Book* (1953).

67. *Amsterdam News*, September 17, 1955, and November 2, 1951; *COGIC "On the Hill" Banquet Program: Banquet Celebrating 50 Years in the Ministry* (September 28, 1974).

68. E. Franklin Frazier, *The Negro Church in America* (New York: Schocken, 1954), p. 56.

69. *Annual Senior Choir Tea Program* (Bridge Street brochure, November 5, 1951); *Twenty-fifth Anniversary of Bridge Street AWME Sunday Bulletin* (February 4, 1958). The sacred even spread into political affairs. In a protest rally sponsored by the Brooklyn branch of the National Association for the Advancement of Colored People (NAACP) in 1959, an invocation was given by Father Julian Dozier of St. Phillip's Protestant Episcopal, and the benediction was given by Rev. Richard Gay of Concord Baptist (Brooklyn Branch of the NAACP, Protest Rally program, May 19, 1959).

70. *Amsterdam News*, May 24, 1941, February 8, 1947, and December 4, 1948; *New York Age*, May 27, 1939.

4. *The Failure to Make Things Better: Brooklyn's Black Ministers and the Deterioration of Bedford-Stuyvesant*

1. There were a few exceptions, such as F. D. Washington and John E. Bryant of COGIC on the Hill. Washington was a noted Republican, and both were active in civic affairs. Hans A. Baer and Merrill Singer, *African-American Religion in the Twentieth Century* (Knoxville: University of Tennessee Press, 1992), p. 176. A list of the Ministerial Alliance of Brooklyn can be found in the Milton A. Galamison Papers at the State Historical Society, Madison, Wisconsin.

2. It should be noted that a close examination of the churches is limited because most black churches did not keep records or evaluate their own social programs. However, the black press serves as a useful source because it reported weekly activities of the churches and ministers. For instance, both the *Amsterdam News* and the *New York Age* provided weekly columns on the various church activities. Moreover, interviews, the directories of the Protestant Council of Churches, and various church publications provided limited but beneficial information on the churches and ministers.

3. David Ment and Mary Donovan, *The People of Brooklyn: A History of Two Neighborhoods* (New York: Brooklyn Arts and Cultural Association, 1980), pp. 6–7.

4. Ment and Donovan, *The People of Brooklyn*, pp. 32–37; Harold X. Connolly, *A Ghetto Grows in Brooklyn* (New York: New York University Press, 1977), pp. 52–55.

5. *Communities Population Characteristics and Neighborhood Social Resource*, vol. 2 (New York: Bureau of Community Statistical Services, Community Council of Greater New York, 1959), pp. 107–109.

6. Ernest Quimby, "Black Political Development in Bedford-Stuyvesant as Reflected in the Origins and Role of the Bedford-Stuyvesant Restoration Corporation," (Ph.D. diss., New York University, 1977), p. 87. A 1929 Welfare Council report asserted that the housing conditions for many blacks in Brooklyn were terrible. Many lived in frame buildings without fire escapes. Some buildings were turned into single-room apartments, causing overcrowding. Toilets were found in the yards of some tenements and in other buildings were located in the halls, forcing families to share them (Connolly, *A Ghetto Grows in Brooklyn*, pp. 118–19).

7. Quimby, "Black Political Development in Bedford-Stuyvesant," p. 111.

8. *Amsterdam News*, October 15, 1938. In one case in 1941, tenants living in a tenement on Myrtle Avenue in Bed-Stuy were so fed up with their living conditions that they launched a rent strike. The tenants asserted that there was no central heating in the building. In addition, the building had loose wiring and gas and oil leaks and was infested with rodents and roaches. *New York Age*, February 26, 1941.

9. Connolly, *A Ghetto Grows in Brooklyn*, p. 119.

10. *Amsterdam News*, September 17, 1949.

11. *Communities Population Characteristics* 2:107–108.

12. Connolly, *A Ghetto Grows in Brooklyn*, p. 119.

13. Ibid., pp. 114–15.

14. "Labor Conditions of American Negroes," Brooklyn Urban League Industrial Department Report, June 15 and 16, 1930 (New York: Brooklyn Urban League, 1930).

15. Connolly, *A Ghetto Grows in Brooklyn*, pp. 186–87.

16. *Communities Population Characteristics* 2:106. Structural changes added misery to the employment situation for blacks in Brooklyn. Manufacturing employment declined as businesses shifted from the Northeast to the South, West, and other parts of the country. Many places closed, relocated, or cut back production. The Brooklyn Navy Yard serves as a good example. Although the Navy Yard was well equipped to build war ships, the federal government attempted to reduce its costs by turning to private shipyards to build ships. The cutback eventually affected thousands of workers, including eight hundred who lost their jobs when laid off from the Navy Yard clothing store. Many were black workers residing in Brooklyn who were the last hired and had the least seniority, Joshua Brown and David Ment, *Factories, Foundries and Refineries: A History of Five Brooklyn Industries* (New York: Brooklyn Educational and Cultural Alliance, 1980), p. 68; *Amsterdam News*, April 4, 1953, and June 27, 1964.

17. *Communities Population Characteristics* 2:106–107.

18. *Report on Hospital Needs of the Bedford-Stuyvesant Area* (New York: Hospital Council of Greater New York, 1953), pp. 5–8; Connolly, *A Ghetto Grows in Brooklyn*, pp. 202–204.

19. Bedford-Stuyvesant Health Congress, *Newsletter* (New York: Health Press, Spring 1953). A copy of the newsletter is found at the Brooklyn Historical Society.

20. *Amsterdam News*, February 2, 1952; Connolly, *A Ghetto Grows in Brooklyn*, 203–204.

21. *Amsterdam News*, November 14, 1945.

22. Kenneth Clark, "Educational Factors in the Prospects for School Integration in New York City" (Speech delivered at the meeting of "Children Together," New York City, December 4, 1956.

23. Parents' Workshop for Equality in New York City Schools, "Fact Sheet on Brooklyn Junior High Schools—Open Enrollment" (January 1961).

24. Parents' Workshop for Equality in New York City Schools, "Fact Sheet on Brooklyn Elementary Schools—Open Enrollment" (January 1961).

25. *The Daily Worker*, June 19, 1956.

26. Diane Ravitch, *The Great School Wars*, (New York: Basic Books, 1974), p. 256.

27. Teachers Union, "Discrimination Against Negro Teachers" (1949); Teachers Union, "Employment in New York Schools in Order to Correct the Situation Revealed by a Survey Conducted by the Teachers Union (June 14, 1955); Jack Greenberg, February 25, 1952. Most of the papers of the Teachers Union are located in the Teachers Union Collection, Cornell Labor Archives, Cornell University (School of Industrial Labor), Ithaca, N.Y.

28. "Report to the Honorable F. H. LaGuardia on the Conditions existing in the Bedford-Stuyvesant Area of Brooklyn in Connection with the Charges made by the Kings County Grand Jury in its Presentment of August 1943: Part One," Police Commissioner, pp. 17–19. A copy of this report is found at the Brooklyn Historical Society.

29. *Bedford Home Owners News* 1, no. 5 (August 1936).

30. *Amsterdam News*, November 20, 1943.

31. Report of the Grand Jury of Kings County (August 1943). A copy of the report is found at the Brooklyn Historical Society.

32. Ibid.

33. *Communities Population Characteristics* 2:103–105; "Report to the Honorable F. H. LaGuardia on the Conditions existing in the Bedford-Stuyvesant Area of Brooklyn, Part One," pp. 17–19.

34. *Communities Population Characteristics* 2:103–105; Report to the Honorable F. H. LaGuardia on the Conditions existing in the Bedford-Stuyvesant Area of Brooklyn, Part One."

35. As early as February 1933 the *Amsterdam News* reported that Bed-Stuy had been selected as a "stamping ground for two hundred additional policemen who began their duties on Monday with purposes of stamping out crime." It was asserted that police went on a rampage, rounding up and arresting innocent people. "Negroes, Puerto Rican and white workers in Harlem and Brooklyn's Bedford-Stuyvesant district seethed with anger yesterday as hordes of detectives and police swarmed into their districts arresting innocent citizens by the scores in a pre-election dragnet ordered by acting Mayor Vincent R. Impelitteri." According to the article, some thirty blacks and Hispanics were arrested indiscriminately in Bed-Stuy on charges of vagrancy. "Police Brutality," Schomburg Clippings, Schomburg Center for Research in Black Culture, New York (Harlem).

36. "Police Brutality," Schomburg Clippings; *New York Age*, August 15, 1936; "The Struggle for Negro Rights in Brooklyn: Report by Carl Vedro for the County Committee." A copy of this report is at Schomburg Center for Research in Black Culture, New York (Harlem).

37. Milton Galamison to Archie Hargraves, Gardner C. Taylor, Henry Hucles, Benjamin Lowery, Henri Deas, and Sandy Ray (letter dated May 14, 1959); "Protest Rally, Tuesday May 19th," Flyer in the Galamison Papers, State Historical Society, Madison, Wisconsin.

38. "Brownsville Boys Club of Brooklyn, City of New York" (New York: New York City Department of Parks, September 1954). A copy of this paper is found at the Brooklyn Historical Society.

39. "Brownsville Boys Club of Brooklyn" (September 1954).

40. *Communities Population Characteristics* 2:113–19; "Reports to the Honorable F. H. LaGuardia, Mayor of the City of New York on Conditions existing in the Bedford-Stuyvesant Area of the Borough of Brook-

lyn in Connection with the Charges made by the Kings County Grand Jury in its Presentment of August 1943: Part Two," Parks Commissioner, pp. 1–3; *Amsterdam News*, July 8, 1944.

41. *Communities, Population Characteristics* 2:116–19.

42. New York City Department of Parks, "Saint John's Recreation Center in Brooklyn" (1956).

43. *Protestant Church Directory* (1945, 1950, 1952); Connolly, *A Ghetto Grows in Brooklyn*, pp. 65–66.

44. *First AME Zion Centennial Celebration Book, 1885–1985* (19??), p. 14; author interview with Rev. Gardner C. Taylor, Brooklyn, August 1, 1988; *Amsterdam News*, October 17, 1936, and October 30, 1948; *New York Age*, November 24, 1936.

45. *Amsterdam News*, September 17, 1949, and November 4, 1950; Connolly, *A Ghetto Grows in Brooklyn*, p. 182n.

46. Sandy F. Ray, *Journeying Through a Jungle* (Nashville: Broadman Press, 1979), pp. 15–23; *Cornerstone Sixtieth Anniversary Book* (1977); *Amsterdam News*, October 2, 1948.

47. Author interview with Gardner C. Taylor; *Amsterdam News*, February 15, 1958, and January 27, 1962. Both Hilton L. James of Berean Missionary Baptist and John M. Coleman of St. Phillip's Protestant Episcopal were also active Democrats (see *Amsterdam News*, July 24, 1948, and July 23, 1955).

48. *Amsterdam News*, April 16, 1949.

49. Andrew Michael Manis, *Southern Civil Religions in Conflict* (Athens: University of Georgia Press, 1987), pp. 53–54.

50. *Amsterdam News*, August 22, 1953.

51. Manning Marable, *How Capitalism Underdeveloped Black America* (Boston: South End Press, 1981), p. 200.

52. *Amsterdam News*, December 9, 1950, and August 3, 1957.

53. Gardner C. Taylor, Speech before the Board of Education Public Hearing, 1959 (the speech is found in the Special Library at Teachers College, Columbia University); Gardner C. Taylor to members of the Board of Education, June 18, 1958.

54. The membership list of the Interdenominational Ministers Alliance is found in the Galamison Papers, State Historical Society, Madison, Wisconsin; author interview with Gardner C. Taylor; *Amsterdam News*, December 26, 1953, and January 14, 1950.

55. *Amsterdam News*, December 22, 1958.

56. *Amsterdam News*, December 26, 1953.

57. *New York Age*, May 22, 1943.

58. Ibid.

59. Connolly, *A Ghetto Grows in Brooklyn*, pp. 93, 102–103.

60. William H. Welty, "Black Shepherds: A Study of the Leading

Negro Clergy in New York City, 1900–1940 (Ph.D. diss., New York University, 1969), pp. 189–93.

61. Welty, "Black Shepherds." pp. 189–93; *New York Age*, March 20 and March 31, 1926.

62. *New York Age*, April 3, 1926.

63. *Amsterdam News*, January 18, 1928.

64. *New York Age*, August 1, 1936.

65. *Amsterdam News*, September 11, 1937; for the Scottsboro Boys see the *New York Age*, September 24, 1938.

66. Welty, "Black Shepherds," pp. 189–94; for the rally see the *New York Age*, September 11, 1937.

67. *Amsterdam News*, February 21, 1942.

68. *Amsterdam News*, June 5, 1948.

69. *New York Age*, August 20, 1938; *Amsterdam News*, July 1, 1939, and February 14, 1942.

70. Connolly, *A Ghetto Grows in Brooklyn*, p. 103; *New York Age*, August 27, 1938; *Amsterdam News*, January 1 and October 15, 1938, and April 29, 1944.

71. *Amsterdam News*, November 19, 1938.

72. Milton A. Galamison, untitled paper on the Cuban Revolution, April 20, 1961 (in the Galamison Papers, State Historical Society, Madison, Wisconsin).

73. *Amsterdam News*, January 28, 1950.

74. Author interview with Rev. Milton A. Galamison, Brooklyn, October 21, 1988.

75. Author interview with Milton A. Galamison.

76. *Amsterdam News*, September 19, 1958, and April 15, 1962; Ravitch, *The Great School Wars*, p. 262.

77. Ravitch, *The Great School Wars*, pp. 273–74.

78. Ministers' Letter, July 19, 1963. A copy of the letter is found in the Galamison Papers, State Historical Society, Madison, Wisconsin.

79. Ravitch, *The Great School Wars*, pp. 278–79.

80. Evelyn Brooks Higginbotham, *Righteous Discontent: The Women's Movement in the Black Baptist Church, 1880–1920* (Cambridge: Harvard University Press, 1993), p. 2.

81. Baxter R. Leach, "Colored Boy Scouts of Brooklyn," WPA Research Papers, Schomburg Collection, Schomburg Center for Research in Black Culture.

82. *Amsterdam News*, July 1, 1925.

83. Herbert V. King became the first African American to hold the post of Commissioner of the Bed-Stuy District Boy Scouts of America. *Amsterdam News*, January 16, 1954; *Brown Memorial Baptist Fiftieth Anniversary Journal* (1966).

84. "Twenty-fifth Anniversary Boy Scouts of Bridge Street" (pamphlet, February 9, 1958); *Bridge Street AWME Anniversary Book* (1980), pp. 129–30.

85. *Amsterdam News*, October 24 and November 10, 1945, January 18, 1954; "Twenty-fifth Anniversary Boy Scouts of Bridge Street" (February 9, 1958); "Boy Scout Family Night" (pamphlet, March 30, 1958); *Bridge Street AWME Anniversary Book* (1980), p. 129.

86. Louis R. Bryan, "Concord Baptist Church Sunday School," WPA Research Papers, Schomburg Collection, Schomburg Center for Research in Black Culture; *Yearbook of the Churches of Brooklyn* (New York: Brooklyn Federation of Churches, 1930–31), p. 70.

87. *Amsterdam News*, November 10, 1945.

88. For Concord see *Amsterdam News*, June 1, 1955; for Bridge Street AWME see *Bridge Street AWME Sunday Bulletin*, "Boy Scout Family Night" (March 30, 1958); "Twenty-fifth Anniversary Boy Scouts of Bridge Street AWME Church" (pamphlet, February 9, 1958).

89. Bryan, "Concord Baptist Church Sunday School."

90. *Protestant Church Directory* (1952); *Amsterdam News*, January 15 and May 28, 1949, and January 14, 1958.

91. *Yearbook of the Churches of Brooklyn* (1930–31), pp. 70–193; *Church Directory of Greater New York* (1939–40), pp. 103–57; *Protestant Church Directory* (1950), pp. 82–138.

92. Author interview with George Beard, Jr., Brooklyn, October 27, 1988.

5. The Ministers' Committee for Job Opportunities for Brooklyn and the Downstate Medical Center Campaign

1. Some of the few works that focus on northern as well as southern civil rights campaigns are David Garrow, *Bearing the Cross: Martin Luther King, Jr. and the Southern Christian Leadership Conference* (New York: William Morrow, 1986); August Meier and Elliot Rudwick, *CORE: A Study of the Civil Rights Movement, 1942–1968* (New York: Oxford University Press, 1973); Alan B. Anderson and George W. Pickering, *Confronting the Color Line: The Broken Promise of the Civil Rights Movement in Chicago* (Athens: University of Georgia Press, 1986).

2. Meier and Rudwick, *CORE*, pp. 199–200.

3. Author interview with Oliver and Marjorie Leeds, Brooklyn, August 11, 1988; Meier and Rudwick, *CORE*, p. 184.

4. Author interview the Leeds; Meier and Rudwick, *CORE*. p. 200.

5. Author interview with the Leeds; *New York Times*, July 11, 1963.

6. Author interview with the Leeds; *New York Times*, July 16, 1963; *Amsterdam News*, July 16, 1963.

7. Same as note 6.

8. Author interview with the Leeds.

9. Author interview with Arnold Goldwag (a member and Public Relations Director of Brooklyn Core from 1962 to 1967), Brooklyn, July 27, 1988; author interview with Gardner C. Taylor, Brooklyn, August 1, 1988; author interview with Rev. William A. Jones, Brooklyn, December 22, 1987.

10. Author interviews with the Leeds and with Gardner C. Taylor. The fourteen ministers were (in order cited in news reports): Gardner C. Taylor of Concord Baptist, Albert Smith of St. Paul Community, Saul S. Williams of Pilgrim Baptist, W. J. Hall of Bethel Baptist, Benjamin J. Lowery of Mount Zion Baptist, Milton A. Galamison of Siloam Presbyterian, Edward Holmes of John Wesley Methodist, Walter G. Henson Jacobs of St. Augustine Protestant Episcopal, Sandy F. Ray of Cornerstone Baptist, Richard Saunders of Stuyvesant Heights Christian, F. D. Washington of Washington Temple, A. W. Wilson of Morningstar Baptist, William A. Jones of Bethany Baptist, and Melvin Williams of Bethany Baptist; *New York Times*, July 16, 1963; *New York Herald Tribune*, July 15, 1963; *Amsterdam News*, July 20, 1963.

11. Author interview with William A. Jones; author interview with Gardner C. Taylor; *New York Times*, July 23, 1963.

12. Author interview with William A. Jones; *New York Times*, July 24, 1963.

13. Executive Committee for Job Opportunities to Gov. Nelson A. Rockefeller (July 28, 1963); the Milton A. Galamison Papers at the State Historical Society, Madison, Wisconsin; *New York Times*, July 24 and August 7, 1963.

14. Author interview with Rev. Milton A. Galamison, Brooklyn, October 21, 1988; *Amsterdam News*, April 7, 1962.

15. *New York Times*, April 1, 1962; *Amsterdam News*, April 7, 1962.

16. *Amsterdam News*, April 14 and April 21, 1962.

17. Clarence Taylor, "'Whatever the Cost, We Will Set the Nation Straight': The Ministers' Committee for Job Opportunities in Brooklyn and the Downstate Medical Center Campaign," *Long Island Historical Journal* 1, no. 2 (Spring 1989): 136–46; *Amsterdam News*, March 24 and 31, April 7 and 14, May 5, 12, and 26, and June 2, 1962; *New York Recorder*, May 7, 1962; *New York Times*, April 1, 1962; and Diane Ravitch, *The Great School Wars* (New York: Basic Books, 1974), pp. 261–62.

18. *New York Times*, July 16 and 24, 1963; author interview (telephone) with Mrs. Sandy F. Ray, October 1, 1987.

19. Author interview with Gardner C. Taylor; *Amsterdam News*, September 2, 1961; Garrow, *Bearing the Cross*, p. 165.

20. Claude Barnett to Gardner C. Taylor (August 22, 1957) and Taylor's reply to Barnett (August 23, 1957) in the Claude A. Barnett Papers, Chicago Historical Society.

21. *Amsterdam News*, June 25, 1960.

22. *Amsterdam News*, September 17, 1960; author interview with Gardner C. Taylor; C. Eric Lincoln and Lawrence H. Mamiya, *The Black Church in the African American Experience* (Durham, N.C.: Duke University Press, 1990), pp. 36–37.

23. Garrow, *Bearing the Cross*, p. 166.

24. Taylor to King (May 19, 1961), in the Martin Luther King Jr. Papers, Special Collections Department, Mugar Library, Boston University; Taylor to Barnett (February 14, 1961), Claude A. Barnett Papers, Box 386, Folder 2, Chicago Historical Society; Garrow, *Bearing the Cross*, p. 166.

25. Taylor to members of the National Baptist Convention (July 1961), in the Martin Luther King Jr. Papers, Special Collections Department, Mugar Library.

26. Author interview with Gardner C. Taylor; *Amsterdam News*, September 9 and 16, 1961.

27. Garrow, *Bearing the Cross*, p. 166; Lincoln and Mamiya, *The Black Church*, p. 37; *Amsterdam News*, September 16, 1961.

28. Lincoln and Mamiya, *The Black Church*, pp. 36–38.

29. Doug McAdam, *Political Process and the Development of Black Insurgency, 1930–1970* (Chicago: University of Chicago Press, 1982), p. 47.

30. *New York Times*, July 22, 1963.

31. Ibid.; *Amsterdam News*, July 27, 1963.

32. Aldon Morris, *Origins of the Civil Rights Movement* (New York: Free Press, 1984), p. 284; *New York Times*, July 23, 1963.

33. Author interview with Milton Galamison; author interview with Gardner C. Taylor; author interview with Gwendolyn Timmons, Brooklyn, April 14, 1988 (Ms. Timmons is a member of Siloam Presbyterian Church and participated in the Downstate demonstrations); *New York Times*, July 16, 1963.

34. Author interview with Samuel and Winifred Fredricks, Brooklyn, May 9, 1990.

35. Author interview with the Fredrickses.

36. *New York Times*, July 25 and 30, and August 1, 1963.

37. *New York Times*, July 30, 1963.

38. Galamison to Richard L. Saunders (December 12, 1963) and Galamison to Dorothy Bostic (July 31, 1963), Galamison Papers, State Historical Society, Madison, Wisconsin.

39. *New York Times*, July 23, 24, 25, 26, and 27, 1963.

40. *New York Times*, July 23, 24, 25, and 26, 1963: *Amsterdam News*, July 27 and August 3, 1963.

41. *New York Times*, July 23, 1963.

42. Press Release dated July 18, 1963 (Thursday) from Robert L. McManus, press secretary to the governor; transcript of a television interview with Gov. Nelson Rockefeller for "In Search of a Solution: Civil

Rights," originating over the facilities of Station WOR-TV, New York, taped on July 31, 1963; *New York Times,* July 18, 23, and 24, 1963; and author interview with Gardner C. Taylor.

43. *New York Times,* August 1 and 2, 1963.

44. Arrest Docket Part 1B—Kings County Book 1 (1963).

45. *New York Times,* August 1 and 2, 1963.

46. Author interview with the Leeds.

47. *New York Times,* August 7, 1963; *Amsterdam News,* August 13, 1963; author interviews with Gardner C. Taylor, the Leeds, William A. Jones, and Milton A. Galamison; Job Opportunities for Brooklyn, letter to Pastors (August 9, 1963), Galamison Papers, State Historical Society, Madison, Wisconsin.

48. *New York Times,* August 7, 1963.

49. Author interviews with the Leeds and with Arnold Goldwag; Leeds to Galamison (August 12, 1963), Leeds to Galamison (no date), Galamison Papers, State Historical Society, Madison, Wisconsin.

50. Meier and Rudwick, *CORE,* p. 231; author interviews with the Leeds and with Arnold Goldwag; *New York Times,* August 8, 1963.

51. Ministers' Committee statement to clarify its position (August 9, 1963) in the Galamison Papers, State Historical Society, Madison, Wisconsin; *New York Times,* August 9, 1963. Galamison would later split with the Ministers' Committee and adopt Brooklyn CORE's position on the legal strategy, urging participants in the campaign who were arrested to plead not guilty. Galamison argued that he understood that many defendants could not afford to miss work and that pleading guilty would only result in a fine; he was also supporting other defendants who felt that they were innocent and wanted to plead not guilty (author interview with Galamison); *New York Times,* February 18, 1964.

52. *New York Times,* August 9, 1963.

53. Ravitch, *The Great School Wars,* pp. 273–79; Miriam Wasserman, *The School Fix NYC, USA* (New York: Simon and Schuster, 1970), pp. 314–15; William A. Jones, *God in the Ghetto* (Elgin, Ill.:Progressive Baptist Publishing House, 1979), pp. 96–101.

54. Robert A. Caro, *The Years of Lyndon Johnson: Means of Ascent* (New York: Knopf, 1990), p. xxi.

55. Caro, *The Years of Lyndon Johnson,* p. xxi.

56. *Amsterdam News,* August 1, 1964; Charles M. Morris, *The Cost of Good Intentions* (New York: McGraw-Hill, 1980), p. 65; *Amsterdam News,* June 3, 1965; Harold X. Connolly, *A Ghetto Grows in Brooklyn* (New York: New York University Press, 1977), p. 189; *Amsterdam News,* November 11 and December 9, 1967; "Homecoming Celebration for Milton Galamison, January 25, 1923–March 9, 1988" (New York: Siloam United Presbyterian Church, 1988).

57. Meier and Rudwick, *CORE*, pp. 204–208, 412–20.

58. David Feingold to Valerie Jorrin (memorandums dated February 6 and 13, 1967), and David Feingold, memorandum on "The Role of the White Worker in CORE" (no date). These memorandums are located in the David Feingold Papers at the State Historical Society, Madison, Wisconsin.

59. Meier and Rudwick, *CORE*, pp. 204–208, 412–20.

60. Author interview with Jeffery Gersen, Brooklyn, July 27, 1988; author interview with Gardner C. Taylor.

61. *New York Times*, August 7, 1963.

62. Leon Fink and Brian Greenberg, *Upheaval in the Quiet Zone* (Chicago: University of Illinois Press, 1989), pp. 24, 78–79.

63. Martin Luther King Jr., "Letter from a Birmingham Jail," in Alex Ayers, ed., *The Wisdom of Martin Luther King Jr.* (New York: Meridian, 1993), p. 78.

6. Driven by the Spirit: African American Women and the Black Churches of Brooklyn

1. C. Eric Lincoln and Lawrence H. Mamiya, *The Black Church in the African American Experience* (Durham, N.C.: Duke University Press, 1990), p. 278.

2. Lincoln and Mamiya, *The Black Church*, pp. 55, 275, 285–86; The Congregational church recognized the right of women to be ordained in 1891. For women in the Congregational church see Marion L. Starkey, *The Congregational Way* (New York: Doubleday, 1966), pp. 295–98; Lois Boyd and R. Douglas Brakenridge, *Presbyterian Women in America* (Westport, Conn.: Presbyterian Historical Society, 1983), pp. 139–56; Alla Bozarth Campbell, *Womanpriest* (New York: Paulist Press, 1978), p. 2; Suzanne R. Hiat, *Woman Priests, Yes or No* (New York: Seabury, 1973), pp. 102–104.

It should be noted that AME churches created an administrative body called the official board, whose duties were to direct the daily work of the church. It also was to give direction to clubs and organizations and to inform church leaders of the needs, achievements, and goals of the church. The pastor was the head of the official board, and stewards and trustees served; however, heads of clubs, class leaders, and stewardesses were also members of the board. Andrew White, "Know Your Church Manual: An Introductory Study of the Local Church for Officers and Members" (Nashville, Tenn.: African Methodist Episcopal Church Publishing House, 1961), pp. 42–44.

3. *Brooklyn Daily Eagle Almanac* (1929), pp. 195–200.

4. *Church Year Book of New York City* (1934), pp. 101–75.

5. *Church Directory of Greater New York* (1936); *Protestant Church Directory of Metropolitan New York* (1942), pp. 90–197; *First AME Zion Centennial Celebration Book, 1885–1985* (New York: Church Publication, 1985), pp. 12–13; *Amsterdam News,* June 4, 1955.

6. *Protestant Church Directory* (1947), pp. 75–133; *Protestant Church Directory* (1948), pp. 76–128; *Protestant Church Directory* (1952), pp. 76–129. The *Church Year Book of New York City* (1930–31), published by the Brooklyn Federation of Churches, listed the names of Siloam's deacons and trustees. All were men. Gwen Timmons, a member of Siloam for over forty years, noted that in spite of the fact that women were elders, deacons, and trustees during the pastorship of Milton A. Galamison, she cannot recall a woman minister occupying Siloam's pulpit. Author interview with Gwen Timmons, Brooklyn, August 29, 1993.

7. Information about Salina Perry's life is found in the *Amsterdam News,* issues of April 29, 1939, June 29, 1946, and October 19, 1963.

8. *Mount Lebanon Baptist Church Jubilee Year Book, 1905–1980* (New York: Church Publication, 1980), pp. 41–50; Jaquelyn Grant, "Black Women and the Church," in Gloria T. Hull, Patricia Bell Scott, and Barbara Smith, eds., *All the Women Are White, All the Blacks Are Men, But Some of Us Are Brave* (Old Westbury, Long Island, N.Y.: Feminist Press, 1982), pp. 141–48.

9. Lincoln and Mamiya, *The Black Church,* pp. 279–83.

10. *Black Churches of Brooklyn,* exhibition brochure (New York: Long Island Historical Society, 1984; the Long Island Historical Society changed its name in 1985 to the Brooklyn Historical Society); *History of the City of New York* (New York: Published by the *Brooklyn Daily Eagle,* 1893), p. 607; *Bethany Baptist Church Centennial Celebration: Commemorating Our History—Celebrating Our Hope, 1883–1983* (New York: Church Publication, 1983), p. 11; *Brown Memorial Baptist Fiftieth Anniversary Journal* (1966).

11. *New York Age,* February 27, 1908, and April 1, 1909.

12. *Amsterdam News,* June 4, 1955; *New York Age,* January 17, 1908.

13. *Bridge Street AWME Centennial Book: 1818–1918* (1919), pp. 45–47.

14. *New York Age,* March 23, 1905.

15. *New York Freeman,* December 13, 1884.

16. *New York Age,* May 8, 1926.

17. *Amsterdam News,* May 12, 1926; *New York Age,* May 15, 1926.

18. *New York Age,* July 11 and August 1, 1925, and January 2 and May 29, 1926.

19. *New York Age,* September 5 and December 26, 1925, and January 2, 1926.

20. Information on the numbers, gender composition, ratio, and function of church organizations and auxiliaries has been gathered on Con-

cord Baptist Church, Cornerstone Baptist Church, and Bridge Street AWME Church. The sources of information varied from church to church, but anniversary books, yearbooks, Protestant church directories, and newspapers have all been researched for this study in order to give a clearer picture of women's roles in the mainline black churches of Brooklyn.

21. *The African Wesleyan Methodist-Episcopal Church Anniversary Book* (New York: Church Publication, 1980), pp. 110–76 (hereafter, *Bridge Street AWME Anniversary Book*); *The African Wesleyan Methodist Episcopal Church Inc. 146th Anniversary Commemorative Journal, 1818–1964* (New York: Church Publication, 1964).

22. *Church Year Book of New York City* (1934), p. 102; *Church Directory of Greater New York* (1939–40), p. 105; *Protestant Church Directory* (1948), p. 80; *Amsterdam News*, June 4, 1955; *Cornerstone Baptist Church Sixtieth Anniversary Book* (New York: Church Publication, 1977), pp. 65–95.

23. *Bridge Street AWME Sunday Bulletin*, "Graduation Day" (June 6, 1951); *Amsterdam News*, July 6, 1954.

24. Cheryl T. Gylkes, "Together in Harness: Women's Tradition in the Sanctified Church," in *Signs* 10, no. 4 (1985): 678–99.

25. *Church Year Book of New York City* (1934), pp. 101–75; *Church Directory of Greater New York* (1936–37), pp. 100–180.

26. *Church Year Book of New York City* (1934), pp. 100–180; *Church Directory of Greater New York* (1939–40); *Protestant Church Directory* (1948 through 1952).

27. *Protestant Church Directory* (1947), pp. 75–133.

28. *Protestant Church Directory* (1947), p. 84.

29. *Amsterdam News*, January 13, 1945, and June 4, 1955; *Mount Lebanon Baptist Church Jubilee Year Book, 1905–1980*, p. 169.

30. *Amsterdam News*, August 22, 1959.

31. *Church Year Book of New York City* (1934), pp. 101–75; *Church Directory of Greater New York* (1936–37), pp. 100–80.

32. Church publications and church directories list numerous children's and youth organizations. For example, see *Brown Memorial Baptist Fiftieth Anniversary Journal* (1966); *Cornerstone Sixtieth Anniversary Book* (1977), pp. 58, 93, 94; *Protestant Church Directory* (1952), pp. 84–129. For Young People's Societies in the black Holiness-Pentecostal churches, see the Protestant church directories.

33. *Brown Memorial Baptist Fiftieth Anniversary Journal* (1966); *Cornerstone Sixtieth Anniversary Book* (1977), pp. 80, 84, 87, 90, 92; *Church of Mount Sinai Sixtieth Year Retrospective* (1979), pp. 38, 49, 103, 105, 106, 108; *First Baptist Church of Crown Heights: Founder's Day* (New York: Church Publication, 1987); author interview with Rev. Clarence Norman Sr., pastor of First Baptist Church of Crown Heights, Brooklyn, February 8, 1988;

Bridge Street AWME Anniversary Book (1980), pp. 146, 150, 152, 159, 160, 170, 173; *Amsterdam News*, June 4, 1955.

34. *Brown Memorial Baptist Fiftieth Anniversary Journal* (1966).

35. Darlene Clark Hine, *When the Truth Is Told* (Indianapolis: National Council of Negro Women, 1981), p. 27.

36. Lawrence W. Levine, *Black Culture and Black Consciousness* (Oxford and New York: Oxford University Press, 1977), pp. 174–89; Michael Harris, *The Rise of Gospel Blues* (New York: Oxford University Press, 1992), pp. 186–87.

37. Wyatt T. Walker, *"Somebody's Calling My Name": Black Sacred Music and Social Change* (Valley Forge, Pa..: Judson Press, 1979), pp. 127–57.

38. *Bethany Baptist Church Centennial Celebration* (1983), p. 79.

39. *Cornerstone Sixtieth Anniversary Book* (1977), p. 70.

40. *Amsterdam News*, November 10 and 17, and December 1, 1945.

41. *Washington Temple Church of God in Christ: Founder's Day Celebration* brochure (New York: Church Publication, September 4, 1988); *Amsterdam News*, June 14, 1958.

42. Robert C. Spellman and Mabel L. Thomas, *The Life, Legend and Legacy of Bishop R. C. Lawson* (Scotch Plains, N.J.: Published by the authors, 1983), p. 11; Robert C. Spellman, "Partial Summary Bibliography of Works Produced by Predominately Black Pentecostals, 1926–1990" (bibliography of a Paper presented at the conference on "African American Religion: Research Problems and Resources for the 1990s," May 26, 1990, Schomburg Center for Research in Black Culture, New York).

43. St. Clair Drake and Horace Cayton, *Black Metropolis* (New York: Harcourt, Brace, 1945), p. 412.

44. *Amsterdam News*, June 20, 1945.

45. *Amsterdam News*, November 13, 1965.

46. *Protestant Church Directory* (1950), pp. 147–49; *Amsterdam News*, September 30, 1940, September 23, 1944, and October 19, 1950.

47. *Church Directory of Greater New York* (1939–40), pp. 163–64.

48. *Amsterdam News*, September 23, 1941, and November 13, 1965; *Protestant Church Directory* (1947), p. 142.

Conclusion: Continuing the Legacy

1. William Julius Wilson, *The Truly Disadvantaged* (Chicago: University of Chicago Press, 1987).

2. Jitu Weusi, "Reverend Herbert Daughtry: Struggling Against Injustice," *Amsterdam News*, January 14, 1978; *Phoenix*, July 13, 1978.

3. Weusi, "Reverend Herbert Daughtry"; *New York Times*, 8/6/78.

4. Weusi, "Reverend Herbert Daughtry."

5. Naomi Levine, *Ocean Hill Brownsville: A Case History of Schools in Crisis* (New York: Popular Library, 1969), pp. 55–84; Diane Ravitch, *The Great School Wars* (New York: Basic Books, 1974), pp. 352–78.

6. *Amsterdam News*, April 8, 1978.

7. Ibid.; *Phoenix*, July 13, 1978; *Amsterdam News*, April 8 and November 25, 1978.

8. Same as note 7 and *New York Times*, August 6, 1978.

9. "Leon H. Sullivan," *Current Biography* (March 1969): 37–38.

10. *Amsterdam News*, September 30, 1978; "Crisis in Race Relations" (flyer from the Black United Front, no date).

11. "Wake Up Black Brooklyn: Can't You See the Handwriting on the Wall?" (flyer from Black United Front, 1978).

12. *Amsterdam News*, December 2, 1978.

13. *New York Daily News*, June 25, 1980.

14. Herbert Daughtry, "Ed Koch and Black Leadership: Part 3," in the *Amsterdam News*, October 13, 1979; *Amsterdam News*, April 8 and September 30, 1978; "Sisters Against South African Apartheid" (House of the Lord flyer, no date).

15. *New York Daily News*, August 28, 1979.

16. Herbert Daughtry, "Black Leadership at the Crossroads," in the *Amsterdam News*, November 3, 1979.

17. Daughtry, "Black Leadership at the Crossroads," *Amsterdam News*, November 3, 1979.

18. Ibid.

19. Basil Wilson and Charles Green, "The Black Church and the Struggle for Community Empowerment in New York City," *Afro-Americans in New York Life and History* (January 1988): p. 66.

20. Both quotes from "Building Nationhood" (APCO brochure, no date); see also Wilson and Green, "The Black Church and the Struggle for Community Empowerment," pp. 66–68.

21. Same as note 20 and APCO Lecture Series brochures (May 1 and 22, 1991).

22. Wilson and Green, "The Black Church and the Struggle for Community Empowerment," pp. 67–68.

23. "Man to Man, Inc." (House of Our Lord Pentecostal Church brochure, no date).

24. *New York Newsday*, April 10, 1988.

25. Ibid.

26. *New York Newsday*, April 10, 1988; *Amsterdam News*, February 11, 1984.

27. Same as note 26.

28. Same as note 26.

29. *Bridge Street AWME Sunday Bulletin* (March 10 and April 21, 1991).

30. C. Eric Lincoln and Lawrence H. Mamiya, *The Black Church in the African American Experience* (Durham, N.C.: Duke University Press, 1990), pp. 385–87.

31. *New York Newsday*, April 10, 1988.

32. *New York Times*, September 5, 1987.

33. *Details* (June 1991): 14–18.

34. "All Male Worship Service" (program for St. Paul Community Baptist Church, May 7, 1991) and Johnny Youngblood's sermon at the service.

35. *First Baptist Church of Crown Heights: Founder's Day* (1987).

36. Ibid.

37. Unless otherwise noted, the following information in the text is from an author interview with Rev. Clarence Norman Sr., Brooklyn, February 8, 1988.

38. Author interview with Clarence Norman; *First Baptist Church of Crown Heights Weekly Bulletin* (September 6, 1987).

39. Author interview with Clarence Norman.

40. Ibid.

41. *First Baptist Church Weekly Bulletin* (September 6, 1987).

42. Author interview with Rev. Wilbert Jones, Brooklyn, May 1, 1990.

43. Ibid.

44. Author interview with Wilbert Jones; author interview with Maritcha Harvey, Brooklyn, May 3, 1990.

45. Author interview with Wilbert Jones.

46. Ibid.

47. *New York Post*, April 11, 1971; Louise Mooney, "Al Sharpton," in Mooney, ed., *Newsmakers* (Detroit: Gale Research: 1991), pp. 383–84; *New York Times*, December 19, 1991.

48. *New York Times*, December 19, 1991; Mooney, "Al Sharpton," p. 383; Robert D. McFadden et al., *Outrage: The Story Behind the Tawana Brawley Hoax* (New York: Bantam, 1990), pp. 109–10.

49. Jim Sleeper, "A Man of Too Many Faces," *New Yorker*, January 25, 1993, pp. 58–60; *New York Times*, December 19, 1991; *New York Post*, April 11, 1971; McFadden et al., *Outrage*, p. 110.

50. *New York Times*, January 13 and December 19, 1991; Mike Sager, "The Sharpton Strategy," *Esquire*, January 1991, pp. 112–13.

51. *New York Times*, December 19, 1991.

52. Sleeper, "A Man of Too Many Faces," pp. 60–61; William A. Jones, *God in the Ghetto*, pp. 98–100; *New York Post*, April 11, 1971; Sager, "The Sharpton Strategy," p. 113; McFadden et al., *Outrage*, pp. 110–11.

53. Jack Robbins, "Daily Closeup," in the *New York Post*, April 11, 1971. In an uncritical biography of Sharpton, National Alliance member Michael Klein asserts that Sharpton's first arrest was after he had gradu-

ated Samuel Tilden High School and formed the National Youth Movement. He and some members of the newly formed organization held a sit-in at New York City's Department of Manpower to demand jobs for youths, Michael Klein, *The Man Behind the Sound Bite: The Real Story of the Reverend Al Sharpton* (New York: Castillo International, 1991), p. 96.

54. Klein, *The Man Behind the Sound Bite*, p. 96.

55. Mooney, "Al Sharpton" *Newsmakers*, pp. 383–84.

56. *Amsterdam News*, September 2 and 9, 1978.

57. Ibid.

58. *Amsterdam News*, November 12, 1983, and September 21, 1985; *New York Daily News*, December 5, 1983.

59. *Amsterdam News*, June 21, 1986.

60. *New York Times*, December 19, 1991; *New York Daily News*, November 2, 1986.

61. Sager, "The Sharpton Strategy," p. 113; Mooney, "Al Sharpton," p. 383; *New York Times*, December 19, 1991; *New York Newsday*, January 22, 1988; McFadden et al., *Outrage*, p. 112.

62. Transcript from *Frontline*, "Don King Unauthorized," produced by Charles C. Stuart, written by Charles C. Stuart and Jack Newfield, Show #1004, air date June 9, 1992 (transcript produced by Journal Graphics), pp. 3–4.

63. Stuart and Newfield, "Don King Unauthorized," *Frontline*, June 9, 1992.

64. *New York Times*, December 19, 1991; Mooney, "Al Sharpton," p. 383.

65. *New York Times*, December 21 through 31, 1986, and January 1 through 10, 1987.

66. Same as note 65; and Mooney, "Al Sharpton," p. 384; McFadden et al., *Outrage*, p. 108.

67. *New York Newsday*, January 20, 21, and 22, 1988; *Jet*, February 8, 1988; *New York Times*, December 19, 1991.

68. Same as note 67.

69. *New York Newsday*, January 20, 21, and 22, 1988. Jim Sleeper reports that Sharpton moved the NYM's headquarters to an office provided free by Spring Records, a company that Pagnano was closely associated with (Sleeper, "A Man of Too Many Faces," p. 61).

70. *New York Newsday*, January 20, 1988, *New York Times*, December 19, 1991.

71. Same as note 70.

72. *Report of the Grand Jury and Related Documents Concerning the Tawana Brawley Investigation*, pp. 7–8 (a copy of the report is found at the library of the State University of New York at Geneseo); McFadden et al., *Outrage*, pp. 11–48; *New York Times*, February 3, 1988.

73. *Report of the Grand Jury*, pp. 68–69.

74. Ibid., pp. 65, 74.

75. Ibid., pp. 69–70; McFadden et al., *Outrage*, pp. 80–84.

76. *Report of the Grand Jury*, pp. 69–70; McFadden et al., *Outrage*, pp. 123–24.

77. *Report of the Grand Jury*, pp. 69–70; McFadden et al., *Outrage*, pp. 124–26.

78. *Report of the Grand Jury*, pp. 69–70; McFadden et al., *Outrage*, pp. 167–69.

79. McFadden et al., *Outrage*, pp. 137–38; *Report of the Grand Jury*, p. 73, and "Abrams to Grievance Committee for the Second and Eleventh Judicial Districts" (October 6, 1988), in *Report of the Grand Jury*, pp. 2–3.

80. *Report of the Grand Jury*, pp. 72–76, 77–84; McFadden et al., *Outrage*, pp. 172–73.

81. *Report of the Grand Jury*, pp. 75–76; McFadden et al., *Outrage*, pp. 175–77.

82. *Report of the Grand Jury*, pp. 75–76; McFadden et al., *Outrage*, pp. 178–79.

83. *New York Times*, February 3, 7, and 10, 1988; McFadden et al., *Outrage*, pp. 183–84.

84. *New York Times*, February 4 and 7, 1988.

85. Ibid., February 5, 10, 18, and 23, 1988.

86. Ibid., February 20 through 23, 1988; McFadden et al., *Outrage*, p. 224.

87. "Introduction," *Report of the Grand Jury*; *New York Times*, February 22 and 25, and March 1, 1988.

88. *New York Times*, June 9, 1988.

89. *New York Times*, June 9, 1988, and March 7, 1988. At the end of April the FBI had ended its active investigation of the Brawley case, asserting that there was no evidence of any civil rights violation (*New York Times*, April 29, 1988).

90. *New York Times*, June 28, 1988.

91. McFadden et al., *Outrage*, pp. 285–95.

92. Ibid., 305–16.

93. *Report of the Grand Jury*, pp. 5–6. Because most of the following summary is from the grand jury's report, page numbers are cited in the text.

94. Ibid., pp. 6–7.

95. "Abrams to Grievance Committee," p. 3.; *Report of the Grand Jury*, p. 77–81.

96. "Introduction," *Report of the Grand Jury*.

97. *New York Newsday*, September 8, 1992.

98. Al Sharpton, "A Letter Written by Reverend Al Sharpton to Mayor David Dinkins" (July 22, 1990), in *Independent Black Leadership in America:*

Minister Louis Farrakhan, Dr. Lenora Fulani, Rev. Al Sharpton (New York: Costello International, 1990), pp. 100–101.

99. Sharpton, "A Letter to Mayor David Dinkins," p. 102.

100. *Al Sharpton, "The Need for a New Alliance," in Independent Black Leadership in America, p. 113.*

101. Speech by Al Sharpton at the "Blacks and Jews Forum," in *Independent Black Leadership in America*, pp. 93–94.

102. Ibid.

103. Bruce Shapiro, "Dr. Fulani's Snake-Oil Show," *The Nation*, May 4, 1992, pp. 585–92.

104. Ibid.

105. Sager, "The Sharpton Strategy," p. 112; *New York Times*, December 19, 1991.

106. Sharpton, "The Need for a New Alliance," in *Independent Black Leadership in America*, p. 114.

107. *New York Times*, February 24, 1988.

108. Cornell West, quoted in Sleeper, "A Man of Too Many Faces," p. 58.

BIBLIOGRAPHY

Primary Sources

MANUSCRIPTS AND PUBLIC DOCUMENTS

Annual Report of the African Civilization Society. Brooklyn Historical Society, New York.

Annual Secessions of the National Baptist Convention USA, Inc. Union Theological Seminary, New York.

Archives of Brooklyn's Black Churches. Brooklyn Historical Society, New York.

Bedford-Stuyvesant Health Congress, *Newsletter* (Spring 1953, Health Press). Brooklyn Historical Society, New York.

Barnett, Claude A. Papers. Chicago Historical Society, Chicago, Ill.

Brooklyn Directories.

Brooklyn Howard Colored Orphan Asylum Annual Report (various years). Brooklyn Historical Society, New York.

Church Directory of Greater New York. New York Public Library.

Church Year Book of New York City. New York Public Library.

Communities Population Characteristics and Neighborhood Social Resource. Vol. 2. New York: Bureau of Community Statistical Services, Community Council of Greater New York, 1959.

Conference Reports of the African Methodist Episcopal Churches. Union Theological Seminary, New York.

"Constitution and By-laws of the Brooklyn Literary Union." Brooklyn Historical Society, New York.

Feingold, David. Papers. State Historical Society of Wisconsin, Madison.

Galamison, Milton A. Papers. State Historical Society of Wisconsin, Madison.

———. Transcript of Oral History Interview. Howard University, Moorland Spingarn Research Center, Washington, D.C.

King Jr., Martin Luther. Papers. Special Collections Department, Mugar Library, Boston University, Boston, Mass.

Kings County Clerk's Office Records of Church Incorporation.

National Alliance Newspapers. Tamiment Library, New York University.

National Association for the Advancement of Colored People Papers. Library of Congress, Washington, D.C.

National Urban League Papers. Library of Congress, Washington, D.C.

New York Teachers News. Tamiment Library, New York University.

Protestant Church Directory of Metropolitan New York. New York Public Library.

Report of the Grand Jury and Related Documents Concerning the Tawana Brawley Investigation (October 6, 1988). Library of the State University of New York at Geneseo.

"Report of the Grand Jury of Kings County" (August 1943). Brooklyn Historical Society, New York.

Report on Hospital Needs of the Bedford-Stuyvesant Area (New York: Hospital Council of Greater New York, 1953). Brooklyn Historical Society, New York.

"Report to the Honorable F. H. LaGuardia on the Conditions existing in the Bedford-Stuyvesant Area of Brooklyn in Connection with the Charges made by the Kings County Grand Jury in its Presentment of August 1943" (Parts One and Two). Brooklyn Historical Society, New York.

Teachers Union Collection. Cornell Labor Archives, Cornell University, School of Industrial Labor, Ithaca, N.Y.

U.S. Census Bureau. *Negroes in the United States, 1920–32.* Washington, D.C.: Department of Commerce, 1935.

———. Ninth Census (1870). Department of Commerce, Washington, D.C.

———. U.S. Census of Religious Bodies (1936). Department of Commerce, Washington, D.C.

Williams, Harry A. Papers. Schomburg Center for Research in Black Culture, New York (Harlem).

WPA Writers Project (1936–1941). Schomburg Center for Research in Black Culture, New York (Harlem).

Bibliography

NEWSPAPERS

Amsterdam News (New York City)
Anglo-African Weekly (New York City)
Brooklyn Daily Eagle (New York City)
Newsday (New York City)
New York Age (New York City)
New York Daily News (New York City)
New York Freeman (New York City)
New York Globe (New York City)
New York Post (New York City)
New York Recorder (New York City)
New York Times (New York City)

Secondary Works

Anderson, Alan B. and George W. Pickering, *Confronting the Color Line: The Broken Promise of the Civil Rights Movement in Chicago*. Athens: University of Georgia Press, 1986.

Baer, Hans A. and Merrill Singer. *African-American Religion in the Twentieth Century: Varieties of Protest and Accommodation*. Knoxville: University of Tennessee Press, 1992.

Brown, Joshua and David Ment. *Factories, Foundries and Refineries: A History of Five Brooklyn Industries*. New York: Brooklyn Educational and Cultural Alliance, 1980.

Caro, Robert. *The Power Broker*. New York: Knopf, 1974.

——. *The Years of Lyndon Johnson: Means of Ascent*. New York: Knopf, 1990.

Clark, Elmer T. *The Small Sects in America*. New York: Abingdon, 1937.

Clark, Kenneth. *Dark Ghetto*. New York: Harper and Row, 1969.

Cleage, Albert. *The Black Messiah*. New York: Sheed and Ward, 1968.

Cone, James H. *Black Theology and Black Power*. New York: Seabury, 1969.

Connolly, Harold X. *A Ghetto Grows in Brooklyn*. New York: New York University Press, 1977.

Curry, Leonard P. *The Free Black in Urban America, 1800–1850*. Chicago: University of Chicago Press, 1981.

Drake, St. Clair and Horace Cayton. *Black Metropolis*. New York: Harcourt, Brace, 1945.

Du Bois, W. E. B. *The Philadelphia Negro* (1899). New York: Schocken, 1967.

——. *The Souls of Black Folks*. New York: Dodd, Mead, 1961.

DuPree, Sherry Sherrod. *Biographical Dictionary of African American*

275

Holiness-Pentecostals, 1880–1990. Washington, D.C.: Middle Atlantic Regional Press, 1989.

Eddy, G. Norman. "Storefront Religion." *Religion in Life* 28 (1958–59).

Ewen, Stuart. *Captains of Consciousness.* New York: McGraw˜2DHill, 1976.

Fauset, Arthur W. *Black Gods of the Metropolis.* New York: Octagon, 1970.

Findley, James F. "Religion and Politics in the Sixties: The Churches and the Civil Rights Act of 1964." *Journal of American History* 77, no. 1 (June 1990).

Fink, Leon and Brian Greenberg. *Upheaval in the Quiet Zone.* Chicago: University of Illinois Press, 1989.

Franklin, John Hope. *From Slavery to Freedom.* New York: Knopf, 1988).

Frazier, E. Franklin. *The Negro Church in America.* New York: Schocken, 1954.

Goff, James R. *Fields White Unto Harvest: Charles F. Parham and the Missionary Origins of Pentecostalism.* Fayetteville: University of Arkansas Press, 1988.

Golder, Morris E. *History of the Pentecostal Assemblies of the World.* Indianapolis, Ind.: Published by Golder and Grace Apostolic Church, 1973.

———. *The Life and Works of Bishop Garfield Thomas Haywood.* Indianapolis, Ind.: Published by Golder and Grace Apostolic Church, 1977.

Hedgepeth, Cynthia E. *Lord Why Me? The Making of an Apostle.* New York: Tabernacle of Prayer Publishing, 1989).

Higginbotham, Evelyn Brooks. *Righteous Discontent: The Women's Movement in the Black Baptist Church, 1880–1920.* Cambridge: Harvard University Press, 1993.

Hooks, Esther. *The Penny Hooks Story: God Specializes.* New York: Hooks Publishing, 1986.

Hughes, Langston and Arna Bontemps, eds. *The Book of Negro Folklore.* New York: Dodd, Mead, 1983.

Independent Black Leadership in America: Minister Louis Farrakhan, Dr. Lenora Fulani, Rev. Al Sharpton. New York: Costello International, 1990.

Jones, Charles Price. "Autobiographical Sketch of Charles Price Jones, Founder of the Church of Christ (Holiness) USA." *Journal of Black Sacred Music* 2, no. 2 (Fall 1988): 52–58.

———. "The History of My Songs." *Journal of Black Sacred Music* 2, no. 2 (Fall 1988).

Jones, G. William. *Black Cinema Treasures Lost and Found.* Denton: University of North Texas Press, 1991.

Jones, William A. *God in the Ghetto.* (Elgin, Ill.: Progressive Baptist Publishing House, 1979.

Levine, Lawrence W. *Black Culture and Black Consciousness*. Oxford and New York: Oxford University Press, 1977.

——. *Highbrow Lowbrow*. Cambridge: Harvard University Press, 1988.

Lincoln, C. Eric and Lawrence H. Mamiya. *The Black Church in the African American Experience*. Durham, N.C.: Duke University Press, 1990.

Manis, Andrew Michael. *Southern Civil Religions in Conflict*. Athens: University of Georgia Press, 1987.

Marx, Gary. *Protest and Prejudice*. New York: Harper and Row, 1969.

Mays, Benjamin and Joseph W. Nicholson. *The Negro's Church*. New York: Institute of Social and Religious Research, 1933.

McAdam, Doug. *Political Process and the Development of Black Insurgency, 1930–1970*. Chicago: University of Chicago Press, 1982.

Meier, August and Elliot Rudwick. *CORE: A Study of the Civil Rights Movement, 1942–1968*. New York: Oxford University Press, 1973.

Ment, David and Mary Donovan. *The People of Brooklyn: A History of Two Neighborhoods*. New York: Brooklyn Arts and Cultural Association, 1980.

Myrdal, Gunnar. *An American Dilemma*. New York: Harper and Row, 1944.

Morris, Aldon. *Origins of the Civil Rights Movement*. New York: Free Press, 1984.

Morris, Charles M. *The Cost of Good Intentions*. New York: McGraw-Hill, 1980.

Nash, Gary. *The Urban Crucible*. Cambridge: Harvard University Press, 1979.

Noble, E. Myron. "Genesis of W. J. Seymour in Perspective," *MAR Gospel Ministries Newsletter* 10, no. 1 (Spring–Summer 1990).

Oliver, Paul, Max Harrison, and William Bolcom. *The New Grove: Gospel, Blues and Jazz*. New York: W. W. Norton, 1986.

Paris, Arthur E. *Black Pentecostalism*. Amherst: University of Massachusetts, 1982.

Peiss, Kathy. *Cheap Amusement*. Philadelphia: Temple University Press, 1986.

Quimby, Ernest. "Black Political Development in Bedford-Stuyvesant as Reflected in the Origins and Role of the Bedford-Stuyvesant Restoration Corporation." Ph.D. diss., New York University, 1977.

Raboteau, Albert. *Slave Religion*. New York: Oxford University Press: 1978.

Ravitch, Diane. *The Great School Wars*. New York: Basic Books, 1974.

Ray, Sandy F. *Journeying Through a Jungle*. Nashville: Broadman Press, 1979.

Rogers, Huey C. [Huie Rodgers]. *The Dynamics of Christian Faith*. New York: Total Truth Publications, 1982.

——. *Power to Turn the World Upside Down*. New York: Total Truth Publications, 1973.

Rozenweig, Roy. *Eight Hours for What We Will*. Cambridge: Cambridge University Press, 1983.

Seraile, William. "Susan McKinney Steward: New York State's First African-American Woman Physician." *Afro-Americans in New York Life and History* 9, no. 2 (July 1985): 27–40.

Sernett, Milton C., ed. *Afro-American Religious History: A Documentary Witness*. Durham, N.C.: Duke University Press, 1985.

Skinner, Arturo. *Nine Gifts of the Spirit*. Newark: Deliverance Evangelistic Center, 1975.

Sobel, Mechal. *Trabelin' On: The Slave Journey to an Afro-Baptist Faith*. Princeton: Princeton University Press, 1979.

Spear, Allan H. *Black Chicago: The Making of a Negro Ghetto, 1890–1920*. Chicago: University of Chicago Press, 1967.

Spellman, Robert C. and Mabel L. Thomas. *The Life, Legend and Legacy of Bishop R. C. Lawson*. Scotch Plains, N.J.: Published by the authors, 1983.

Spencer, Jon Michael. *Protest and Praise*. Minneapolis: Fortress Press, 1990.

Synan, Vinson. *Aspects of Pentecostal-Charismatic Origins*. Plainfield, N.J.: Logos International, 1975.

Tyler, Mary. *The Bridegroom Songs*. Indianapolis, Ind.: Christ Temple Bookstore, n.d.

Wade, Wyn Craig. *The Fiery Cross: The Ku Klux Klan in America*. New York: Simon and Schuster, 1987.

Walker, Wyatt T. *"Somebody's Calling My Name": Black Sacred Music and Social Change*. Valley Forge, Pa.: Judson Press, 1979.

Washington, Joseph R. *Black Religion*. Lanham, Mo.: University Press of America, 1964.

——. *Black Sects and Cults*. Lanham, Mo.: University Press of America, 1984.

Wasserman, Miriam. *The School Fix NYC, USA*. New York: Simon and Schuster, 1970.

Williams, Melvin. *Community in a Black Pentecostal Church: An Anthropological Study*. Pittsburgh: University of Pittsburgh Press, 1974.

Wilmore, Gayraud S. *Black Religion and Black Radicalism*. Maryknoll, N.Y.: Orbis, 1986.

Wilson, Basil and Charles Green. "The Black Church and the Struggle for Community Empowerment in New York City." *Afro-Americans in New York Life and History* (January 1988).

Woodson, Carter G. *The History of the Negro Church*. Washington, D.C.: Associated Publishers, 1945.

Wynes, Charles E. "T. McCants Stewart: Peripatetic Black South Carolinian." *South Carolina Historical Magazine* 80 (1979): 311–17.

INDEX

286

Designer: Audrey Smith
Text: Palatino
Composition: Columbia University Press
Printer: Maple-Vail
Binder: Maple-Vail